WOMEN'S UTOPIAS IN BRITISH AND AMERICAN FICTION

NAN BOWMAN ALBINSKI

ROUTLEDGE
London and New York

First published in 1988 by
Routledge
a division of Routledge, Chapman and Hall
11 New Fetter Lane, London EC4P 4EE

Published in the USA by
Routledge
a division of Routledge, Chapman and Hall, Inc.
29 West 35th Street, New York NY 10001

© 1988 Nan Bowman Albinski

**Printed and bound in Great Britain
by Billing & Sons Ltd, Worcester**

British Library Cataloguing in Publication Data

Albinski, Nan Bowman
    Women's utopias in British and American fiction.
    1. Fiction in English. Women writers,
    1800–1985. Special subjects Utopias.
    Critical studies
    823′.009′358
    ISBN 0-415-00330-X
Library of Congress Cataloging-in-Publication Data
ISBN 0-415-00330-X

Contents

Acknowledgements

The original research on this topic was completed for a PhD degree in the English Department at Monash University, Australia, which included study in the British Library, and the utopian collection of the Pennsylvania State University. I wish to acknowledge the assistance of both Monash Department of English and the Monash library staff.

Additional research has continued at the Pennsylvania State University, where members of the Pattee Library have given sterling assistance; my thanks to Charles Mann and Sandy Stelts, and Noelene Martin and their staff.

Henry Albinski's contribution has been a constant and interested support: best friend and critic, he has lightened the load with books and meals and much more. My thanks.

Introduction

Why a separate study of women's utopian fiction? Basing a literary analysis on writers' gender assumes that gender plays an important role in subject or style, an assumption that stands on the firmest ground in utopian fiction. Making concrete a vision of utopia is a highly personal, even idiosyncratic, act, yet firmly anchored in the writer's social reality. William Golding reminds us that: 'when a utopia glitters all gold in the memory it does so against a background of social darkness, of misery, want, deprivation at every level'.[1] The nature of one's 'social darkness' may be dictated by race, colour, creed — or gender. They do not merely influence one's position in society, but constitute different social realities. For those who face legal disabilities and other entrenched barriers against membership in the institutions of dominant culture based on 'scientific' explanations of their essential difference that justify exclusion, then the 'social darkness' is bound to be a distinctive shade.

The subject of this study is a comparison of the historical development of utopian writing by British and American women. Chapters 1 (British) and 2 (American) discuss works published before 1920. The same alternating sequence of British and American writers is continued in Chapters 3 and 4, which cover the period 1920–60, and Chapters 5 and 6, which cover 1960–87.

Exclusion from the institutions of dominant culture is most clearly marked for British and American women before 1920. Without a vote in national politics, often debarred from higher education and admission to professional bodies, they also faced legal discrimination in the matrimonial courts. Although life was not uniform for all women in both countries — for class and race must also be considered — exclusion and discrimination transcended other distinctions, affecting them equally as women. When political suffrage was gained and many of the legal disabilities gradually expunged, writers faced the extension of gender-based 'marriage bars' (compulsory retirement on marriage) during the years of economic depression; and they also found that the price of emancipation included subtler pressures to choose between career and family. The modern period has brought the identification and rejection of the 'feminine mystique', but still such a basic principle as equal pay for equal work has yet to be attained; and, as we enter a period already labelled

1

'post-feminist', difference still has its meaning.

Over the generations these changing circumstances have brought a healthy crop of utopias from women writers: there are visionary and satirical utopias, and utopias both urban and pastoral. Some are small-scale urban or rural communities that examine ways of living together harmoniously, and others depict national or international social transformation. Those depicting nations or communities of women only are in a minority (perhaps the best-known of these is Gilman's *Herland*, 1915), and for both British and American women writers, utopia, variously though it may be interpreted, is an egalitarian society composed of both women and men, free from discrimination in both public and private life. Utopia is sometimes segregated from the known world by space: it may be on Mars or Venus, in a hidden valley in South America, somewhere near the North Pole, or on a remote island. It may likewise be isolated in time. Overall, fantastic voyages to other planets are outnumbered by journeys to the future, where utopia awaits; or perhaps dystopia, an increasing twentieth-century fear. Whatever setting the writer may choose, whatever forecast she may make, the focus of attention is always on her own society, with its propensities for good and evil, and its possibilities of fruitful change.

As recently as 1970 a feminist theorist expressed her concern that 'there is not even a *utopian* feminist literature in existence' (original emphasis).[2] Contemporary feminist scholarship, particularly in America, has shown this to be historically inaccurate, for there is a strong tradition of utopian writing by women — much of it being feminist — which has been restored to critical attention.[3] Simultaneously with this process of rediscovering the past, contemporary American feminist writers have considerably augmented the lost tradition with new works. The utopian writing of Angela Carter, Doris Lessing, Joanna Russ, Marge Piercy and Ursula Le Guin, to name the most prominent of recent writers, has been the most innovative new wave of the utopian genre. However, the tradition of women's utopias has persisted, largely unbroken, in Britain as well as in America, as indicated by the number of works — over 260 — listed in the primary bibliography appended herein — a list that does not claim to be exhaustive.

Women's utopian visions (and nightmares) are widely diverse, as are those of men. Beneath the social fabric lie prevailing definitions of human nature and of female and male. In creating new societies, utopian writers must either accept and build on these prevailing definitions or, challenging them, offer alternatives.

Despite historical and cultural differences in the definitions on which their challenges are based, women utopians have more consistently questioned the status quo of gender relationships than have their male counterparts. An insightful analytical vantage point for examining these challenges is outlined by anthropologist Sherry Ortner in 'Is female to male as nature is to culture?' Ortner examines the ways in which women have been distanced from the power structures of dominant (male) culture physiologically (through their role as childbearers); sociologically (through their role as child raisers); and psychically (through a realm of symbols and images that may be so polarised as to contain the *elevation* of women through an association with the supernatural — yet also exclude them as marginal and peripheral). Ortner argues that:

> The culture/nature distinction is itself a product of culture, culture being minimally defined as the transcendence, by means of systems of thought and technology, of the natural givens of existence . . . Woman's physiology, more involved more of the time with 'species of life'; woman's association with the structurally subordinate domestic context, charged with the crucial function of transforming animal-like infants into cultured beings; 'woman's psyche', appropriately molded to mothering functions by her own socialization and tending toward greater personalism and less mediated modes of relating — all these factors make woman appear to be rooted more directly and deeply in nature. At the same time, however, her 'membership' and fully necessary participation in culture are recognized by culture and cannot be denied. Thus she is seen to occupy an intermediate position between culture and nature.[4]

How does this help us to understand women's utopian literature? The definitions of male = culture, female = nature, have a long history, and it is one in which not only these definitions, but also assaults upon them, have changed. If we begin with the second half of the nineteenth century we find the justification of the 'angel in the house', women's 'proper sphere', the associations of motherhood and womanliness, all related to the concept of nature, and buttressed with the principles of history, religion, anthropology and sociology. The religious justification for female subordination was not eroded by secular theories which gathered strength from the mid-Victorian period, merely supplanted: misogynist interpretations of Darwinian theory found 'scientific' bases (woman's 'child-like nature', which placed her in the same category as the unevolved and primitive). Freudians were later to step into the same breach.

> Had Enlightenment thinkers identified women with nature, then females would have been hailed as the embodiment of order and reason. But it was not the *philosophes*, but the Romantic thinkers of the first half of the nineteenth century and those who were later influenced by Romantic thought, who equated woman and nature. For them, nature was not a realm of decorum and rationality; it was a condition to be overcome and controlled — the very antithesis of civilization.[5]

Given these assumptions, it is small wonder that British Victorian women utopian writers totally rejected all the elements of their 'natural' roles. For the most part they worked from a feminist model of theories of biological and social evolution to justify their inclusion in the public domain of 'culture', focusing on their right to enter political institutions. To this end they emphasise their decorum and rationality in order to disassociate themselves from the inferior status of their 'natural' roles. Their utopias are national in scope, highly urbanised and politicised, and generally limited to the public ('male') sphere: reference to the domestic world of marriage and family is almost exclusively limited to a demand for easier divorce laws.

US women had a different social and political reality. There were fewer legal and political disabilities to chafe them, and educational and professional pathways were easier to open, due mainly to the advantage of forming 'an esteemed minority in a new country'.[6] While the main institutions of power were as male-dominated as those in Britain, American women were regarded as the 'guardians of culture', but 'culture' defined in terms of aesthetics and morality rather than in the wider sense of thought and technology. The women of both countries relied on popular conceptions of their higher moral natures to determine their utopias, but within different frameworks — the British women, secular, often socialist; and the American women, religious. American women's utopias are also most often urban: they are set closer in time to the writers' present; and the primary transformation role is not political but social — and these utopias are likewise generally communal rather than national. British emphasis on social evolution over generations is replaced by a vigorous individualism (found also in male American writers' work), which often ascribes the development of utopia to internal change, and which emphasises the social influence of individuals rather than legislated change.[7] The often spoken text for these utopias is 'the kingdom of God is within you' Luke, XVII.xxi), and they are imbued with the same ideals of perfectionism that inspired the religious communities of the early and mid-nineteenth century: where these as the subjects of utopian fiction are examined and shown wanting, it is through the failure of particular leaders rather than that of their utopian idealism. Belief in social rather than political change, in internal rather than external influences, and in religious and moral rather than secular evolutionary principles, defines the major differences between women utopists of the two countries. Also important is the absence in America of a rigid class system which tabooed association with 'trade', and also the worst excesses of the association of women with 'nature'. It is interesting that many of the women who work in these utopias have outdoor jobs; these are not regarded as defilement through association with nature, but instead are dignified avenues through which women can achieve economic independence: the terms 'floriculture' and 'horticulture' show a revealing mediation.

The 1920s and 1930s were the first decades of women's suffrage, from which so much had been expected. British and American women respond in quite different ways to this, as they do to the two world wars, despite the similarity of feminist activists' experience. British writers of the period 1920–60 (Chapter 3) wrote very few single-issue feminist utopias during this period, but their work throughout these four decades is highly political, changing in response to international circumstances (these novels show a consistently high usage of male pseudonyms). The 1920s were the years of anti-utopian satire and anti-communist dystopia; the 1930s of anti-Fascist dystopia; the wartime 1940s of the spiritualist, highly nationalist utopia common also in America during the war; the post-war 1940s and early 1950s show a return to the post-war phenomenon of the 1920s, political anti-utopian satire. The almost complete silence on gender distinctions and the absence of any need to defy the equation with nature show an almost total preoccupation with the intellectual and political implications of culture. The optimism of the Victorians' belief in the inevitability of an upward march of evolutionary progress had received a bitter blow from World War One: the growth of totalitarian regimes founded on the conflicting ideologies of communism and Fascism added to the erosion of this optimism. These are the decades of the three great dystopias: Zamiatin's *We* (1924); Huxley's *Brave new world* (1934); Orwell's *Nineteen eighty-four* (1949). While these monuments of the genre are male-authored, there is no dearth of political dystopias by women — quite the contrary. For both, the strength of Western culture was threatened by revolution and the rise of the totalitarian state; but its values were also being questioned from within, and one of these values was the concept of utopia. Some of these writers openly question its viability as a goal, and others go beyond this to regard it in the same light as Berdiaeff (whom Huxley quotes in his epigraph to *Brave new world*), as a dangerously misleading idealisation of conformity and a pattern for repression. This, now one of the commonplaces of twentieth-century thought, went through its anguished birth in the literature of the 1920s and 1930s.

Women's activism through these years centred on the conflict between women's 'natural' role as childbearers and rearers, and their professional lives: too often the choice was family or career. It is noteworthy that in the one 1930s feminist utopia that recalls the figure so familiar in Victorian novels, the woman Prime Minister, she is faced with this choice: although politics wins fairly easily over domestic anonymity, it is a conflict not faced, nor even glimpsed, by earlier writers.

US feminists of this period shared similar goals: equal pay, legislative protection of mothers and children, access to birth control information. Even fewer of the utopian novels by American women, however, reflect these issues. They are conservative, often anti-feminist, although they remain markedly optimistic: the 'feminine mystique' far outweighs any radicalism. The early 1920s produced several feminist works, but mostly spiritualist (and sometimes theosophical) utopias, sometimes contrasted in the same work with a socialist dystopian society. The same trend continued from the mid-1930s until the late 1940s, when a spate of anti-socialist and anti-technological dystopias reflect immediate post-war concerns including the question of nuclear technology. (Nuclear concern also appears in British post-war writing.) A most interesting change here is a greater awareness of America as a nation rather than as a series of communities, and with this a greater awareness of her international role. In the 1920s and 1930s, involvement in World War One surfaces in depictions of disaster on a vast scale, originating in Europe and spreading to America (revolution, war or natural catastrophe.) These dystopias usually convert to utopias as a consequence of religious belief: sometimes the destruction leads to Armageddon and the establishment of a new Earth through the

Second Coming; sometimes it merely acts as a clearing-house without divine intervention.

The economic depression of the 1930s is reflected differently in the two countries. The American New Deal does not enter the literature until after World War Two, where it becomes, in hindsight, the foundation of a dangerous, unAmerican socialism. British reaction appears in the fiction of the 1930s, mainly founded on the fear that the economic situation in Britain might lead to a parallel of the political situation in Germany, so tipping the balance towards British Fascism or dictatorship.

The decades since 1960s show other themes, other differences (Chapter 5, Britain; Chapter 6, the US). The resurgence of feminism has infused the utopian genre with a new and vigorous wave. The British writers of the 1960s and early 1970s produced many satires (wry alternative perspectives on the cold war, on American involvement in international affairs, and on the nature of utopia). Feminist utopian novels begin to reappear in greater numbers overlapping with these. Although they lack the clarity of the visions of American feminist utopias, these works are engaged in the same debate. Once more the nature/culture distinction is important, though the British writers show a much higher, continuing degree of scepticism on the subject of Western culture, defending it while questioning its directions. There is a sense of impending crisis (in this, nuclear holocaust does play a role, but only as part of a spectrum of changes), and the city as the centre of culture is often depicted as embattled by a decline into barbarianism; and there is no sign of interest in the form of the small, pastoral community so enticing to American writers. The political realist strain of the past is increasingly submerged as women writers turn increasingly to allegory or ambiguity of setting, character and narrative. Where realism survives, it is in dystopian images of grey bureaucracy and urban decay.

American writers produce more clear-cut images of their dystopian targets: militarism, patriarchal hierarchy, and the repression and exclusion of women in an aggressive, materialistic society. Established religion, which had been such a sustaining force for women in earlier periods, now becomes their enemy, as a religious fundamentalism adds justification to the military-industrial complex. Their dystopias usually result from nuclear accident or war, which sometimes serves the same clearing-house function that European conflicts did for writers of the 1920s and 1930s. Although more dystopias have been written in this period than before, the balance of optimism is maintained, one exciting new development with these novels being the frequency with which they present multiple societies. As a narrative device, this heightens their writers' social message by comparing tendencies in modern society, polarised into utopia and dystopia, and emphasises the urgent need for present action to determine our future.

The utopias themselves are generally of a small scale — that is, once more communal rather than national. Their writers are aware of the nature/culture debate, and the utopias are models of mediation. Nature is no longer the enemy, nor is it inferior to culture: it has risen to a point of equal importance with 'thought and technology', re-evaluated through the ecological movement's concern with pollution of the environment, and increasing disillusion with urban life. The need to respect, rather than conquer, nature, has removed the stigma from the old association: equilibrium is maintained in the utopias by selective use of the most advanced technology. Likewise, in these utopias there is complete gender equality, for not only is there an outstanding number of women physicists and astronauts, but also an emphasis on men's nurturing qualities. These utopias develop the shared, 'human' characteristics of us all.

One small, but important, group of works exempt in part from this analysis is that of the lesbian separatist utopias. The claims of 'biology is destiny', so often used in the past by misogynists to exclude women, are here accepted and transformed into the definition of women as truly different and inherently superior to men. These writers joyfully claim nature as women's own province, and see all vestiges of contemporary culture as male-dominated and therefore unacceptable: their own utopias are predicated on a woman's culture that is derived from the natural world. These utopias are pastoral, often relying upon heightened development of the senses and 'natural' power to replace technology (i.e. using extra-sensory perception for long-range communications), and their role models are the legendary Amazons.

Thus we come full circle from the British Victorian writers. They also had inverted 'biology is destiny' as a justification of women's exclusion from circles of power, though, by taking gender difference and using it to argue *for* women's inclusion, they were not rebelling against the status quo. Modern lesbian separatists, on the other hand, do reject the institutions of dominant culture that Victorian women were so eager to enter. Hester Eisenstein has summed up the three options of feminist theory since 1970:

First, there is the option of agreeing to compete in the male-defined world of politics on its own terms, in the manner of Margaret Thatcher. Second, there is the option of withdrawing from that world, out of pessimism as to its essentially patriarchal nature, creating instead an otherworld of female retreat . . . Finally, there is the option of entering the world and attempting to change it, in the image of the woman-centred values at the core of feminism.[8]

Responses to these three options are observable throughout the history of women's utopian fiction. Late nineteenth-century British women walk a balance between the first and the third options: they do not challenge political institutions, although they wish to change the world through them. Of earlier writers, only Clyde (1909), Lane (1880–1) and Gilman (1915) join the separatist group of the 1970s in choosing the second option.

The third has proved attractive to the majority of writers: it offers a model for change in which those values or objects which they wish to preserve, whether located in the present or in the certainties of the past, are infused with new elements. These writers create societies which combine reverence for life and a harmonious balance with nature with consciously chosen aspects of culture: the peaceful use of low-resource technology to relieve drudgery and pain, and psychological and sociological understanding to forge new community bonds. All the unwanted elements of our society — aggression, pollution, sexism, ageism, alienation — are the components of dystopia.

Before we begin a closer examination of women's utopian fiction, the issues of terminology and definition call for explanation. The history of utopia in English literature begins with Thomas More's novel of that name (1516), and since then the word 'utopia' has carried several, much argued meanings. Lewis Mumford writes of 'The distinction that More, an inveterate punster, made when he chose the word utopia, as an ambiguous midterm between outopia, no place, and eutopia, the good place'.[9] Something of this original sense of ambiguity has been usefully drafted by American scholars as a means of avoiding ambiguity:

Utopia may be used as a general term covering all the various classes of utopian literature. Eutopia — although the word has unfortunately fallen out of favor — or the positive utopia refers to presentations of good places. Dystopia or the negative utopia refers to presentations of bad places. The satirical utopia refers to works where the satire is the focus of the work.[10]

I have found this distinction between utopia (genre) and eutopia (a vision of the good place) most useful, and I have therefore used it throughout the following discussion. I have also followed Sargent's lead in using anti-utopia to describe utopian satires, 'that large class of works, both fictional and expository, which are directed against utopia and utopian thought', because it describes not merely the form of these novels, but their intent.[11] If used interchangeably with dystopia, although many dystopias are explicitly anti-utopian, it masks several very real differences between them, in particular their view of human nature, and their temporal focus.

'Eutopia', or the good place which is no place, is used to describe those visionary works which depict a social state which the author presents as desirable. These imaginary societies are:

> all presented as better than any existing society because of the rationality, harmony, utility, and order prevailing within them. Furthermore the imagined social systems they embody are better in the sense that men [*sic*] living in these regimes are either morally better people, happier, more self-fulfilled, or freer because conflicts have been eliminated from their environment and personality. Utopian writings have been one expression of the belief that given reasonable, natural, and truly just institutions man's [*sic*] lot can really be immeasurably improved.[12]

The eutopia's golden age was the late nineteenth century, when the social evolutionist movement in Britain and its concomitant belief in progress (though associated with orthodox Christianity) in the US promised reform of social injustice. The utopian novels that resulted were models of prescriptive change. They differ from most of the earlier eutopias in that their visions are set in the future rather than in isolated areas of the Earth or on another planet, and that their authors made a direct connection between the imperfect world in which they lived and the more perfect world of the future. The gulf between present and future is spanned by a bridging history, in which they describe how this more perfect world might come about. Common to all writers of eutopias of this type is the belief in the malleability of human nature. Given the right conditions, human nature as it is constituted has within it the ingredients possible for change, and most eutopias of this period do not describe their perfect worlds as peopled by those so spiritualised that they are not recognisably human.

Dystopia, on the other hand (a term first used by John Stuart Mill in 1868), is a society demonstrably worse than the known world; if eutopia is the dream, dystopia is the nightmare. Dystopian writers share eutopian writers' belief in the malleability of human nature, but, while the eutopian writer depicts human nature changing for the better, the dystopian writer depicts it being manipulated for the worse. Because this manipulation is often undertaken in the name of eutopian improvement, particularly by tyrants and demagogues, the dystopia presents a warning against gullibility, and also against the utopian vision itself. As narratives, dystopias are more successful than eutopias, their tensions sustained by the psychological conflict stemming from characters' realisation of the true nature of their society, and the drama of their subsequent rebellion. (Eutopia, by contrast, suffers from literary stasis: discovered by a visitor from the 'real world', or described by an omniscient narrator, the lack of tension in eutopian society is its abiding literary flaw.) The dystopia was the dominant form of the genre in the 1920s and 1930s, and in the years after World War Two; and it continues to be so for male writers. Women writers (particularly in the US) have reversed this trend, and, moreover, through the growing practice in the 1970s of incorporating alternative societies in one novel, balance their dystopias with contrasting eutopian visions.

The anti-utopia differs from the dystopia in that its central focus is satire, rather than warning: as the name implies, it is sceptical about utopia and utopian societies. Although it may share the dystopia's view of eutopia, there is one basic disagreement between them — their attitude to human nature. Against the inherent changeability of the utopian or dystopian writer, the anti-utopian writer regards human nature as fixed and unalterable and by implication at least tainted with original sin. Yet this scepticism about human nature can be the anti-utopian's saving grace, for the very imperfections of human nature become a defence against the imposition of conformity. Much of the humour of these satires lies in the failure of attempts to pour perverse and stubborn humanity into the moulds of the perfect utopian state. There is a difference, too, in the main reference points of these two negative utopian forms. The dystopia warns of a future that the present may be

11

incubating; the anti-utopian satire concerns itself more with what is, than what may be. Anti-utopias are more commonly a British form of the genre than an American one, and most frequently appear in women's fiction in the 1920s and 1960s. While the model of the anti-utopia is Samuel Butler's *Erewhon* (1872), it is most certainly not a tradition that died with him; it has had many women proponents, and its scepticism is still heartily alive.

One of the delights of utopian fiction is the range that these three forms offer. They encompass varying narrative forms, and include concrete realism, satire and speculative and science fiction. Much can be discerned by observing not just the change in subject matter, but also the change of tone. Women writers of utopian fiction have exploited the genre's wide spectrum of possibilities, and have depicted their utopian women as heroes, not as heroines, passive and inactive. For, as Joanna Russ, utopian science fiction writer, asks: 'Our literary myths are for heroes, not heroines. What can a heroine do? What myths, what plots, what actions are available to a female protagonist?'[13] As Russ points out, however, science fiction is one of the genres that has been able to avoid the stereotyping of mainstream fiction, and the first woman writer she mentions in her *How to suppress women's writing* (1983) is Margaret Cavendish, the Duchess of Newcastle, whose *Description of a new world called the blazing world* (1666) is the first utopian work in English by a woman. Few followed in her footsteps for over a century and a half, but those who eventually did so were a lively bunch, interested in creating their own female 'heroes' and remaking the world.

While the names included in the primary bibliography of this book include many accomplished mainstream writers and most of the distinguished names in recent science fiction, there are also major and minor writers in other genres, and many authors of single works. One of the pleasures of research has been that of making new acquaintances and seeking recoverable biographical material, much of which has been included in footnotes and the bibliography. In addition, at the conclusion of each chapter there is a short section devoted to discussion of those writers, one or sometimes two, who exemplify the essential concerns of their periods, and whose interest is reflected in their writing of at least two works which examine aspects of utopianism. Perhaps it is no accident that they are also among the most persuasive writers of their periods: Lady Florence Dixie (Chapter 1); Charlotte Perkins Gilman (Chapter 2); Katharine Burdekin/Storm Jameson (Chapter 3); Ayn Rand (Chapter 4); Angela Carter/Doris Lessing (Chapter 5); Joanna Russ/

Ursula Le Guin (Chapter 6). The diversity of this list is obvious. The famous and the forgotten, polemicists of left and right, they epitomise the changes and preoccupations of over a century of women's utopian fiction. Behind them stand a multitude of other writers, each with her own visionary gleam of gold lighting the shadows of her world.

Notes

1. *A moving target* (Farrar, Straus, Giroux, New York, 1982), pp. 172–3.
2. Shulamith Firestone, *The dialectic of sex* (Jonathan Cape, London, 1970), p. 256.
3. Most particularly, Carol Farley Kessler's pioneering anthology *Daring to dream. Utopian stories by United States women 1836–1919*, (Pandora, Boston, 1984), with its annotated bibliography (1836–1984). I wish to acknowledge my own indebtedness to Kessler's work, and also to that of Daphne Patai, 'British and American utopias by women (1836–1979): an annotated bibliography, Part 1', *Alternative Futures*, vol. 4, nos. 2–3 (1981), pp. 184–206. Also invaluable have been Lyman Tower Sargent's *British and American utopian literature 1516–1975: an annotated bibliography*, 1st edn (G.K. Hall, Boston, 1979), and the manuscript of the 2nd edn (forthcoming, 1988); Glenn Negley, *Utopian literature: a bibliography with a supplementary listing of works influential in utopian thought* (Regents Press of Kansas, Lawrence, Kansas, 1977); Richard Gerber, *Utopian fantasy: a study of English utopian fiction since the end of the nineteenth century* (Routledge and Kegan Paul, London, 1955); Paul Brians, *Nuclear holocausts: atomic war in fiction, 1895–1984* (Kent State University Press, Kent, Ohio, 1987).
4. 'Is female to male as nature is to culture?' in Michelle Rosaldo and Louise Lamphere (eds), *Woman, culture and society* (Stanford University Press, Stanford, 1974), p. 84.
5. Abby Wetten Kleinbaum, *The war against the Amazons* (McGraw-Hill, New York, 1983), p. 169.
6. Rebecca West, review of *Jailed for freedom, Time and Tide*, 1927, in Dale Spender (ed.), *Time and tide wait for no man* (Pandora, London, 1984), pp. 68–9.
7. This point is made in Lyman Tower Sargent, 'English and American utopias: similarities and differences', *Journal of General Education*, vol. XXVIII, no. 1 (1976), pp. 16–22. Although there is little overlap between Sargent's pre-1900 bibliography in this short paper and mine, his points of difference hold true for women writers: the British are less technologically inclined, less anti-urban, more inclined to believe in reform and education as agents of change, and more inclined to write dystopias and satires than the Americans.
8. *Contemporary feminist thought* (Unwin, London, 1984), p. 144.
9. 'Utopia, the city and the machine' in Frank E. Manuel (ed.), *Utopias and utopian thought* (Houghton, Mifflin Co., Boston, 1965), p. 8.
10. Sargent, *Annotated bibliography*, 1st edn, p. xi.

11. Ibid., p. x.

12. Roger L. Emerson, 'Utopia' in Philip P. Wiener (ed.), *Dictionary of the history of ideas* (5 vols) (Charles Scribner's Sons, New York, 1973), vol. 4, p. 458.

13. 'What can a heroine do?' in Susan Koppelman Cornillon (ed.), *Images of women in fiction: feminist perspectives* (Bowling Green University Press, Bowling Green, Ohio, 1972), p. 7 .

1

A Nation Transformed

Some of the most remarkably independent women in fiction come to life in the British women's utopias of the late nineteenth and early twentieth centuries. Forthright yet dignified women of the future, they enter traditional political institutions, and through them transform the nation. The bibliography for this chapter is comparatively short, yet its contents introduce late-Victorian feminism in a context of one of the greatest debates of the age. Most of these writers are permeated with Victorian faith in progress, particularly through the upward movement of evolution: the conflict is between science and socialism (the secular faiths) on the one hand, and religion on the other.

However, the evolutionary feminists are in the ascendancy. Their interpretation of evolutionary theory is based on emancipation from primitive stages of society when physical force ensured power, it accepts 'biology is destiny', inverts the acknowledged role of morality in society, and, by placing women in the unique position of guardians of the future race, turns justification for exclusion into justification for involvement by asserting women's moral leadership. Their eutopias do not fit Showalter's definition of

> flights from the male world to a culture defined in opposition
> to the male tradition. Typically the feminist utopias are
> pastoral societies, where a population of prelapsarian Eves
> cultivate their organic gardens, cure water pollution, and run
> exemplary day care centers.[1]

The role model for British women utopian writers is certainly not the mythic (and guilt-laden) figure of Eve. They refuse to identify themselves with nature, and one doubts that any of these women

15

either knew about organic gardening, or would have cared for it if she did. Typically, British women's utopias are urban societies (usually a future Britain) where a handful of democratically inclined Boadiceas or Queen Elizabeth the Firsts are Members of Parliament, cure poverty and crime, and run exemplary social welfare legislation through the House of Commons. The 'progressive' role of science and technology is only challenged by religiously inclined writers, and even they are less concerned about their products than the increasing secularisation of the age, and the substitution of science for religion.

The conquest of nature is as much woman's as man's ideal, whether sanctioned by religious text or by Darwinian theory. Thoroughgoing products of their age, these women endorse the industrial revolution: where its defects are acknowledged, as in the air pollution caused by domestic or industrial coal burning, the cure is the use of more sophisticated technology, rather than less. Even a tentative, Morris-like medievalism is placed within a technological framework. The most medieval of these novels, *Mercia, the astronomer royal; a romance* (1895) set in the year 2002, suggests Trial by Champions as a means of solving international disputes, and the medieval flavour extends (tediously) into the language of the characters. Yet this is also a world of solar energy, robotised servants and flying machines, where Mercia (true Victorian that she is) looks forward to a Golden Age of Science, 'when even the elements of Nature are tamed'. (p. 167).

For so long preached the doctrine of their 'proper (domestic) sphere', late-Victorian women were far more interested in asserting their right to be co-inheritors of the power structures of current male-dominated culture than in claiming versions of a domestic-based, devalued, restrictive moral guardianship as their own visionary ideal. Victorian stereotypes of women were saturated with images of childishness, irrationality, the primitive, all elements to be overcome.

> Much of the anthropology in this period was given to documenting and glorifying the triumph of man over nature. Rousseau's savage was no longer noble, rather a living testament to civilised man's rude origins; Victorians gloried in the fact that economic, technological and cultural progress in the West had all but vanquished the remnants of natural man.[2]

'Natural woman' confined to her domestic role is equally vanquished from the sphere of culture: her mythic associations with the sub-conscious and irrational, while offering a view of woman as 'other' which is the polar opposite of the demure, self-sacrificing 'angel in the house', are likewise marginal to the male world of culture and power. They transcend the association with nature into the equally excluding status of myth.[3]

These cultural assumptions are partly shared by Victorian women utopists, who in redefining their social role scrupulously avoid identification with nature. An interest in child-care, for instance, would reinforce this association, and it is noteworthy that, in the few instances where children are discussed in these works, they are defined as 'primitive' creatures who must be disciplined in order to civilise them (the Amazons underwent the same treatment). Clapperton's *Margaret Dunmore; or A socialist home* (1888), for instance, recommends the use of a 'prison' for naughty babies: she disapproves of corporal punishment, but condones isolation to curb wilfulness (p. 143). These writers' silence on the subject of children almost matches their silence on the family generally. Although easier divorce is a constant in their eutopias, they offer no radical alternative to marriage, completely ignoring the domestic life that they were told was their 'natural' place in favour of an active, heroic public life.

Because women wish to enter rather than to challenge existing institutions, their utopias are more conservative than those of men. Male writers describe future worlds in which all social institutions *but* marriage have been radically changed; women utopians are radical only insofar as they mention marriage only in the context of a near-unanimous interest in easier divorce. Sylvia Strauss comments on the depiction of women in men's utopias of the period:

> It must have come as a shock to many women that their vaunted allies could not entertain the thought of them as other than sex objects. These iconoclasts were ready to fling aside political traditions of a thousand years' duration; challenge religious doctrines deeply imbedded in the collective unconscious; put to the test all accepted dogmas — except those that related to women's proper sphere. Whatever else women might be able to do, what contributions they could make to society, would have to take a backseat to their primary function of wifehood and motherhood.[4]

An example (and one that Strauss quotes) is that of William

Morris in his otherwise delightful *News from Nowhere* (1890). Morris so thoroughly rejects contemporary political institutions that he uses the Houses of Parliament as a repository for dung (as More's Utopians had shown *his* contempt for gold by using golden chamber pots). Yet Morris embodies Victorian attitudes to women:

> Don't you know that it is a great pleasure to a clever woman to manage a house skilfully, and to do it so that all the house-mates about her look pleased, and are grateful to her? And then, you know, everybody likes to be ordered about by a pretty woman: why, it is one of the pleasantest forms of flirtation.[5]

However, Lady Florence Dixie's *Gloriana, or The revolution of 1900* (also published in 1890) has a different ideal of the 'clever woman': she is not interested in housework or flirting, but in emancipating her sex through education, physical exercise and discipline, and through political leadership. The only house that Gloriana aspires to manage is the House of Commons.

The difference between Morris and Dixie, and their utopias, is directly related to their circumstances. Morris, impelled by the most laudable humanitarian impulse, writes as an 'insider' impatient with a world of privilege; while Lady Florence, for all her aristocratic connections, remains an 'outsider'. Oscar Wilde's definition of utopia in 'The soul of man under socialism' (again, 1890) offers a useful metaphor: 'Utopia . . . is the one country at which Humanity is always landing. And when Humanity lands there, it looks out, and, seeing a better country, sets sail. Progress is the realisation of Utopias.' Men, securely ensconced in traditional power structures, could discard them in favour of new forms of organisation; women, locked outside, needed to land on those islands. Thus, while it may be disappointing that women of this period did not challenge cultural assumptions and forge a radically different alternative to the world they knew, their focus is understandable. The tantalising, unreachable island was political suffrage, and it was there that the early feminists located their eutopias.

These works fall into three separate categories. Most numerous are the primarily feminist eutopias (14 of 20 titles = 70 per cent): Clapperton (1888); Swanwick (1888); Corbett (1889); Bevington (189?); Dixie (1890); Schreiner (1890); Wolstenholme-Elmy (1893); Mears (1895); Coleridge (1900); de Bury (1904); Dixie (1905); Hamilton (1908); Clyde (1909); Minnett (1911). The two smaller groups (each of three titles = 15 per cent) are related by common religious themes: the first group depicts alternative eutopias, the second, dystopias. The religious eutopists are Hearn (1892); Drane (1898); Nichol (1908). Two of the three dystopian works which share their principles, opposing scientific materialism in the name of religious orthodoxy, are Cobbe (1877) and Bramston (1893); and the third is an early anti-communist dystopia, Thomas (1873). Most, if not all, of these writers are feminists. Their eutopian societies, usually of a future and transformed Britain, reflect the feminist movement's priorities and its values, the effect of those battles won, and those still to be fought.

The publication dates of these novels span three decades. The mid-1880s to the first decade of the twentieth century was a period of little progress towards suffrage, the main target of the women's movement. However, although a time of feminist aspiration rather than achievement, it was a period of intense activity in the history of the utopian genre. There were many more male than female utopists during these three decades, although publication figures show an almost identical surge of interest in the genre, i.e. a burgeoning in the 1880s, which peaks in the 1890s, although thereafter women's writing declines to almost complete silence in the years immediately preceding World War One.[6] It is important to remember that these women writers were part of a flourishing literary movement, although their themes are so often different from those of men.

The classical Amazons interested many late-Victorian male writers: several feminist utopians invoked them, but with quite different results.[7] The legendary nation of women offered a desirable model of women's autonomy, although, of course, some aspects of Amazon life were either tempered or ignored. Their warlike nature was largely unacceptable when most feminists were pacifists, their aggresssive mating with male slaves inadmissible. Amazons hardly seemed fitted for a complex, urbanised, technologically advanced future society based on social reform. However, 'Amazonian' was eagerly adapted to describe larger than life women characters, compounds of impressive physical size and Victorian dignity. While 'civilising' the Amazons meant eliminating their basest associations with sensual nature (which most attracted male writers), they offered a model of female governance, untainted by associations with domesticity. Auerbach quotes the speech of an Amazon from Herodotus' *The Persian wars*: 'To draw the bow, to hurl the javelin, to bestride the horse, these are our arts — of

womanly employments we know nothing.[8] Victorian feminist
writers found in the Amazons raw material for their women citizens
of the future, equally alien to 'womanly employments'.

The first of these was Elizabeth Corbett in *New Amazonia: a
foretaste of the future* (1889). Written at the height of the 'surplus
women' debate, it provides an ingenious solution: not shipment
of women to existing colonies where there were 'surplus men', but
the government's grant of Ireland (and £50 million) to women and
their children so that they might establish their own colony. Universal suffrage is the necessary precursor to this feminist emigration
(which presumably also puts paid to the 'Irish question'), reliev-
ing pressure in a future England in which women outnumber men
by three to one and are exploited as sweated labour.[9] (Perhaps
Corbett was familiar with Jessie Boucherett's exasperated wish for
'a new planet alongside for us to export our superfluous women
to'.)[10] Six centuries after settlement, the most notably 'Amazonian' feature of the women is their size (some are seven feet tall).
Corbett is unusual in providing two time-travellers to her utopia,
one female, one male: the woman rejoices that here her 26-inch
waist is not regarded as a deformity, but the male (an effete and
weedy misogynist) sees the feminist eutopia as a dystopia. 'The men
here seem to be fools. They let the women grow up as strong and
healthy as themselves, and it would be difficult to reduce them to
civilisation again' (p. 64). Like the recidivist male of Gilman's
Herland (1915) he longs for feminine, flirtatious, impressionable
women, not feminist Amazons. However, far from lacking the
cultural imperative to 'mould civilization from the land', these
women live in a technological society: there are 'railways, water
companies, and similar great undertakings' owned by the state ('the
mother of the people'), there are electric cars and smokeless fires,
and the servants available through the 'Domestic Aid Society' carry
out their work with the latest scientific equipment. Here, where
the major cities are renamed after suffrage leaders (Besantville,
Beecherstown, Fawcetville), the uneven balance of the sexes in
England has been reversed; there are few men in this society —
just enough to provide marriage partners and to father children.

Corbett's misogynist would probably have felt equally
intimidated by the eponymous Mercia, even though she would not
have towered over him to quite the same extent:

In former times Mercia would have been considered too tall
for the ideal of womanly beauty, for she was five feet, ten

inches in height . . . Her breadth of chest indicated also that the physical part of her training had reached fullest perfection. (pp. 42, 44)

While Corbett's society is identified with the Amazons mostly through its title and through her women's size, Dixie's *Gloriana* (1890) spells out associations with the Amazons more fully. Several times in the course of the narrative the author refers to the popular writer Whyte-Melville, who

> declared in his writings, 'that if a legion of Amazons could be rendered amenable to discipline they would conquer the world'. He was right. The physical courage, of which men vaunt so much, is as nothing when compared with that greater and more magnificent virtue, 'moral courage', which women have shown that they possess in so eminent a degree over men; and hence physical courage would come as an agreeable and welcome visitor where hitherto it has been forcibly denied admission. (p. 92)[11]

Her Gloriana teaches discipline to the women of England in institutions in which

> women and girls can meet each other, and for a mere nominal fee learn to ride, to shoot with gun and rifle, to swim, to run, and to indulge in the invigorating influences of gymnastics and other exercises, calculated to strengthen and improve the physique of those taking part therein. [Also in] volunteer companies, who are drilled by the hand of discipline into smartness and efficiency. (pp. 50–1)

These are nineteenth-century counterparts of the warrior occupations of the Amazons, and intellectual pursuits are added to them, especially in Gloriana's great 'Hall of Liberty' for 'women students from all parts of the world' (p. 84). This energy is not expended for conquest or power, however — rather, in the name of feminism and of democracy, 'which means progress, comfort, and happiness for the toiling millions' (p. 182).

Clyde's considerably later *Beatrice the sixteenth* (1909) moves away from contemporary problems. Her nation of women, Armeria, is located somewhere in Asia Minor. It is a slave-owning monarchy ruled by a queen, whose women fight with sword, javelin and dart, and who speak a language compounded from Greek and Latin. The utopian traveller, Mary Hatherley, MB, explorer and geographer, finds the unfamiliar configuration of the night sky suggestive only of an era before Christ. She has stepped out of time into the world of the classical Amazons.

Despite their warlike abilities, these women live settled, civilised lives: agriculture is no stranger to them, and neither is government. Mary Hatherley symbolically rejects her own world in the decision to stay in Armeria, contracting marriage ('conjux') with an Armerian woman. Yet Clyde does not suggest a sexual relationship between these women — rather, one of love and friendship.[12] This eutopia, found 'ready made' rather than created from the known world, shows that Clyde has abandoned British society as beyond reform.

Something closer to male stereotypes of the Amazon, including identification with untamed Nature, symbolic of the threatening, if seductive, 'other', is found in Mary Coleridge's short poem, 'The white women' (1900). A footnote attributes her 'lovely, wild white women folk' who 'never bowed their necks beneath the yoke' and 'when they fight . . . cry/The war-cry of the storm' to a Malayan legend. The male narrator finds them disturbingly sensuous — they 'fling their girdles to the Western wind/Swept by desire' — but there are perils in voyeurism:

> One of our race, lost in an awful glade,
> Saw with his human eyes a wild white maid,
>   And gazing, died.

These women are 'creatures of an imagined golden age of the past, not models for the future'.[13] The same images recur in a very different context in her 'Marriage', where the 'wantonly free' maiden must die so that the sedate matron may exist.[14]

In numerical terms, the explicit or inferential Amazons are not a major development in these novels, but they are important; they show Victorian women's awareness of a stereotype often used by male writers, which they appropriate for a quite different purpose, one that emphasises their strength and independence, and their associations with culture, while male writers generally stress the fragility of Amazon government and the strength of their associations with nature.

While the Amazons appear peripherally in these novels as a symbol of female power, questions of how utopia should be constituted, and how it might be achieved, are central to the period.

The following themes emerge as the most important, and we will examine them in order: evolutionary thought and its offshoot, Reform Social Darwinism; politics and women's suffrage; the public lives of women (work); the private lives of women (sexuality, marriage and family); and religion, science and technology.

Evolution/Reform Social Darwinism

Excepting only the three religious novels of the period (Drane, Hearn, Nichol) and Clyde, the eutopias are set in a future Britain far enough from the present to allow social reform, a transformed environment and a modified programme of eugenics to have worked their changes on human nature.

Evolutionary theory was translated from biology to sociology in several ways, depending on whether conflict or co-operation was seen as the motor of progress. The Spencerian, conflict-based model underwrote *laissez-faire* capitalism, and regarded poverty and crime as the inevitable sign of lack of fitness to survive. The Reform Social Darwinists, on the other hand, emphasised the beneficent role of co-operation: they stressed the role of social cohesion in preserving and aiding the progress of the human race, and eagerly proposed means of accelerating its ascent. The malleability of human nature is an integral principle in expectations of successful social engineering through the elimination of undesirable factors in the environment. Reform Social Darwinists applied a socialist co-operative prescription to capitalist ills. The utopian genre was the perfect vehicle for illustrating and popularising their social theories, and their philosophy revived and renewed it in the 1880s and 1890s.

What were the implications of this for women? Fee argues that male anthropologists and historians interpreted the past as a series of stages leading to patriarchal authority, the monogamous family, and women's restriction to a domestic role. The conclusion was 'an interpretation of Darwinism which made the sexual division of labor part of the evolutionary process and therefore necessary for progress':[15] male-authored utopias projected this into the future with little change. Feminist writers drew different conclusions, however, interpreting evolutionary theory to form 'a model for the enforcement of female influence'.[16] Although their critique of marriage is restricted to calling for an escape hatch, they slashed at its root, presenting a view of evolution traced from primitive societies. The male had gained superiority through his physical strength, and consolidated his monopoly on public life by experience and success. However, feminist evolutionists suggested that the brute force so vital in nomadic and agricultural stages of history was now atavistic: the future required intellectual vigour and (most importantly) that 'greater and more magnificent virtue, "moral courage"' lauded by Dixie. As through the industrial and scientific revolutions the secrets of evolutionary progress had now been 'decoded', humanity held the key to the future, and was no longer blindly subservient to the laws of nature. In this sense, many late Victorians, not only feminists, felt that they stood at a crossroads of history. Technology reduced the value placed on sheer physicality; understanding of natural laws led to a higher premium on intellect; and accelerating evolutionary progress required selfless decisions based on the highest ethical standards. The role of the 'new woman' was to carry the moral burden, undertaking her mission not for the narrow world of a single family, but for a limitless horizon of future generations.

At this point, of course, the main justification for women's exclusion from public life became the main justification for their inclusion: feminists adroitly turned the restrictions of the angel in the house' in their own favour, redefining, in the name of evolution, the male-defined status quo: 'Having confined all those virtues inappropriate within the stock market or the boardroom to the hearts of their women-folk, middle-class men were then left free to indulge in all those unfortunate vices necessary for successful bourgeois enterprise.'[17] Now feminists declared these virtues essential to the new age. This argument underlies all of the utopian novels of this period except, naturally enough, those few by religious writers, and is most clearly articulated in the works of Clapperton, Dixie and Schreiner. The latter's allegorical 'Three dreams in a desert' (1890) illustrates it so graphically that hunger-striking suffragettes regarded it as 'a bare literal description of the pilgrimage of women. It fell on our ears more like an ABC railway guide in our journey than a figurative parable'.[18] In the first 'dream' the figure of woman is discovered on the ground, 'a great burden on its back'; and beside it, the figure of man, immobilised (p. 68). Her bonds crack as she strains to rise, and he explains:

> The Age-of-muscular-force is dead. The Age-of-nervous-force has killed him with the knife he holds in his hand; and silently he has crept up to the woman, and with that knife of Mechanical Invention he has cut the band that bound the

burden to her back. The Inevitable Necessity is broken. She
might rise now. (pp. 71–2)

Through the second and third dreams woman struggles alone
through a barren land, until she reaches the utopia of 'brave women
and brave men, hand in hand. And they looked into each other's
eyes, and they were not afraid. And I saw the women also hold
each other's hands' (p. 84). Woman as the modern pilgrim has not
only saved herself; she has led the salvation of '*the entire human race*'
(p. 83, original emphasis).

Jane Hume Clapperton expressed the same philosophy, but at
greater length. Her utopian novel, *Margaret Dunmore, or, A socialist
home* (1888), is sandwiched between two major theoretical works:
Scientific meliorism and the evolution of happiness (1885) and *A vision of
the future, based on the application of ethical principles* (1904). In *Vision*,
she states that 'Unconscious evolution has carried us forward from
savagery through many transitions to a state of civilisation which,
though grossly imperfect, contains within it a new element of advance.'[19] The new element is knowledge of the evolutionary process, which makes the progress of evolution possible. *Margaret Dunmore* puts Clapperton's principles into action, emphasising the role
of women as educators of men in the values of the new age, and
as the agents of evolution:

Now, one of the characteristics of an expanded domestic life
is its facilities for comparison . . . It affords a new field for
conscious natural selection. Here all the delicate relations of
human life with the inherited manners and customs that cling
about these relations will be closely observed, and put to the
test, and only such will survive as broadly merit survival by
ministering to man's social wants in promoting his greatness,
goodness, and happiness. (p. 120)

Women promote this natural selection by the choice of husbands to father their children, and it is a woman of this society
who lectures her husband on the necessity for birth control to defer
her pregnancy until she considers that her husband is ready for
fatherhood.

Dixie's *Gloriana* allots women the same role as custodians of the
future:

I believe that with the emancipation of women we solve

[over-population] now. Fewer children will be born, and those that are born will be of a higher and better physique than the present order of men. The ghastly abortions, which in many parts pass muster nowadays . . . as men, women, and children, will make room for a nobler and higher order of beings . . . who will come to look upon the production of mankind in a diseased or degraded state, as a wickedness and unpardonable crime. (p. 137)

We will return to the subject of birth control in the context of sexuality and the family: its relevance to the subjects of evolution and reform is through women's 'moral guardianship' and its role in developing a spontaneous programme of eugenics.

Other novels share this point of view, if less outspokenly. Corbett's *New Amazonia* stresses moral responsibility in a mostly female world in the care taken in breeding and educating future (and better) generations. The prologue to *Mercia, the astronomer royal* (1895) ascribes a utopian future to women's emancipation: here, mothers choose the number and sex of their children, and select intellectual and scientific pursuits for their prenatal influence. Minnett's *The day after tomorrow* (1911), although working in a shorter evolutionary time-span (1975), presents another world, in which enormous changes have occurred as a consequence of women's emancipation, although these are the result of economic change rather than selected breeding. The extent to which environmental or hereditary influences are emphasised varies with individual writers, but with all the utopians there is the sense of moulding future generations on an ascending scale of physical and intellectual health and well-being.

One of the strongest (and strangest) evolutionary messages is in the second of the poems included here — *Woman free*, by 'Ellis Ethelmer' (1893) (Elizabeth Wolstenholme, later Mrs Elizabeth Wolstenholme-Elmy).[20] She theorises that menstruation is a legacy from brutal rapes of prehistory (Schreiner's 'Age-of-Physical-Force'), which, with the aid of science, can be eliminated, transforming 'woman slave' to 'mother free'. Ethelmer's poem is doubly interesting because, apart from this fascinating thesis, she sees this utopian event as accomplished by woman combining natural wisdom and science, 'Source of the light that cheers this later day' (Stanza I).

Man's counsel helpful in that track shall be
For all his learning rich return and fee;

His philosophic and chirurgic lore,
To her imparted, swell her innate store;
Till, clothed with majesty of mind she stand,
Regent of Nature's will, in heart, and head, and hand.

(Stanza LVIII).

'Ethelmer's' seriousness can be gauged by her extensive footnoting: 32 pages of poetry carries 190 pages of footnotes, citing historians, anthropologists, and other feminists (including Dixie).[21]

What women writers contribute to the genre is a more humanised version of the eugenics argument that so propelled many male writers. Giving expression to women's traditional nurturing roles, but in a societal rather than a familial context, adds validity and weight to their evolutionary theories: it subverts, without openly violating, Victorian expectations about woman's true nature, and also furthers their claims to political emancipation.

Of course the evolutionists had their critics. The two minor sections of the genre, both orthodox Christian eutopias and anti-scientific dystopias, attack the underlying evolutionary thesis of feminist eutopias — their forms may differ, but their principles are the same. The main target of Frances Power Cobbe [Merlin Nostradamus] in *The age of science: a newspaper of the 20th century* (1877) and Mary Bramston in 'The island of progress' (1893) is scientific materialism. Another connection linking them is anti-vivisectionism. Cobbe's targets are more clearly defined: a Simian Educational Institute, the practice of euthenasia (the ashes of the dead are used to manufacture water-filters), vivisection not only of animals (there are only twelve dogs left in England), but also people (parents who do not have their children inoculated). Bramston repeats this last dystopian fear: on her 'island of progress', social deviants are submitted to the Scientific Experimenters for torture. In Cobbe's world 'infidelity respecting the sacred doctrine of Evolution' is a more serious crime than murder: the relation of the vivisector to this 'sacred doctrine' in both these works is as the inquisitor of the new faith.

During Frances Power Cobbe's long life (1800?–98), she was associated with many avenues of feminist reform; and she was also the founder (1876) of the Society for the Protection of Animals Liable to Vivisection. Coral Lansbury, in her fascinating *The old brown dog*, credits her with an unusually clear awareness of 'the connections between vivisection, pornography, and the condition of women'; and Lansbury's analysis of those connections, when applied to Cobbe's dystopia, helps to explain why the women are oppressed, excluded from culture and silenced by being denied literacy.[22] Rather than male-dominated science freeing women, it equates them with animals, thereby reducing them to that 'natural' state subservient to science. In Cobbe's future the suppression of all humanitarian values is symbolised by the coming death of the world: the 'newspaper' reports the death of the sun, and a new (eternal) Ice Age. Interestingly, she forecasts devolution, inverting the historical progression of the evolutionists.[23]

Another antagonistic view is that of Drane (Mother Francis Raphael, OSD), in *The new utopia* (1898). In her eutopia of Roman Catholic renewal she specifically rejects party politics of Whigs and Tories, Darwinian theory, and the 'new woman', condemning her for an 'affectation of learning' and 'a peculiar style of dress which finds favour in proportion as it is manly' (p. 111). With a monastic order as its spiritual core, the community in its shadow is called 'Utopia'. Drane's novel shows concern for the spiritual welfare of the working classes, and is a catholic version of the medievalism so appealing to the Victorians.

Politics

During the years when most of these novels were published the suffrage campaign moved with glacial slowness. The first debate in the House of Commons on the subject took place in 1867, the year of the Second Reform Bill. Henceforth:

> Nearly every year for the remainder of the nineteenth century, woman suffrage was debated in the House of Commons. Three times, a bill to enfranchise propertied women won a majority vote, but the bill never reached a second reading because of government indifference.[24]

Throughout the period, women had tried to work through the channels of party politics, but were betrayed without discrimination by all the major parties. Small wonder that Ray Strachey, in her history of the women's movement, *The cause* (1928), entitles her chapter on 1870–1900 'The deceitfulness of politics'.[25] Lady Florence Dixie wrote an acid letter to *The Times* (17 May 1892), pointing out the moral to be drawn from a recent Liberal betrayal: women should only canvass for political candidates who will pledge their support in writing for women's suffrage. Others learned the same lesson, and, when the militant suffrage Women's Social and Political Union (WSPU) was reorganised in 1907, renunciation of party-political affiliation became a condition of membership. It is not astonishing, therefore, that few of these writers advocate a particular political ideology, and certainly none of them meddle with party politics. The only avowedly socialist work was written before the disillusion of the 1890s (Clapperton, 1888). *Margaret Dunmore*'s partisan political basis declares socialism 'the legitimate child of freedom, although as yet a mere babe in swaddling clothes' (p. 21). Furthermore, the socialist home, 'La Maison', is an ex-nunnery donated by a woman to the socialist cause: it is built in Manchester on the site of the Peterloo Massacre (1819). It is therefore the inheritor of three traditions: a community of women, a superseded religious tradition (to be replaced by socialism, the secular 'religion'), and a landmark in English working-class radicalism.[26]

Bevington's anarchist pamphlet appeared some time in the 1890s: *Liberty: a journal of anarchistic communism* lists her as a co-contributor with Morris, Shaw and Kropotkin. One of the few British women anarchists to write a utopia, albeit a short one (the next was Edith Mannin, 1945), hers is mostly devoted to extolling the virtues of a postcapitalist society without money where poverty and crime are unknown. Mme Blaze de Bury's *The storm of London* (1904) is a fantasy based on the levelling consequences of the distintegration of all cloth through an (unexplained) supernatural cause: class divisions are swept away along with real or assumed modesty, producing a more egalitarian society. Daphne Patai draws attention to *Storm*'s source; a 'variation of Carlyle's *Sartor Resartus*', it is aimed at the 'total reform of society along socialist-anarchist lines'.[27]

The satirical 'Vision of communism' (Thomas, 1873), on the other hand, is opposed to such levelling tendencies, and presents a society where, in the interests of equality, beauty is disguised, intelligence suppressed: it is a dystopia of the lowest common denominator, of a kind to appear more frequently in the mid-twentieth century (for example, L.P. Hartley's *Facial justice*, 1960).

The transfer of the WSPU from Manchester (where it had been formed in 1903) to London (1906) began a new era, one of public demonstration, civil disobedience and confrontation which turned government indifference a variety of reactive colours. During the years of increasing militant suffrage activity there was a decline in the publication of utopias, both male- and female-authored. Yet there was one 'wonderfully witty cautionary tale', a play written by two WSPU members, Cicely Hamilton and Christopher St John (Christabel Marshall), which was very successful in the West End.[28] *How the vote was won* was based on a Women Writers' Suffrage League pamphlet by Hamilton (1908), and although the play does not examine a utopian society, its outcome is certainly utopian. Women act out men's 'pious fraud about women's place in the world' (p. 24): they go on strike, hand over their possessions to the WSPU, and quarter themselves either on male relatives or in the workhouses. As a result, the men are soon actively campaigning for votes for women, anxious to get their wives back to work, and remove their sisters and aunts from an unwelcome dependence. One of the few works that presents women's collective action to achieve a goal (see also Waisbrooker, Chapter 3), it is a thoroughly modern farce, reminiscent of Aristophanes' *Lysistrata*.

However, most of the earlier works dealt with a world in which women have gained the vote, and women politicians have gone into action. It is obvious that women of this period were not interested in political suffrage simply for their potential influence as voters, but to take an active hand as Members of Parliament. Details of the passage of legislation rarely form the substance of these novels: the changes leading to a utopian future are usually described after the fact, and ascribed directly to the women's vote and the action of women Members of Parliament. Some writers use special prefaces to explain them: Corbett, 1889; Mears, 1895; Minnett, 1911. Corbett takes her stand for suffrage on the current controversy between 'women' and 'ladies'.[29] In the novel she explains the society that women would found, with nationalised industries, bans on tobacco, alcohol and meat-eating, rejuvenation of the aged, free education, and relaxed divorce laws. Mears's introduction describes women's political influence in the future bringing easier divorce, birth control, 'servant' machines and professional employment for women (although the job description of the Mercia of her title looks backward rather than forward). The narrative applauds the action of 'lady MPs' who, assisted by 'influential wives', aid the liberation of Turkish women. Minnett's list of legislation directly attributable to women includes divorce reform, national insurance, tariff reform, heavier taxation of the rich, an improved, free colonisation scheme and a peace charter.

Dixie's *Gloriana* (1890) is the woman politician *par excellence*. She enters Parliament as a male, Hector L'Estrange (a subterfuge that she has successfully carried off at both Eton and Oxford), and once elected she uses her considerable rhetorical powers to argue for women's emancipation. Although she fails initially she is (as Hector) offered the Prime Ministership, but here the exigencies of a rather melodramatic plot intervene. Later she becomes the first woman Prime Minister in her own name. The final chapter, a retrospective from 1999, introduces the reader to a utopian world that women have made, where 'poverty and misery are things no longer known' (p. 345).

Much of *Gloriana* reads like an uncanny forecast of the militant suffrage movement, for their 'precision, their regalia, their marshals and captains, had a decided military flavour'.[30] The *Daily Express* (14 June 1908) described a suffrage parade as 'one of the most wonderful and astonishing sights that has ever been seen since the days of Boadicea'. Dixie's novel is quite prescient, including as leader of her women's quasi-military corps Flora Desmond, 'The Captain', forerunner of the WSPU's Flora Drummond, 'The General' (c. 1879–1949) given her nickname 'because of her pugnacity, and her habit of riding a horse at the head of the suffragette processions, in paramilitary dress'.[31]

Work

The first women's colleges opened in London at mid-century (Queen's, 1848; Bedford, 1849), although the conferral of degrees at the older universities did take some time (Oxford, 1919; Cambridge, 1947). Professional recognition for women was almost as slow (British Medical Association (1875), Dental Association (1895), the Institutes of Chemistry (1892) and Architecture (1898)); and legal and engineering professional societies did not admit women until after World War One.[32] Expanded opportunities for teaching with the beginning of compulsory secondary education for both sexes (1870), the professionalisation of nursing, and the role of philanthropic activities in the transition to paid social work, all increased the opportunities for middle-class women to enter public life, and they became, as Holcombe concludes, 'an essential part of the country's labour force' by 1914.[33] Just how essential is the nub of Hamilton and St John's *How the vote was won*. After all, argues a suffragette:

the majority of men in this country shouldn't for years have kept alive the foolish superstition that all women are supported by men. For years we have told them it was a

31

delusion, but they could not take our arguments seriously. (p. 24)

The women who strike are a cook, housemaid, governess, writer, owner of a dressmaking business, music-hall singer and boarding-house proprietress. The list is hardly one of professional women, though perhaps to include them would have tempered the comic effect of a most successful play.[34] It also raises the question of class, for not only men lose their employees in this strike of working- and middle-class women: 'The duchesses are out in the streets begging people to come in and wash their kids. The City men are trying to get taxi men in to do their typewriting' (p. 30).

There is a general absence of professional women in earlier novels, apart from the teachers in *Margaret Dunmore* and *The new Amazonia*. One suspects class bias, especially as American utopias of the same period offer a fascinating range of occupations for women. The biographer of Barbara Bodichon, an organiser of the Society for the Promotion of Employment for Women (founded 1859), comments on prevailing attitudes:

> In England custom still ruled supreme, and it required great courage on a woman's part to earn a living at all, let alone to adopt some quite original manner of doing it. 'Propose any new work for women,' said one of the pioneers, 'and you are sure to be encountered by a sneer.' To earn money was to lose social caste. It was an inexorable law.[35]

Although, as Holcombe points out, the situation had changed very much by the beginning of the twentieth century, there was still a stigma associated with 'trade' that was bound to limit the imaginations of the mostly middle-class women writers. The woman Member of Parliament therefore steps into an appropriately prominent public role: she has power, respectability and status — and, furthermore, these are untainted by payment. This suited the 'moral mission's' aim of applying feminist principles to government, and did so without any suggestion of pecuniary self-interest.

One recurrent theme of American women's writing during this period, the exploitative nature of *laissez-faire* capitalism, particularly as it oppressed working-class women, is mentioned only in Hearn's religious utopia, *1900? A forecast and a story* (1892). She berates a callous millionaire industrialist who employs women at 50 per cent of the male wage: 'A woman is well off if she gets ten shillings a week, and she does as much work as a man will do for a pound' (p. 22).

Like American women writers she is equally strong in condemning socialist agitators (whom she considers just as exploitative), and advocates the establishment of co-operative communities, where both women and men will work with dignity and have proper rewards for their labour.

Meanwhile, what occupations for women do these writers portray? Of course, a woman doctor and lawyer can have little to do in an achieved utopia, but a woman scientist and engineer should find ample scope for their talents. *Mercia*'s introduction describes women of the future learning chemistry and other sciences in order to influence their unborn children; but Mercia herself is astronomer royal, a rank that in the novel's quasi-medieval context suggests court astrologer (particularly as celibacy is a requirement of the post, whether the incumbent is female or male).

Minnett introduces the admirable social effects of 'women legislators'. Clyde's 'Mary Hatherley, MB, explorer and geographer' is a more original creation, but her profession seems important mostly as a plausible narrative device to explain her presence alone in an isolated area of Asia Minor.

Sexuality/Marriage/Family

Once political power for women is imaginatively assumed, its exercise carries a nurturant aspect. Late Victorian women were not eager to reverse the roles assigned to male and female, or to adopt the worst aspects of masculine behaviour. Their reaction against the double standard of morality was never as strong as that of American women (see Chapter 2), and never enters the contentious areas of marital fidelity or prostitution.

The strong, autonomous women of these novels are often single; if married, they are childless, and their husbands are distanced by some narrative device. Only Clyde (1909) is prepared to step into a moral quagmire by proposing any alternative to marriage (other than easier divorce), but her 'conjux' is platonic monogamy between two women. She overcomes the problems of sex and reproduction: her women adopt daughters from nearby 'barbarian' tribes, thus evading the tradition that Amazons had intercourse with expendable male slaves, and killed their sons.

Although one might not reasonably expect sexuality to be a

discussed element of future women's lives during this period, veiled references to birth control might be expected. Of course, the evolutionary reformers foresee fewer births, and one of women's roles in the new future is to choose not only their husbands, but also the number of their children. By every criterion known to woman, in eutopia every child must be a wanted child. This form of 'spontaneous' eugenics, control by women's moral choice, underwrites most of these eutopias. 'Natural selection' passes naturally to women, and underwrites their hopes for the future. The birth control movement of the late nineteenth century was associated with 'free love' and dominated by men. Feminists proposed instead 'continence and psychic love', which emphasised the spiritual components of marriage, and de-emphasised sexual intercourse: 'It may be that because bodily integrity was a basic human right for which men had never had to strive and would probably not understand.'[36] Prostitution, incest, the low legal age of consent for girls, and 'sex-slavery' in marriage were enemies fought by feminists and some male reformers of the period, all social evils which are a consequence of male sexual predation. Their appearance in these works is limited to Wolstenholme-Elmy's footnotes, and some brief references in Dixie's *Izra*. It was not artificial birth control that women proposed, but greater self-restraint by men. Annie Besant 'in spite of her feminist views has never become one of the heroines of the movement'.[37] But then, Besant was at variance with other feminists, promoting artificial birth control because she believed that 'men were incapable of self-control and that prostitution was inevitable'.[38] The only one of these writers to so much as hint at anything other than moral sanctions is Clapperton, who discreetly refers to lessons on physiology for the members of her commune, and the use of 'unhurtful scientific methods' to defer conception (p. 126).

Wolstenholme-Elmy and Dixie (1903–5) are the most outspoken about 'voluntary motherhood', continence and psychic love. Wolstenholme-Elmy, as a sex education pioneer, suggested in her booklets the use of the safe period; and in *Woman free* she proposes the separation of intercourse (for conception only) and psychic love. So too does Dixie, who, although she does not exclude marriage from *Izra*'s eutopia, declares that 'woman must be given perfect sexual freedom and acknowledged as owner of herself' (26 August 1905, p. 132). However, it is freedom, not licence.

In this land there is no enforced motherhood. Women are free.
It is their prerogative to give life to another only when they

choose, and it is their aim and glory to create perfection in
each being conceived. Wander where you will in Loveland,
you will find no sign of the prostituted married slave . . . Over-
reproduction in the human species is unknown. (5 December
1903, p. 356)

For the other women writers we can probably safely assume that,
once women have political power and their moral power increases,
this will produce its healthful effect on women's sexuality and
reproduction. From the response in the novels it seems that their
likely choice is celibacy. It is notable that the only one to marry
within the bounds of the fiction is Gloriana (named after Elizabeth
the First, the Virgin Queen); that she is separated from her fiancé
shortly before their intended wedding, and that the narrative breaks
off with their reunion, resuming with a retrospective chapter after
their death.

Within this eutopian context, marriage as an ideal (if not a practice) is purified and takes on new meaning, but only within the context of easier divorce. Whatever the dystopian writers may have
to say about undesirable contemporary attitudes, they can find no
radical alternative to marriage to satirise, not even the subject of
easier divorce. Inequalities still existed in the law in spite of the
changes effected by the Matrimonial Causes Act (1857, with succeeding amendments), and divorce was not only harder for women
to obtain, but the expense was often beyond them.[39]

One *literary* difference between the utopian works of female and
male writers is directly attributable to this attitude to marriage. The
female 'hero' may marry, but, if this is the case, it usually occurs,
in true romantic style, at the conclusion to the narrative. There
is one further safeguard. Male writers usually use first-person nar-
rators, nineteenth-century males who travel to the future, examining the new society with the help of an older male, their utopian
mentor; and more often than not the mentor has a young daughter,
whom the traveller courts. His education into utopian values
parallels his love affair, adding the romantic interest to an often
static discussion of the economics, government, etc. of the ideal
world.

Women writers, on the other hand, intent on exploring the role
of the woman of the future as an active 'hero' rather than submissive
heroine, cannot introduce an unevolved Victorian male as a fit
partner for the emancipated woman of the future. Women writers
therefore commonly use omniscient narration: the romantic interest,

where there is one, is between a woman of the future and her male counterpart, who has evolved to her moral level. (Clapperton calls for a 'New Man' to partner the 'New Woman', but does not create him herself.) Notably, the only woman writer in this group to use the 'dream' formula of time travel so popular with male authors is Corbett, but she does not conclude her novel with a romance.

Although husbands may linger on the margins of these utopias, children are banished. References are several times made to them, by Corbett and Clapperton, but each time it is in relation to their discipline and training. Children, because they must be 'civilised' like other aspects of nature, are important only as products of the new age, the result of conscious 'natural selection'. Within this context, birth control is not a means of emancipating individual women, but a social benefaction, calculated to space births and to improve the quality of the next generation.

Science and technology

In the late nineteenth century science was viewed as the great emancipator, Schreiner's 'Knife-of-Mechanical-Invention' and Elmy's cheering light. Although many women had been enslaved by the Industrial Revolution, many had also been emancipated by it: it was, of course, largely a matter of class. Barbara Bodichon (of the Society for the Promotion of Employment for Women) hailed in lyrical terms the first sewing-machine that she ever saw, declaring that: 'life in slop-shops would be revolutionised', though she recognised that it made new occupations for women 'even more necessary to find'.[40] While the society did not have an enormous impact on women's unemployment, it did take advantage of the new technology, training women to use printing presses and typewriting machines.

The majority of writers find increased technology and urban life to be the way of true progress. Mechanical servants, electric railways, flying machines, clean air — all are far from original in Victorian futuristic literature, but their presence shows that women, like men, accepted the role of technology, and rejected the non-technological pastoral utopia. These marvels are accepted as natural to eutopian future, but there is a remoteness about scientific advance: no working women chemists, pilots or inventors take their places in these future worlds. Absent also is domestic feminism, the interest of American women writers in co-operative housework, except for a fragmentary reference by Clapperton. However, the other women utopists are only too keen to remove themselves from the domestic sphere, rejecting its limitations for the political world of power and influence.

Also absent is any feeling for eutopian communities of women. None of the many communities of women in existence offered appropriate settings (religious houses, women's colleges, settlement houses).[41] It is, as Auerbach observes, America where 'the idea of female communities seems to have been more amorphously glorious, less potentially threatening than it was in England'.[42] The settlement movement, in which some women were actively involved (though far fewer, for instance, than in America), is reflected only in Anna Swanwick's pamphlet *An utopian dream* (1888), the text of an appeal for money to purchase the freehold of the Royal Victoria Hall (the 'Old Vic') for use as a 'People's Palace' for the poor of South London.[43] Separatist communities of women would not only have been too marginal to the dominant culture and its power structures to suit most women, but 'potentially threatening' in several ways. Until quite recently the only British utopian novel to propose a women's community has been the eighteenth-century *Millenium Hall* (1762) by Sarah Robinson Scott [A Gentleman on His Travels]. A country house college and refuge for gentlewomen, this community extends its charity to the surrounding countryside. Popular enough to go through four editions between 1762 and 1778 (and recently re-issued by Virago), its pious, reformist character undoubtedly appealed to those committed to establishing women's colleges, without the conventual taint that their opponents found so distasteful.[44] Its nineteenth-century equivalent, sadly, was Tennyson's *The princess* (1847, written shortly before the first women's college opened in 1848), which ridicules the women's university as 'unnatural', Amazonian (in the pejorative sense) and condemned to failure once its moving spirit falls in love with a man.

The communitarian impulse in Britain, particularly compared with that in America, was never strong. It emerges most consistently in the work of eutopian religious writers. Hearn shows distrust of the city and its vices, setting her model town for workers in the Welsh countryside, isolated from the contagion of the slums. No Luddite, she does not propose the destruction of factories, merely their relocation in healthier surroundings. Nature does play a regenerative role, but education has a much greater one; the town is equipped with libraries, reading rooms and meeting halls. Drane's

Roman Catholic *The new utopia* (1898) provides the same kind of regeneration in a community outside London, but through the spiritual association with a monastery.

If the work of any one woman sums up the dominant tone and preoccupations of this period it is Lady Florence Dixie (1855–1905). An ardent feminist, author of two eutopias, *Gloriana* (1890) and the shorter 'Loveland' embedded in her later *Izra* (1902–5, serialised in *The Agnostic Journal*), she creates strong women characters who transcend the boundaries of gender and put her reforms into action.[45] A rebel against injustice wherever she saw it, Lady Florence (younger sister of the Marquess of Queensberry, Wilde's 'screaming, scarlet Marquess'), wrote and spoke for a variety of causes. She was not a member of any of the influential suffrage organisations, and from at least 1900 lived in her native Scotland and so was away from mainstream politics; but she continued to write. The reforms that she proposes in *Gloriana* are political and physical, and her active, courageous hero Gloriana, who as Hector L'Estrange leaves Eton and Oxford a national hero (as both cricketer and writer), is the *alter ego* of Lady Florence, explorer (Patagonia), war correspondent (South Africa), crack rider and self-styled 'female Nimrod' (until her later opposition to blood sports), travel writer, novelist and political pamphleteer.[46] Her emphasis on the need for women's physical activity as a means to emancipation is similar to that of her contemporary, the American Charlotte Perkins Gilman, but Dixie (although far from wealthy herself) does not share Gilman's interest in women's economic independence.

From the political and quasi-military world of *Gloriana* to *Izra*, some changes take place. Although she is still interested in government her later view is more socialist (in 'Loveland' 'all land is administered by the state . . . and no single being or company can amass wealth on the toil of others' (6 February 1904, p. 84). Evolutionary progress is still a central point, but its end is far removed from the transformed yet familiar London of the earlier book. The dream vision of 'Loveland' will not be reached 'until we have cycled over Evolution's track, and risen to its plane' (20 February 1904, p. 115). The people of 'Loveland' are spiritually much further advanced than *Gloriana*'s Londoners of 1999, even being able to communicate through extra-sensory perception. Dixie has not only moved towards the esoteric in her later years; the distancing of eutopia from the real world in her later novel is a sign of her declining optimism as the possibility of reform retreats. This declining optimism was a general trend during the Edwardian years. The number of utopias published fell off rapidly in the first two decades of the century. When it rose again after World War One, it was with a very different temper indeed.

Notes

1. Elaine Showalter, *A literature of their own. British women novelists from Brontë to Lessing* (Virago, London, 1979), pp. 4–5.

2. Elizabeth Fee, 'The sexual politics of Victorian social anthropology' in Mary S. Hartman and Lois Banner (eds), *Clio's consciousness raised* (Harper Colophon, New York, 1974), pp. 86–102. Fee examines the theories of Maine, Bachofen, McLennan, Lubbock, Morgan and Spencer as they traced social evolution from primitive to contemporary society. With the exception of the American, Morgan, all consider the patriarchal model of the monogamous family 'inextricably linked with the progress of civilization' (p. 101).

3. For a complex analysis of these, see Nina Auerbach, *Woman and the demon, the life of a Victorian myth* (Harvard University Press, Cambridge, Mass., 1982).

4. 'Women in "utopia"', *The South Atlantic Quarterly*, vol. 75 (1976), pp. 115–31.

5. *News from Nowhere, or, An epoch of rest* (Monthly Review Press, London, 1966), pp. 76–7.

6. Lyman Tower Sargent, *British and American utopian literature 1516–1975: an annotated bibliography*, 1st edn (G.K. Hall, Boston, 1979), lists 57 British entries for the period 1890–9 (including most, but not all, of the novels discussed here), and 52 for the period 1900–9, which are mostly by male writers, and are predominantly anti-socialist or anti-feminist.

7. These usually involved the arrival of a single male on an Amazon island where males are kept for stud purposes; the irresistibility of that male for the ruling Amazon, and the restoration of 'normal' relationships on the island, or the elopement of the male and his (suitably adoring) Amazon princess.

8. *Communities of women: an idea in fiction* (Harvard University Press, Cambridge, Mass., 1978), p. 4.

9. The true ratio was never this high. A. James Hammerton, *Emigrant gentlewomen: genteel poverty and female emigration, 1830–1914* (Croom Helm, London, 1979), gives figures of 1,042 females per 1,000 males in 1851, 1,055 in 1881, 1,068 in 1901 (England and Wales), Table 2, p. 29. Hammerton also notes that 'From 1880 to 1914 a variety of female emigration organisations came into being, whose leaders, although women, emphatically were not feminists' (p. 148).

10. 'How to provide for superfluous women' in Josephine E. Butler (ed.), *Woman's work and woman's culture. A series of essays* (Macmillan, London, 1869), pp. 27–48. Boucherett's real suggestion here is the emigration of more men, to raise the employment opportunities for women at home.

11. G.J. Whyte-Melville's *Sarchedon, A legend of the great queen* (1871; 188?);

1899) is a Babylonian romance in the same style as Rider Haggard's *She*.

12. Twenty-five years after *Beatrice*, Clyde published *Eve's sour apples*, a polemical work in which she condemns sexual relations as demeaning and vulgar, substituting artificial reproduction, and advocates close relationships between women, but *not* homosexuality.

13. Showalter, *A literature*, p. 192.

14. Theresa Whistler, Introduction, *The collected poems of Mary Coleridge* (Hart-Davis, London, 1954), p. 50.

15. Strauss, 'Women in "utopia"', p. 127.

16. Showalter, *A literature*, p. 185.

17. Barbara Taylor, *Eve and the new Jerusalem: socialism and feminism in the nineteenth century* (Virago, London, 1983), p. 126.

18. Lady Constance Lytton, quoted in Martha Vicinus, *Independent women: work and community for single women, 1850–1920* (Virago, London, 1985), p. 273.

19. (Swan Sonnenschein, London, 1904), p. 328.

20. Wolstenholme (1834–1918) was an active feminist, particularly engaged in education and the suffrage movement. She is author of one of the earliest sex-education books for children, *The human flower* (1892). Sensitive discussion of her life and work may be found in Lee Holcombe, *Wives and property: reform of the married women's property law in nineteenth century England* (Martin Robertson, Oxford, 1983), pp. 118–25, and Sheila Jeffreys, *The spinster and her enemies: feminism and sexuality 1880–1930* (Pandora, London, 1985), pp. 28–35.

21. She quotes from McLennan, Mill and Darwin on the evolution of society, and on women's position in tribal and technological communities. In describing how the violence of earlier societies has been replaced by greater understanding, she places social evolution at the service of her feminism.

22. *The old brown dog. Women, workers and vivisection in Edwardian England* (University of Wisconsin Press, Madison, 1985), p. 129.

23. In the title essay of her later book *The scientific spirit of the age and other pleas and discussions* (Smith, Elder, London, 1888), p. 4, Cobbe distinguishes between Science (with which she has no quarrel) and the 'Scientific Spirit' (with which she has). She quotes from Darwin's admission, in his then recently published *Life*, of the gradual loss of his aesthetic and religious sense as his studies progressed.

24. Andrew Sinclair, *The better half. The emancipation of the American woman* (Harper and Row, New York, 1965), p. 281. For a complete analysis of suffrage and party politics, see Constance Rover, *Woman's suffrage and party politics in Britain 1866–1914* (Routledge and Kegan Paul, London, 1967).

25. (1928; reprinted by Virago, London, 1978.)

26. Peterloo was a 'constitutionalist reform demonstration' of between 60,000 and 100,000 that ended in violence. The historian E.P. Thompson calls the two most important points about it 'the actual bloody violence of the day' and 'the sheer *size* of the event, in terms of its psychological impact and manifold repercussions. It was without question a formative experience in British political and social history' (original emphasis). *The making of the English working class* (Penguin, Harmondsworth, 1974), pp. 752, 754.

27. 'British and American utopias by women 1836–1979), *Alternative*

Futures, vol. 4, nos 2–3, Spring-Summer 1981 p. 192. The National Union Catalogue lists for Mme de Bury (whose full listing is Blaze de Bury, Marie Pauline Rose (Stewart) Baronne) a number of critical works on Molière, Racine, Byron and Shelley.

28. Carole Hayman, 'Note on performance' in Dale Spender and Carole Hayman (eds), *How the vote was won and other suffragette plays* (Methuen, London, 1985), p. 21. Cicely Hamilton (1872–1952), actress, playwright, essayist and journalist, was closely identified with the suffrage campaign, having formed the Women Writers' Suffrage League. Her best-known work is *Marriage as a trade* (1909).

29. An anti-suffrage letter to the *Nineteenth Century Magazine* signed by 104 'ladies' drew a suffrage reply to the *Fortnightly Review* signed by 2,000 'women'. Corbett upbraids the ladies for treachery, and contrasts them ('idle parasites of men') with women ('independent fighters for women's rights'). Preface, unpaginated.

30. E. Sylvia Pankhurst, *The suffragette movement: an intimate account of persons and ideals* (1931; reprinted as a Kraus Reprint, New York, 1971), p. 266.

31. Olive Banks, *The biographical dictionary of British feminists* (Wheatsheaf, Brighton, Sussex, 1985), pp. 70–1.

32. Charlotte Haldane, *Motherhood and its enemies* (Chatto and Windus, London, 1927), p. 109.

33. Lee Holcombe, *Ladies at work: middle class working women in England and Wales, 1850–1914* (Archon, Hamden, Conn., 1973), p. 20.

34. The Methuen edition quotes an (undated) review from the *Pall Mall Gazette*: 'The fact that it is so acutely controversial is not at all against it — is, in fact, a virtue rather than a defect, for the Theatre of Ideas is upon us' (p. 20).

35. Hester Burton, *Barbara Bodichon* (John Murray, London, 1949), p. 112.

36. Jeffreys, *The spinster*, p. 33. 'Continence and psychic love' is the title of her second chapter.

37. J.A. and Olive Banks, *Feminism and family planning in Victorian England* (Liverpool University Press, Liverpool, 1964), p. 97.

38. Jeffreys, *The spinster*, p. 33.

39. Many women therefore accepted legal separation with maintenance as an alternative. In *Wives and property*, Holcombe cites an average of 800 petitions for divorces and decrees of nullity in the early twentieth century, while 'magistrates courts were issuing well over 7,000 maintenance orders annually' (pp. 99, 107).

40. Burton, *Barbara Bodichon*, p. 137.

41. Vicinus, in her *Independent women*, documents their history.

42. Auerbach, *Communities of women*, p. 23.

43. Swanwick (1813–97) was with Cobbe a co-signee of Mill's 1866 petition for female suffrage, and associated with Queen's, Bedford and Girton (Cambridge) Colleges.

44. Scott, with her companion Lady Barbara Montagu, lived a muted variant of *Millenium Hall*, restricted by their modest income (the fictional Hall has combined assets of £86,000). For an account of Mary Astell's attempt to found a women's college, see Ruth Perry, *The celebrated*

Mary Astell (University of Chicago Press, Chicago, 1986).

45. In 1890 Dixie also published *Aniweee; or the warrior queen: a tale of the Araucanian Indians*. A rattling adventure yarn, it contains three heroic young women, British Topsey, Araucanian Indian Aniweee, and a nameless queen of the Trauco tribe. It is truly 'a feminist tale with female heroes . . . in which Indians are the "good guys"'. Catherine Barnes Stevenson, *Victorian women travel writers in Africa* (Twayne, Boston, 1982), p. 82.

46. For a feminist interpretation of her life and work, see Stevenson, *Victorian women*; and for one noticeably less so, although a valuable source of information on the entire family, see Brian Roberts, *The mad bad line. The family of Lord Alfred Douglas* (Hamish Hamilton, London, 1981).

Bibliography of Primary Material

Note: * denotes works cited in other bibliographies, but not located or read. Works are cited in chronological order of publication. References to works included in the chapter-specific primary bibliographies are cited internally in the text.

Thomas, Bertha (1873) 'A vision of communism', *Cornhill's Magazine*, September, pp. 300–10

Cobbe, Frances Power [Merlin Nostradamus] (1877) *The age of science: a newspaper of the 20th century*, Ward, Lock and Tyler, London

Clapperton, Jane Hume (1888) *Margaret Dunmore, or, A socialist home*, Sonnenschein, Lowrey and Co., London

Swanwick, Anna (1888) *An utopian dream and how it may be realised*, Kegan Paul, Trench and Co., London

Corbett, Elizabeth Burgoyne (1889) *New Amazonia: a foretaste of the future*, Tower Press, London

Dixie, Florence Caroline (Douglas) (1890) *Gloriana, or The revolution of 1900*, Henry and Co., London

Bevington, L.S. (189?) *Common sense country*, James Tochatti, Liberty Press, London

Hearn, Mary Ann [Marianne Farningham] (1892) *1900? A forecast and a story*, James Clarke, London

Schreiner, Olive (1890) 'Three dreams in a desert' in *Dreams*, T. Fisher Unwin, London

Bramston, Mary (1893) 'The island of progress' in *The wild lass of Estmere*, Seeley and Co., London

Wolstenholme-Elmy, Elizabeth C. [Ellis Ethelmer] (1893) *Woman free*, Women's Emancipation Union, Congleton

Mears, Amelia Garland (1895) *Mercia, the astronomer royal; a romance*, Simpkin, Marshall, Hamilton Kent and Co., London

Drane, Augusta Theodosia (Mother Francis Raphael OSD) (1898) *The new utopia*, Catholic Truth Society, London

Coleridge, Mary (1900; reprinted 1954) 'The white women' in Theresa Whistler (ed.), *The collected poems of Mary Coleridge*, Hart-Davis, London

de Bury, Mme F. Blaze [Francis Dickberry] (1904) *The storm of London:*

a social rhapsody, John Lang, London

*Kingscote, Adelina Georgina [Lucas Cleeve] (1905) *A woman's aye and nay*, John Lang, London

*Young, F.E. (1905) *The war of the sexes*, John Long, London

Dixie, Florence Caroline (Douglas) (1906) *Izra, a child of solitude*, John Lang, London (All references are to the serialisation in *The Agnostic Journal*, September 1902–November 1905.)

Hamilton, Cicely and Christopher St John (Christabel Pashall) (1908; reprinted 1985) *How the vote was won*, Methuen, London

Nichol, Mrs C.A. Scrymsour (1908) *The mystery of the North Pole*, Francis Griffiths, London

Clyde, Irene (1909) *Beatrice the sixteenth. Being the personal narrative of Mary Hatherley, M.B., explorer and geographer*, George Bell and Sons, London

Minnett, Cora (1911) *The day after tomorrow*, F.V. White, London

*Harrison, Eva (1915) *Wireless messages from other worlds*, J.N. Fowler, London

2
Individualism and the Ties
of the Community

American women's utopias of the late nineteenth century are much more numerous than the British, so that individual characterisation is more difficult. Charlotte Perkins Gilman's *Herland* (1915), *the* classic feminist eutopia of an all-female nation, is included in this period, as are her two other less well-known genre novels, that of America 30 years hence (*Moving the mountain*, 1911) and *Herland*'s sequel of a visitor from eutopia to the contemporary world (*With her in Ourland*, 1916). They are part of a lively, voluminous literature that includes satires, off-world romances, role reversals (both feminist and anti-feminist), classic utopias of the hidden valley or other planet, proposals for co-operative industrial villages and urban settlements, spiritualist future-worlds — the range is broad, and the ideal societies extraordinarily inventive.

There is, however, a distinctive tone to American utopianism which emerges quite sharply on comparison with British works. The same egalitarian, feminist impulse is evident in both, but the forms of its expression are quite different. The political, national, futuristic, evolutionary, secular eutopias of the preceding chapter are replaced by religious, communal, present or near-future urban or rural eutopias. Rather than silence on marriage and the family, American women suggest a spectrum of equalising reforms: they wish to rewrite the marriage service and eliminate the double standard of morality, and advocate the sharing (or automation) of domestic tasks. In the absence of a long-scale, evolutionary, eugenic perspective, their smaller-scale utopias are more often set within one generation, and their background of social darkness, deprivation and want is more frequently described in detail. Class bias is less important, and commercial employment for women more acceptable. Although tension might be expected between the strong note of individualism and an interest in functioning communities, this is resolved by locating the source of such groups in inspirational belief. These writers were undoubtedly influenced by the millennial communities of the earlier nineteenth century, and the utopian literature of the turn of the century echoes their optimistic belief in perfectionism.

The genre during this period was at its zenith in America: 190 utopian works were published during the period 1890-9, as against 70 in Britain.[1] The sheer numbers are indicative of the primarily optimistic strain of native interest. It is the optimism of the American Dream, of Locke's 'In the beginning all the world was *America*'. This was the ethos of American settlement, and of the many utopian communities founded there. It was also manifested early in American literature: Charles Brockden Brown's *Alcuin* (1798), one of the earliest American novels, includes a feminist eutopian vision, and American women were writing short utopian pieces in the first half of the nineteenth century.

There is one difference between male/female writers in the US during this period. Male writers (for example, Bellamy in his seminal *Looking backward*, 1888) favoured futuristic metropolitan utopias which indicate their interest in social evolution, although they accommodate this to orthodox Christianity rather than Darwinian theory. Women writers often adopt urban settings, but these are generally localised, and show change occurring in contemporary, rather than a future society. On one major point there is no divergence. Bellamy staunchly denied that his future Boston was socialist, a political ideology that smacked too strongly of Old World decadence, and which he summarised as 'the red flag' 'sexual novelties' and 'an abusive tone about God and religion'.[2] American writers generally are far more religiously inclined than the British, and share Bellamy's horror of socialism. Take the attitudes of several reformers of the late nineteenth century as an illustration. Jane Hume Clapperton writes favourably of the eugenic practices of the Oneida colony in Indiana, but she rejects their millenarian beliefs as 'childish theology' (*Margaret Dunmore*, p. 41). On the other hand, an otherwise favourable *Nationalist* review of a British novel includes a long paragraph regretting that it is 'outspokenly Atheistic'.[3]

One of the American women writers of the period, Lucia Mead, introduces a young woman millionaire who is criticised for combining belief in evolutionary theory with a less than literal reading of the Bible: she offsets the secular implications of this in her

45

discussion with an English socialist (friend of William Morris), a 'straw man' for socialism, whose theory she considers will: '[do] away with individuality and [crush] out some of the deepest human instincts' (*Memoirs of a millionaire*, p. 91). In the eutopian novels of the 1880s and 1890s, socialist or anarchist agitators frequently make their appearance, and are more often English troublemakers than they are native-born Americans. The time-frames of the two matriarchal societies discussed here, *Mizora* and *Herland*, are revealing. They depend on long evolutionary scales to establish their new societies of women (and, incidentally, to place men as 'atavistic') and so their histories are pre-dated 3,000 and 2,000 years. This time-frame also handily makes their societies pre-Christian, avoiding any charge of atheism. They thus manage to include longer evolutionary vistas than any of the British women, but without a conflict between religion and theory.

American women writers more often locate their utopias within a remarkably short time-frame. Whereas a utopia in the future is quarantined in time, one in isolated areas of the Earth or on another planet is quarantined in space; and both of these distancing devices are frequently used. However, so too is a native domestic setting, which reveals the highest optimism about achieving eutopia. How long might this take in the United States? Bellamy's *Looking backward* (1888) moves almost 120 years into the future, from 1887 to 2000. Yet in the first issue of *The Nationalist*, the official organ of the Nationalist Clubs which formed in the novel's wake, the editorial quotes him from 'a late letter':

> We must do all we can to shut the mouths of those who talk of needing centuries to make over society. No sort of talk, not even open opposition, is so foolish or so demoralizing as this. Fifty years will see our entire programme accomplished.[4]

Women writers obviously felt the same way. Waisbrooker (1894) thought it would take 50 years; Cooley (1902) 100 years (she dates her story from the dawning day of the twenty-first century, which makes 100 years the natural 'jump'); and Gilman (1911) placed the wholesale regeneration of the United States at 30 years. All three of these women are also writing of change on a national rather than a limited communal scale. Against this background of optimism, it is less surprising that women who propose more localised reforms should suggest the possibility of immediate, not deferred, change.

The twin strains of American pragmatism and idealism are admirably demonstrated by their utopias.

The social criticism of all these writers addresses not only middle-class problems of a division of labour, inequalities in marriage and the results of a double standard of morality, but also the sweated labour of working-class women, unemployment for both sexes during the depression, prostitution, venereal disease and alcoholism, and the disruption caused by increased immigration. Their descriptions of dystopian reality contrast with their eutopian visions of independent business and professional women, and of women philanthropists involved in education and reform. The protagonists of these novels, committed to ideals of equality and social justice, are role models for their readers, combining economic independence and the responsibilityy of a job, with a refined social conscience and the abilty to change society.

The cultural patterns of British and American life are reflected in their very different utopias. As noted, the belief in theories of biological and social evolution that require postponement of utopia to such a distant future in British utopias is replaced by a belief in the possibility of immediate, inspirational change. The associations that affected British women were of less consequence, particularly the invidious association with 'nature' as compared with 'culture'. Indeed, American women (particularly in the pioneering states in the West) were regarded as the guardians of culture, though this was defined in an aesthetic and moral sense, rather than that more embracing definition of 'thought and technology' given in the introduction. Rebecca West, reviewing Doris Stevens's *Jailed for freedom* in *Time and Tide* in 1927, examines cause and effect:

> The American struggle for the vote was much more difficult than the English for the simple reason that it was much more easy . . . In England there existed in abundance forces which made it easy for women of no special spirit but of ordinary character to become militant . . . But the American women had not nearly so many of these primary incentives to passion. They formed an esteemed minority in a new country. Though the common law of the United States is the child of English common law, it had cheerfully modified itself in the direction of treating women fairly; the professions were open to them; the tradition of underpayment was not nearly so strong . . . They had a just cause but no intoxicating provocation.[5]

Yet in spite of the absence of a 'scientific' justification for restrictions on women's public role (in America, Freud was later to be more influential in justifying this than Darwin ever was), and such legal and professional disabilities as those which affected British women, the common notion of the separate 'proper sphere' remained an obstacle. American women imaginatively surmounted this with the same principle (that of the 'moral mission'), but by different means — the religious and sociological rather than the political. Where British women eschewed any symbolic contact with nature because it would reinforce arguments against their role in public life, American women were not under the same constraint, and in fact they quite often elevated association with the natural world into a commercial virtue. Working with nature ('horticulture', 'floriculture') brings individual characters financial success and serves a social function in the early utopias; and, in those of a later date, women working out-of-doors are even more common, but in traditionally male preserves, as geneticists, mechanics and sailors. Both early and late works stress means of gaining autonomy: nature could be an avenue to economic independence and status, and provide an entry into power structures. The fact that so many of the women workers in the later eutopias have taken on traditionally male occupations, but work outdoors rather than indoors, shows an increasing awareness of women's ability successfully to combine the worlds of nature and culture.

The period covered by this chapter begins, approximately, with the first Women's Rights Convention at Seneca Falls (1848). The Convention's five targets for equality — access to higher education and to the professions, property rights, the vote, and the elimination of the double standard of morality — had variable rates of success between then and the passage of the 19th Amendment in 1919. Progress on the first three aims was piecemeal and gradual, but gains were made without damaging confrontation. Being an 'esteemed minority' resulted in an early (often unsought) state vote for women of the West: Wyoming, 1869; Utah, 1870; Colorado, 1893; Idaho, 1896. The North and Midwest were to follow later, and for different reasons: Washington, 1910; California, 1911; Oregon, Arizona and Kansas, 1912; Nevada and Montana, 1914. Flexner's description of the years from 1896 to 1910 as the 'doldrums' of the suffrage battle is borne out by these figures,[6] which are mirrored exactly in the frequency (or infrequency) with which women's suffrage appears in utopian novels. Corbett (1869), Cridge (1871), Howland (1874), Lane (1880–1) and Shelhamer

(1885) are optimistic about the vote; and so too are Gilman (1911) and Bruere (1919). The only eutopia dependent on women's suffrage in these doldrums is Cooley (1902).[7] (The anti-suffrage, antifeminist works by women appear only during the earlier period: Wood (1882); Dodd (1887); Tinckner (1892).)

The truly utopian dream of eliminating the double standard of morality was (is) the most elusive. It is rather out of place among the Convention's legal and political aims, although perhaps not uncharacteristically American in the context of two later attempts to legislate morality, the Comstock Act and the Volstead Act (prohibition) (20th Amendment). The suffrage movement in the US was, and continued to be, less directed at political parties than a moral crusade; the extent of the Women's Christian Temperance Union (WCTU) influence may be disputed, but the causes of temperance and suffrage were inextricably intertwined.

However, if the pervasive political context of the British suffrage movement and women's eutopias is absent in America, interpretations of the Amazons are not. Their size remains important, but they are noticeably less militant. A nation barely a generation removed from the implacable division of civil war is in no state of mind to champion militancy over the virtues of peace and conciliation. Mary Livermore's 'millennial' 'Cooperative Womanhood in the State' (1891) calls for a republic of women 'within the national government' where the women shall sit 'side by side in government and the nations shall learn war no more'.[8] A feminist-inspired pacifism is the core of many of these early utopias: the most outspoken is anarchist Lois Waisbrooker's *A sex revolution* (1894), in which women avert another civil war by insisting on *accompanying* the men into battle. Common to both of the matriarchal eutopias are wars in the distant past which have killed all the men, leaving women to control their own destinies.

These two nations of women are set in remote and hidden places on the Earth (legendary Hyperborea at the North Pole, and in South America). The pre-history of Mizora shows an amazing similarity with the recent history of the United States: 'This first Republic had been diseased from its birth. Slavery had existed in certain districts of the nation . . . Enmities arose . . . which culminated in another civil war' (p. 96). Subsequently, the nation is factionalised, ultimately leading to the men's downfall and the rule of women, which may have been Lane's view in 1889 of a eutopian aftermath to the American Civil War. The Mizorans (an incomplete anagram of Amazons) wait until male aggression has left only a remnant of their number alive, and that remnant, excluded from public life (like traditional women), withers away. 'Ironically, women rendered men extinct simply by depriving them of activity.'[9] Paradoxically, these women are also marked by inactivity: 'Although Mizora is a mechanized society designed by female scientists, built by female carpenters, and governed by female politicians, all the women are represented as virtually asleep.'[10] This lassitude is most marked (as Pfaelzer notes) in the early chapters: it wears off only slightly once the narrative picks up speed. They do, however, run exemplary elections, and regard science as their mother (with some justification, for their devotion is rewarded with the secrets of reproductive technology), and they are so dissociated from nature that they eat only artificial foods in order to avoid contamination by contact with the soil. The Mizorans are most Amazonian in their size; their 30-inch waists and pride in their lung power equals that of the British Amazons.

Gilman's *Herland* has a similar pre-history of a two-sex world and male violence, complicated by natural disaster: those men surviving war had mostly been male slaves, who kill their masters, old women and boys, 'intending to take possession of the country with the remaining young women and girls'. However, the 'infuriated virgins . . . rose in sheer desperation and slew their brutal conquerors' (p. 55). With a more active (and Amazonian) beginning, Herlanders are never afflicted with Mizoran lassitude: Kleinbaum considers them 'truly an Amazonian community, a self-sustaining female nation'.[11] Although the Herlanders are neither aggressive nor nomadic, they are extremely agile and hardy, able to outrun and outclimb as well as outwit the three men who enter their country.[12] Unlike the Mizorans, Gilman's Herlanders worship nature (who likewise rewards them by the miraculous gift of parthogenetic reproduction, the gift of science in *Mizora*) and venerate motherhood.

A somewhat different view of Amazons occurs in the anti-feminist *Pantaletta: a romance of Sheheland* (1882), by Mrs J. Wood. This anti-feminist satire is about a land of 'terrible beardless men', whom the intrepid male traveller finds are mannish women (freaks of nature), who have instituted a role-reversal society — the men caring for the children. As one might expect, the double standard of morality is reversed in theory, yet, as the women are mostly ugly 'old maids', it proves hard to put into practice, particularly for Captain Pantaletta, driven to murder to try to get a man. The male traveller, as in most men's Amazonian fantasies, finds himself besieged by frustrated women.

However, if American women did not often turn to the legendary Amazons, where did they turn? They looked at their own history, their own lives, and nourished their idealism with hopes of changing the inequality they found at home and in the marketplace. The growing settlement movement in the cities also offered a model, as did earlier millennial communities in America, planned industrial communities (particularly those of the Fourierists) in France, and even the co-operative movement in England (although English socialists have such a bad name, several works favourably cite the experience of the successful Rochdale co-operative). Because American rural and urban communities play such an important role, their historical context and appearance in utopian fiction should be examined first: subsequent themes identical with those in Chapter 1, although much different in substance, will be discussed in the same order, with the exception that a section on religion will replace that on evolution.

Communitarianism

Intentional communities were declining in number and popularity towards the century's close, but their experience was a useful model of reform, and their radicalism, particularly in sexual or gender role experiments, was frequently re-examined by turn-of-the-century feminists. Some of these communities were groups that came from Europe seeking religious freedom, like Rapp's colonies at Harmony, New Harmony and Economy (1804–1905), and the Shakers (founded in 1780). Some were attempts to replicate industrial-based secular communities already successful in Europe, like Owen's New Harmony, 1825–7, or the several American Fourierist colonies. Some were native-born communities — the Transcendentals at Fruitlands (1843–4) and Brook Farm (1840–1) and the Oneidan Perfectionists (1848–80).

There were also newer models. The late 1880s and early 1890s, a time of economic depression and labour disputes, also saw an influx of migrants from eastern and south-eastern Europe, swelling the cities, changing the familiar composition of American life. The changing balance of population brought a response in the urban settlement movement; the exemplar was Jane Addam's Hull House in Chicago. Women writers produced several variants on these, which thrive through the members' piety and their commitment to hard work. They also introduced a rural model, the New England industrial town that has fallen on hard times but is revitalised by co-operative ownership.

Firstly, the historical communities: Davis (1866) Rappite; Alcott (1873) Fruitlands; Brodhead (1891) Kentucky Shakers; Wiggin (1909) Maine Shakers; Snedeker (1917) Owenite Harmonists. Howland (1874) depicts fictional Fourierists, Kinkaid (1903) a German Pennsylvania town similar to the Rappites; Orpen's Midwest *Perfection city* (1897) is secular and socialist, and Mason's (1900) a small Christian socialist community ('Fraternia') in North Carolina (no directly parallel community is made explicit for these secular communities).

The two stories about patriarchal German societies (Davis, Kinkaid) condemn repressive attitudes to women and sensuality. Davis's celibates (particularly the women) compensate for sex with food, and the entire settlement has an air of sterility and listlessness that drives away an idealist (male, with child) who had expected to find there a new Eden.[13] Kinkaid's Walda, young, beautiful and intelligent, lives in a society that, while not celibate, adopts a Pauline attitude to marriage — better than burning, but only by the smallest of margins. Walda rejects the role of prophetess, and chooses to marry an outsider and leave the unhealthily repressive community: she is condemned as a Jezebel, presented with a scarlet cloak, and narrowly misses a stoning.

These attitudes to patriarchal celibacy contrast with attitudes to the celibacy of Shaker communities: founded by a woman, Mother Ann Lee, the Shakers offered women autonomy, an equal voice in their hierarchy, separate and independent living quarters. Shaker practices are far more joyous than those of patriarchal sects: they are founded not on fear and repression, but on love and tolerance, of which Shaker dancing and singing are a visible sign. Although the writers of novels with Shaker settings (Brodhead, Wiggin) are equivocal about the adoption of life-long celibacy because of their own commitment to motherhood, nonetheless they depict it as a most favourable training ground or refuge for women. If unable fully to endorse Shaker celibacy, they are attracted by its short-term appeal. Brodhead's *Diana's livery* describes the Shaker settlement in Kentucky, through the eyes of a 'worldly' suitor for a Shaker girl, as 'sterile'. Yet the main character, Naamah, is ample justification of the benefits of Shaker life for women: she is independent, responsible and intelligent. Although the community is eventually disbanded because of the duplicity of its male leader, leaving Naamah free to enter the world and marry, Shaker ideals remain intact in her character.

Wiggin's Shaker community in Maine is a refuge for an unhappy wife. Once again the community's values are questioned (mostly through the author's examination of the motives that would lead men and women to choose a celibate life) but not discredited, and, though it seems inevitable that the visitor should leave, her presence there is vital to her self-respect and leads to the salvation of her marriage.[14]

One reason for the success of Shaker settlements was that women became members as individuals, not as conscripts. Women who entered communities only to fulfil their husband's ideals found life quite different, and a high proportion of unwilling participants undermined the communities that accepted wives as part of the husband's baggage, albeit a useful domestic part. One observer of the exploitation and misery this situation could bring in a rural co-operative is Louisa May Alcott. An involuntary member (at the age of 11) of her father's short-lived community, 'Fruitlands', she is retrospectively bitter about her mother's role as the practical woman who had to work from dawn to dusk, not only to feed the commune but also to bring in the crop when 'some call of the Over-soul wafted all the men away' ('Transcendental wild oats', p. 67). She wrote of 'Fruitlands' in the same year as her novel *Work*, and their themes of economic independence and exploitation overlap.[15]

Another group of unwilling women appear in Snedeker's *Seth Way*. Snedeker also had a family connection with the community of which she wrote, for she was socialist Robert Owen's great-granddaughter. Because of her affectionate memories of Harmony (where she was raised on her grandmother's stories of settlement days), her sympathies are with the founders: she writes with admiration of the women who independently joined the community, but is critical of the restlessness of the involuntary women members. Feminist historians portray their lot more sympathetically: frequently without a voice in community affairs, the women had a double load of work (including all the housework). The total lack of male comprehension of their situation contributed to the early demise of both the American and the British Owenite communities.[16] Snedeker introduces several independent women into the community, including the feminist Frances Wright. However, Snedeker manages a degree of historical accuracy without confronting Wright's notoriety: she assigns to a fictional character her 'acceptable' activities, particularly as a negro emancipist.[17]

Orpen is much more sceptical of the egalitarian virtues of socialist utopian communities. Her *Perfection city* takes many side-swipes at the idea of co-operation and sharing, feminism and pacifism: most

members are hypocritically selfish and lazy. The young wife con-
scripted into this poor and struggling Kansas community is relieved
when it fails. We can compare the young wife in Mason's *A woman
of yesterday* (1900), another who finds communal life a refuge from
an unwise marriage, and learns the independence and self-confidence
she needs when, freed by her husband's death and the community's
failure, she can return to the world and resume her vocation as a
missionary. Orpen's is a secular community, and Mason's a Christian socialist one: this division along religious principles is generally
typical of contemporary attitudes. Clarke's *Co-opolitan* (1898) presents
a successful community, but one in which the major figure is a
woman, who makes the choice to join, and whose own success as
a novelist is reflected in the community's success.

Historical communities offered one avenue of approach to communitarian utopianism, and contemporary settlements and
industrial villages another. Most popular during the late 1880s and
1890s, these urban/industrial utopian settlements are often woman-
instigated, sometimes funded by a woman philanthropist, and are
usually successful. They offer suggestions for economic self-help,
make proposals for increased public health through better housing
and nutrition, sometimes to effect explicitly the 'Americanization'
of lower-class immigrants from eastern and south-eastern Europe.
The novels of this group are Howland (1874); Douglas (1880); Mead
(1889); Woods (1889); Bartlett (1891); Winslow (1893); Sherwood
(1895). While these novels prescribe means of improving the lives
of both women and men, women are very clearly delineated as the
prime social agents. The reformist impulse is 'domestic feminism',
discussed in detail in Dolores Hayden's *Grand domestic revolution*,
illustrating her thesis that 'the overarching theme of the late
nineteenth and early twentieth century feminist movement was to
overcome the split between domestic life and public life created by
industrial capitalism, as it affected women'.[18] The one area of life
shunned by British women becomes an important bridge to utopia
for many Americans.

Although discussion of domestic feminism properly belongs with
the sections on work, and on science and technology, its contribution to these urban eutopias cannot go unremarked. It provided
a blueprint for architectural, economic and social reform based on
somewhat revolutionary proposals for the commercialisation of
housework, particularly cooking. This benefited women (and
society) in many ways: it provided economic support for those who
founded and ran wholesale catering/housework companies and co-

operatives; it saved time and money for the individual housewife, freeing her for paid work; it improved national health through placing nutrition in the hands of specialists; and it prevented waste and dirt. In Cridge's role-reversal *Man's rights; or, How would you like it?*, for instance, men are first emancipated from housework through co-operative kitchens and labour-saving devices, *then* they have the time and energy for their political siege. Gilman was one of the leading proponents of 'domestic feminism', and Hayden devotes a complete chapter to her influence. Although this is not central to *Herland*, it is a cornerstone of her first eutopia, *Moving the mountain* (1911), where she argues for its organisation on a national basis (her novel of the previous year, *What Diantha did*, describes how one woman builds up a thriving business, and transforms the lives of other women in the process).

Most of the earlier writers, however, used smaller groups in order to concentrate on the details of planning and show the transformation of individual lives. Marie Howland was also a staunch proponent of domestic feminism, and her *Papa's own girl* (1874; 1918), modelled on the Fourierist community established by industrialist Godin at Guise, France, incorporates the domestic arrangements that she saw in action there. This is a utopia started from scratch, and endowed by a male philanthropist. It is also architecturally the most lavish of any of these utopias: its Social Palace (where members work and live) has '4 immense buildings, with a vast glass-covered court in the centre, about 200' square. Each quadrangle also was to have a glass-roofed court' (p. 407). Within this grand setting she replicates the co-operative domestic arrangements at Guise (communal kitchens and laundries).[19]

Douglas (1880) prescribes co-operation in a different way: by grafting a coffee palace (to promote temperance) and cooking schools on to her New England village, she educates the women and promotes co-operation between them, in a parallel to the industrial co-operation fostered among the men in the mill. Winslow's *Salome Shepard* (1893) follows the same model of a mill town transformed by co-operation, and by a concomitant domestic renewal: Salome is the owner who instigates the reforms. In an urban context, Bartlett (1891) sets her women to work educating the poor, operating classes in home management, and combating socialist agitators who wish to make political capital from the workers' exploitation. This philanthropic strain of 'domestic feminism' is a legacy of such organisations as the earlier American Female Moral Reform Society.[20]

Of the urban societies, Woods's (1889) very detailed novel

describes how self-help among the poor grows into a large self-supporting residential co-operative movement. They begin by sharing meals to save money, and women's labour and organisational ability gradually become the foundation of a residential community, providing the residents with good, nutritious and economical meals. Further commercialisation (a successful catering service) contributes to the community's economic base.

Mead goes even further than this, providing actual plans for sanitary housing for immigrant workers in New York, with her plans including 'kitchenless houses' with a central catering service. Mead sees domestic feminism as a means of 'Americanising' these families through improving (and standardising) their housing and nutrition.

Religion

The strength of religious belief can be gauged already through responses to both religious and secular communities. Although both may fail, secular ideals are usually pilloried in a way that religious principles are not (with the exception of those of the rigid, patriarchal groups). Attention to historical communities is only one way in which religion influences American women's utopias; it also permeates present and future. In the present, it is the principle behind the urban settlements and the industrial villages. The future is not a golden age to be reached through secular means, but a heavenly after-life. It is sometimes literally heaven, sometimes an abstract spirit world, but always a place where there are lessons to be learned (education is a major occupation in the after-life) and from whence they are often conveyed to those still on Earth. Shelhamer's *Life and labor in the spirit world* (1885) even claims to have been dictated by 'spirit guides' (the author is medium of the 'Banner of Light, Public Free Circle, Boston'). Spiritual growth and understanding are the theme of these novels: Phelps (1874, 1883, 1887); Shelhamer (1885); Rogers (1905); Fisher (1916). A small subgroup which offers advice to those still on Earth on how to achieve domestic harmony and maintain morality, these heavenly utopias collapse the boundaries between this life and the next, transforming earthly suffering for those still alive; and extending understanding for those in the after-life.

Politics

'Can it be possible that women vote nowhere but in Utopia?'
(Corbett, 1869, p. 202). As far as national American elections were
concerned, the answer stayed 'yes' for another 50 years. The long-
worked-for women's suffrage amendment was delayed, while three
others were passed following the post-bellum 15th (enfranchising
negro males). It is possible to account for American suffragists'
relative lack of militancy during much of this time by citing such
historical factors as the absence of an established party system or
a tradition of parliamentary rule, and the effect of the American
Civil War, and such geographical factors as the difficulty of
communication over vast distances, or the want of a centre of concentrated power/population. To these can be added the effect of
piecemeal franchise in the states, and the environment described
by Rebecca West. These utopias express faith in internal, rather
than external, change, and are definitely not single-issue (suffrage)
prescriptions: electoral franchise enters utopia as part of a *spectrum*
of reforms — sometimes the least, and the last.

Yet despite the differences between British and American
circumstances, and British and American suffrage campaigns, there
were similarities between the two national movements — the
doldrums of the 1890s, for instance. Disappointment in political
parties played a role in America as in Britain. Women's alliance
with the (rural-based) Populist Party (which had strong temperance
associations) Buhle describes as having an 'ideological continuity,
from the WCTU to Populism, almost precisely parallel to that
between the urban-based women's movement and Nationalism'.[21]
When Populism ceased to be a movement and was officially
constituted as the People's Party in 1892, however, it failed to
endorse the women's ballot: the prominent suffragist Willard experienced the same sense of disillusionment as Dixie had with the
Liberals in the same year, but accusing them of giving in to 'the
craft of the liquor wing' and Southern conservatism.[22] Populist
influence was soon over, its reformist role passed to the Progressive
Party after 1900, though directed at the problems of the growing
cities (particularly immigration and prostitution). Often accused of
sensationalist journalistic exploitation of these, Progressivist concern
at least made its mark on a national, rather than a regional, front.

Generally, the major parties avoided commitment (or betrayal)
on the subject of women's suffrage. American Harriet Staton Blatch,
returning with Emmeline Pankhurst from the suffrage 'front

line' in England, complained of American politicians:

> Why, they blandly admit us before the legislative commit-
> tees, listen to all we have to say, treat us with perfect courtesy
> . . . and then never so much as bother to answer our
> arguments. As for voting on our measures, they simply pocket
> them without a word. They won't bar us from the streets.
> They won't so much as put us in jail. It's distressing, I tell
> you. Yes, highly insulting![23]

After the invigorating (to say the least) scene that she had left
behind, one can understand her impatience — and the trenchancy
of Rebecca West's comments about American women's difficulties.

One woman who did seek political power was the flamboyant
Victoria Woodhull, a candidate for the Presidency in 1872 (when
she was supported by the Equal Rights party until scandal alienated
them), in 1876, and again in 1880. Her eutopian 'Constitution of
the United States of the World' (1870) was part of an early campaign address delivered in Lincoln Hall, Washington, DC. It contains a 'declaration of interdependence', and guarantees not only
individual but community rights. It proposes universal suffrage,
social welfare payments, and the nationalisation of railways and
mineral-bearing lands, free trade and the encouragement of the
international federation of the title. Woodhull reappears as the title
character in Wood's *Pantaletta* (1882), where anyone familiar with
her history can recognise her as the 'Apostle of Free Love' who

> put on the robes of an angel of purity and, in a foreign land,
> imposed upon one of the greatest men of letters (unfortunately
> approaching his dotage) and at his hands received the nomina-
> tion of perpetual candidate for the Presidency of Petticotia
> (p. 129).[24]

Meanwhile, somewhere in eutopia, women voted. Although the
vote is accepted as 'natural' in Corbett's (1869) utopia, the changes
mentioned are less the consequence of legal action than of a change
of attitude in domestic relations: likewise, the changes in the division of labour are not legislated but 'natural' changes, based on
a sensible basis of physical strength (men do the scrubbing and
heavy cleaning). Cridge's role-reversal satire (1871) focuses in its
final sections on men's seemingly endless struggle to an impossible
goal, the vote:

Evidence within *Man's rights* suggests that Cridge's motivation for writing came from a discouraged sense of how long the women's suffrage movement had been active and how little change had been made in American society. When the narrator in her dreams sees the men's rights leaders twenty years later, the plainly dressed 'Susan Anthony' figure is gray-haired, and although the movement has some more supporters . . . the issues are still the same.[25]

Cridge was writing in 1870; and the road ahead was to be even longer than she feared. In her parody are all the familiar anti-suffrage arguments (used by woman against man): 'No,no, my dear . . . Nothing is more disgusting than feminine men. We don't want men running to the polls, and electioneering: what would become of the babies at such times?' (p. 89). The trivialisation of men's names by these dignified women — Sammie, Johnnie — points up the condescension of the self-justifying ruling sex.

Howland (1874) introduces suffrage only towards the conclusion of *Papa's own girl* (1874). It is linked with temperance. After Clara's conservative mother is told by an earnest young working man that 'the ballot in women's hands would shut up the rum shops' (pp. 434–5), she withdraws her opposition to women's suffrage. Her radical daughter, Clara, although a suffrage worker, has forged her own economic independence and helps to create a new community without the vote.

Mason (1889) comments on the American political process, where elections are run by 'the rum-selling and the rum-drinking masses' (p. 219); her female hero, like Clara, prefers economic to political power. Suffrage and temperance also combine in Mizora, whose women are adamant on the sobriety of their voters and the orderliness of political campaigns run solely by and for women (p. 70). Yet the conflict between suffrage and temperance on the one hand, and all-male elections and alcohol on the other, in a period when 'most polls . . . were set up in saloons and barber shops' suggests that, although the issue of electoral reform does not figure largely in a majority of these novels, their strong temperance bias may be a political statement.[26]

Cooley (1902), in her socialist future, is one of the few who dates a changed society from universal franchise. Her women, 'when given political freedom', 'went to work with enthusiasm, using the "influence" *necessary* to effect transformations — the ballot. And so we have a fine sanitary condition and a healthful race' (p. 513, original emphasis). Hand in hand, however, with political and economic reform (the nationalisation of industries) is moral reform by the new 'Religion of Humanity' (p. 515). Gilman's first eutopian novel, *Moving the mountain* (1911), shows some similarities. Her narrator, after 30 amnesiac years in Tibet, returns to an America transformed by the women's vote, the nationalisation of much of its industry, and a moral reform movement based on the 'laws of nature'. The shock to his system is extreme.

There are few other women's voices in favour of suffrage, though some decidedly against. Tinckner (1892), in her religious utopia, flatly states that 'woman as a lawmaker is meddlesome and tyrannical. She goes too much into detail' (p. 301). She proposes a strictly domestic sphere for women, a strictly public sphere for men. Dodd's *The republic of the future* (1887) is a socialised future America in which equality has de-feminised women (a common complaint in the 1920s) and de-stabilised public life:

> Whatever slight inequalities may still exist between men and women in the matter of muscular energy or physical strength is more than counterbalanced by the enormous disproportion between them, numerically, as voters. [The ratio is 10 females to 1 male.] Some very curious and important political changes have been effected by the preponderance of the woman's vote. Wars, for instance, have been within the last fifty years declared illegtal. Woman found that whereas she was eminently fitted for all men's avocations in time of peace, when it came to war she made a very poor figure of a soldier. (pp. 42–3)

(Note the dystopian reference to miliary women, as in *Pantaletta*.) Dodd's dismissal of 50 years of peace as the unwelcome result of women's vanity strikes the reader as ludicrous, though her tone does not invite an ironical interpretation.

The orientations of these women writers, even when they propose 'socialist' forms of government control to curb *laissez-faire* capitalism, are generally more nationalist than radically socialist — that is, when they propose nationalisation, it is not explicitly associated with socialist theory. Margaret, the heroine of Bartlett's *The new aristocracy* (1891), for example, gives an impassioned speech to a political meeting, in which she faces down the anarchists, preaching individual responsibility in what could be an epigraph for this period: 'In the breast of each individual lies the power of bettering himself, and as we better ourselves intellectually and morally, as well as materially, by so much we better the world' (p. 71). Sherwood, who in an *An experiment in altruism* (1895), finds settlements a little too detached from the real issues of reform (a woman doctor, and a woman philanthropist who dedicates her life to reclaiming prostitutes are her heroes), declaims against 'the businessmen of the country, who refuse to make concessions, and leave the workers prey to outside agitation' (p. 169). She underscores her message in the character of the 'anarchist': having given up work to devote himself to political agitation (which includes encouraging exploited needlewomen to strike for a living wage), he is content to be supported by his wife's sewing (p. 157)! Woods's *Metzerott* is that rarity, an anarchist and a good and moral man: the martyred death of his son (a Christian believer) at the end of the novel shocks and then converts his father from his atheism.

Work

Utopian visions by American women show increasing concern with the problems of working women, and one of their surest prescriptions for emancipation is economic independence. Uninhibited about associations with 'trade', they admire the successful business woman as much as the woman engineer. The earlier utopias deal mainly with criticising the trivialities of occupations suitable for middle-class women, or of the drudgery of housework and difficulties with servants. Later utopias consistently introduce the exploited working-class woman, whose poverty makes her a prey to moral danger. This growing awareness acknowledges one of the consequences of economic depression, the employment of women in shops and factories at starvation wages. It also shows increased awareness of and contact with this problem, due to settlement work. The British middle-class women's battle on behalf of the prostitute had taken place half a century earlier; and, with the rise of the cities, the American women were to find that the problem was theirs too.

Firstly, the gleam of gold. What were the occupations of women in Utopia? Cridge puts the women to work 'in colleges, as students and professors, as lawyers, judges and jurors' (p. 16). Towards the close of this period Gilman's 'amnesiac' male (1911) reacts with ascending levels of horror on finding that, firstly, his little sister is a qualified medical practitioner; secondly, she is president of a co-educational college; and, thirdly, the pretty young woman whom he has been admiring is a civil engineer. ('It's perfectly horrid! Aren't there any women left?' — p. 25.)

One can see the effects of change over these decades in one most important area — a gradual familiarisation witih the substance of 'men's work' as women's horizons expand. Facing the somewhat stiff and generalised laboratory workers in *Mizora*, one feels inclined to the opinion expressed by the author: 'Science had hitherto been, save by a *very* few, an untrodden field to women; but the encouragement and rare facilities offered soon revealed latent talent that developed rapidly' (p. 134). The outstanding women of the earlier novels are the business women, whether running a 'horticulture' business, or a wholesale catering firm. There is a freedom and openness in these eutopias that values women's work, and that moves easily from the worlds that women knew to one confidently imagined and understood. There is more than that, however. There is a longing for fruitful, satisfying, well-paid, socially useful work, a sense of energy to be expended: Ford, rebelling against the paternalism of the Nationalists, produced a woman character who declares: 'If I had to choose between being a blacksmith and doing nothing, I should certainly be a blacksmith!' (p. 253). Mead's woman millionaire advocates evening classes in carpentry for girls: 'it would do more for them physically than a course at the gymnasium' (p. 312). Given this energetic attitude, American women take on a variety of occupations in eutopia: Ford's, Mason's, Howland's and Gilman's (1911) business women, Douglas's and Woods's caterers, Jones/Merchant's banker, Sherwood's doctor, Cooley's and Waisbrooker's sociologists/settlement workers, even Wiggin's Shaker women who worked their herb gardens and historically began the seed trade have their place in a bustling world of working women. The novels of the later decades include Gilman's (1915) hardy foresters and geneticists, Bennett's sea-captains, and Bruere's tractor-drivers (and designers) taking part in the 'world's first experiment in industrial democracy' (p. 179). All of these women are seen actively engaged in their occupations: Bruere's woman mechanic gets her hands well and truly soiled, and barriers of class and sex come down here and in *Herland* in a way unimaginable in *Mizora*.[27]

In Cridge's role reversal, trivial underpaid 'women's work' becomes the work of men, who spend their time (once emancipated from housework) sewing and doing 'all the delicate nothings that interest only ladies in this waking world of ours'. The narrator of this story has enormous problems with her own (nineteenth-century) household help, and wakes from her dream visions of the alternative society (on Mars) to domestic problems. These are solved in Corbett's eutopia, with reasonable cooks and complacent husbands. In later novels the servant problem ceases to *be* a problem: within the context of domestic feminism, service is acceptable employment (one of Bartlett's protagonists takes employment as a cook at $20 per week, and performs a social function by educating the other servants in hygiene and nutrition).

Later utopias have a consistent dystopian image of sweatshop labour at appalling rates of pay, and of the slide into prostitution that was so often its end. Throughout there is an awareness of the inequity of female/male pay differentials. Cridge mentions men being paid one-third of a woman's wage; and Gilman does not dwell on the exploitation of women in any detail in her utopias/dystopias, but in *Herland*'s Chapter 6, 'Comparisons are odious', the American men admit that at least one-third of American women work, and that 'they are all *poor*' (p. 62). In Mead's *Memoirs* (1889), her millionaire endows a missionary fund, on the condition that women administer the sacrament and that they receive equal pay. Howland's Clara, making economic independence the key to her own liberation, also gives work to other women.

As the economic depression of the 1890s worsens, however, the gulf between the two sexes widens. With more women entering the work-force as cheap labour, a more specific sense of exploitation enters these utopian works.[28] One of the first is Woods's *Metzerott, shoemaker* (1889), which mentions the sewing women who work for 'Grind and Crushem', sewing shirts for 5 cents a dozen. She also refers to the temptations that befall shop girls and servants who are subject to an undignified surveillance, and are forced to 'live-in', yet must bear with the low morals of the other women who supplement their starvation wages with casual prostitution. Although praising the independence of the American girl, she deplores the snares of the big city: her urban commune is begun by women who had chosen starvation rather than immorality.

The reformer in Bartlett's *The new aristocracy* (1891) also sticks to principle, refusing to marry her wealthy fiancé, because he does not share her social commitment. Devoting herself to work in the slums, his independent decision to found an industrial village leads to their reunion. Sherwood (1895) remarks on 'the great shops, where women worked and starved on two dollars a week' (p. 21): the fate of these is exemplified by two cautionary tales of the striking tailoress and the young woman from the country whose work as an underpaid shop assistant leads her into prostitution. It is this moral quagmire referred to in Cooley's future world (1902) which has abolished the sweatshops, and 'a thousand other evils once considered almost a requisite of trade' (p. 512).

Although this may seem to be the stuff of sentimental, sensationalist literature, the fact of women's exploitation by nineteenth-century capitalism is being told in these regenerative eutopias. The most outspoken statement on this subject comes from Lois Waisbrooker, an anarchist. In *A sex revolution* (1894) women's problems are defined in economic terms and an economic solution proposed. Waisbrooker's novel takes up where George Noyes Miller's *The strike of a sex* [1890] leaves off. Miller's book proposes a successful strike by women who refuse 'involuntary motherhood': it is written by a member of the Oneida community to publicise their birth control method, male continence.[29] Waisbrooker, also identified with the campaign for sexual reform, contends that birth control alone will not emancipate women.[30] Her narrator goes to sleep reading Miller's book, and sees first the strike that puts an end to another civil war as 'Lovella' leads women in insisting that, if men will go to war, they will accompany them. This is sufficient to ensure peace. She sees then an immense multitude who 'plied a needle, a sewing machine, or both': 'a hungry, gaunt, sorrowful multitude, many of them working upon rich garments, while the plainest, coarsest of those upon which others stitched were better than they themselves could wear' (p. 100). There are also prostitutes, also victims of an inequitable economic system. Lovella and the women are conceded 50 years' rule to try to overcome these evils.

Sexuality, marriage and family

'"Marriage as of old?" I timidly ventured. "That depends on what you consider was in vogue in your time. Monogamy was officially recognized but not universally practised, we have been told . . . it is almost universal with us"' (Cooley, p. 513). This change has been brought about by the adoption of 'one standard of purity — and that the highest — for men and women' (ibid., p. 515).

The attitude of American women to marriage is one of reform, rather than dissolution. Divorce was, after all, much easier to obtain in the United States; increasing 'drastically after the Civil War', it doubled roughly each two decades, from 1.2 per cent of 1,000 marriages in 1860 to 2.2 per cent in 1880, to 4.0 per cent in 1900, to 7.7 per cent in 1920.[31] The escape-hatch was always wider and easier to reach in America than in Britain.

First of all, American women are quite outspoken on the subject of sexuality, particularly where the double standard of morality is concerned. Over time there is a change in this: it begins as a matter of personal justice, which later expands to include the social evils, venereal disease and prostitution. Feminists were insistent that the equality they sought did not imply their willingness to adopt male standards of morality (although some of their opponents were quick to suggest this — Wood (1882) and Dodd (1887), for example). Feminists in the USA, as in Britain, were irrevocably tarnished by any suggestion of moral 'laxity': Victoria Woodhull was to suffer for her support of 'free love' (like Annie Besant); both went into self-imposed exile and regained some respectability, Besant in America, and Woodhull in England. Almost every eutopian writer stipulates moral reform like that proposed by Cooley. Some show women leaving unfaithful husbands for eutopian communities of various kinds: Howland's Clara does so to start in business with Susie, another victim of the double standard (she bears Clara's brother's illegitimate child); Pittock (1890) includes a wife deserting her unfaithful husband to live in a Hawaiian eutopia. In Evans (1905) women from Venus leave their earthly husbands — able to bear hard work and neglect, they refuse to accept infidelity as well.

Waisbrooker's procession of women includes not only prostitutes but 'unhappy wives — wives who submitted to husbands rather than incur greater evils' (p. 97). She reinforces her message of the need for economic independence by showing how women's poverty supports the double standard. These husbands may make 'no demands', but

> with a sort of lordly indifference they have said, by their manner, if not in words, do as you please, I make no claims. But if you are free, I am; I can find other women who will accept me, women who need my aid and I cannot support more than one. (p. 98)

Waisbrooker presents what is a strikingly frank awareness of rape within marriage, and of the relationship between economics and sexual behaviour. In *Moving the mountain*, Gilman (1911) shows how enfranchised women may strike at the root of this situation. When her dreamer returns, one enlightening chat that he has is with his new brother-in-law, who tells him of events in the intervening 30 years:

> The young women learned the proportion of men with syphilis and gonorrhoea and decided that it was wrong to marry them. That was enough. They passed laws in every State requiring a clean bill of health with every marriage license. Diseased men had to die bachelors — that's all. (p. 138)

Although this decreased the incidence of marriage, leaving many women single, it does not have the effect the dreamer thinks — increase prostitution. This, which he considers the 'social necessity, as old as Ninevah!', is no more: women legislators have wiped it out by reversing normal practice, passing laws against the women's male customers, rather than the women themselves (p. 306).

The absurdity of women adopting the single (male) standard is explored in Jones/Merchant (1893) where in the 'lower' alternative society 'emancipated' women reject marriage: 'Why should the free wish for fetters? . . . [Passion] may be satisfied without entailing such tremendous possibilities' (p. 172). After a glimpse of this world, 'where women have the same rights, privileges and vices as an upper-class American man',[32] the visitor from Earth (an upper-class American male) is horrified: he subsequently visits another, more spiritualised world, where the standard of morality is the single standard of purity.

There are a number of references in these works to the marriage ceremony: what women most want is for it to reflect *partnership*, not patterns of dominance/submission. Mason (*Hiero-Salem*, 1889) introduces the marriage motto of a couple who quite happily reverse/combine roles, he being the father/mother, she the mother/father: 'Each individual is a unit, and has to execute in life a part characteristic of his cause of being. Each is an absolute idea and identity' (p. 20). With this as their guide, there is no conflict between her devotion to business, and his to raising and educating their children. Gilman (1911) accentuates the voluntary nature of marriage for women in eutopian America: 'she is the wife of her husband in that she is his true lover, and that their marriage is legally recorded; but her life and work does not belong to him' (p. 136). The marriage vows in *Herland*, made at the Altar of Motherhood and attended by ritual procession, dancing and anthems, must be far removed from the traditional Christian wedding ceremony.

A completely new form of marrige contract is reproduced in Phelps (1874) and in Snedeker's *Seth Way* (1917). This is an amended copy of that actually written by Robert Owen's son, marriage reformer Robert Dale Owen, in which the husband divests himself of 'the *unjust rights* which, in virtue of this ceremony, an iniquitous law tacitly gives me over the person and property of another' (p. 400).[33] Both fictional and historical documents bear the wife's signature. For nineteenth-century women eutopia truly is a place where men share responsibility for home and children, where they cease to regard their wives as labour, and regard them as friends.

Science and technology

While there is as general an agreement here as in British novels that science and progress are equivalent, and equally good, the absence of futuristic eutopias reduces opportunities to forecast how these marvels will work. The co-operative housekeeping schemes do have some in-built technology, sophisticated kitchen equipment and delivery devices, but these are not greatly detailed. In Mizora and *Herland*, worlds without man, science is of course the business of women. The remoteness of Mizoran science has been commented upon, as has the emphasis on plant genetics and biology in *Herland*, which has the most detailed emphasis: this again is a form of domestic feminism, concerned as it is with Gilman's theme of the need for the elimination of waste, and for good nutrition.

Gilman's work has much the same place here as Dixie's in the previous chapter. It, too, is a microcosm of contemporary feminism. Gilman's works of theory are feminist perspectives of religion, economics, work, family: all of her social theories are worked out in her utopian fiction. Although unusual for an American in her interest in socialism, and in the distinctive biological and evolutionary role of women, she epitomises the domestic feminism of the time, its optimism, its belief in individual change within a co-operative community. Her theories on evolutionary history, and in particular on how this has affected the relationship of the sexes, are identical with those of pioneering American sociologist Lester Ward, a position that led her, like most of the British women, to emphasise women's future role as leaders in a new, moral evolution.

Although her first eutopian novel, *Moving the mountain*, presents an America transformed in only 30 years by a new moral outlook that influences legislation, the long range of history in *Herland* makes it an ideal vehicle for an alternative evolutionary span, one entirely determined by women's nature. Its dystopian sequel, *With her in Ourland*, the voice of purely evolved woman comments on our unevolved state, and she concludes that, whatever apparently superior technological progress we might have to offer, it cannot compensate for the violence of war and the misery and exploitation of women and (some) men. Gilman's position as the best-known American woman utopist of this period rests mainly on the strength of *Herland*, but her other two novels are supporting pillars of her feminist philosophy: the three supplement each other.

Gilmans three novels were not written in a vacuum, however. There was a slight decrease in publication during the first two decades of this century, but these novels take on an increasing militancy. Evans (1905) and Irwin (1914) describe worlds of men bereft of women; women come to them through some supernatural means, but they soon take them for granted. Evans (whose women come from Venus) has already been discussed; Irwin's *Angel Island* presents an even more painful story. The women who come to her men are creatures of the air, whom the men woo, luring them closer to the earth, finally trapping them, and cutting their beautiful wings. (This is analogous to the initial attempt of the three men who enter Herland to capture the women, who are observing them from safety in the trees: the women are likened to colourful, free-flying birds, and they are tempted with colourful trinkets. Gilman's women retain their freedom, however; Irwin's lose theirs, and are trapped.) Their wings kept trimmed, the women are not able to move far until one gives birth to a winged daughter. When the father insists that her wings will be cut at puberty, the women in combination secretly toughen their tender feet and learn to walk, then go on strike, moving away until men agree that their daughters' wings will be left alone. Subsequently a boy is born, the first to have wings. The parable is obvious. Taken together with Gilman's three novels, Bennett's story 'Friend Island' of a world of women sea-captains and pilots, where a shipwrecked male's stubborn refusal to control his temper so alienates a sensate island that its two inhabitants are almost drowned, and Bruere's *Mildred Carver* (1919), Evans's and Irwin's novels add up to a series of strong statements on women's growing independence. The changing occupations of these women are one sign of this; and their new self-assertion in the years surrounding the final gain of the franchise is another. Significantly, they speak not only of women's need to develop their own abilities and to have confidence in them, but also of the necessity for women to co-operate to achieve their goals.

Bennett's other work, *The heads of Cerberus* (1919), while not specifically feminist, does lead into the period that is to follow. The tale of a dystopian future Philadelphia, it warns of the dangers that lie in isolationism, for here America has turned its back on the world, has even turned its back on the sense of itself as a nation, and this parochialism has led to tyranny. This is a dire warning on a newly developing theme. The major transitions occurring at the end of this period are, for feminists, women's suffrage, and for the nation, an increased awareness of its identity, both in a domestic and an international context:

the principles of cooperation and socialism which [experimental and literary utopians] advocated never applied immediately to the larger American scheme. Only in the twentieth century did such would-be reformers break with the utopian tradition and turn to the slow transformation of that creaking, infinitely complex but apparently viable structure to which they must belong.[34]

Notes

1. Lyman Tower Sargent, *British and American utopian literature 1516–1975: an annotated bibliography*, 2nd edn (G.K. Hall, Boston, 1988).

2. Letter to W.D. Howells, quoted in Sylvia Bowman (ed.), *Edward Bellamy abroad: an American prophet's influence* (Twayne, New York, 1962), p. 31.

3. Vol. 1, no. 6 (October 1889), p. 223.

4. Vol. 1, no. 1 (May 1889), p. 21.

5. Quoted in Dale Spender, (ed.), *Time and Tide wait for no man* (Pandora, London, 1984), pp. 68–9.

6. Eleanor Flexner, *Century of struggle: the women's rights movement in the United States* (Belknap Press of Harvard University, Cambridge, Mass., 1959), p. 271.

7. About Cooley (*c.* 1875–after 1955), daughter of social activist, Ida Husted Harper, little is known. See Carol Farley Kessler (ed.), *Daring to dream. Utopian stories by United States women, 1836–1919* (Pandora Press, Boston, 1984), p. 205, for an introduction to this 'journalist, lecturer, and teacher'.

8. *The North American Review*, 153 (September 1891), p. 295. Nina Auerbach, *Communities of women: an idea in fiction* (Harvard University

Press, Cambridge, Mass., 1978), pp. 161–2, notes the paradox of learning from war the lessons necessary for peaceful co-operation. Carol Kessler, 'The heavenly utopia of Elizabeth Stuart Phelps' in Marleen Barr and Nicholas Smith (eds), *Women and utopia* (University Press of America, Lanham, Maryland, 1983), notes that Phelps (1874) also reacts against the Civil War.

9. Jean Pfaelzer, *The utopian novel in America 1886–1896. The politics of form* (University of Pittsburgh Press, Pittsburgh, 1984), p. 149.

10. Ibid., p. 148.

11. Abby Wetten Kleinbaum, *The war against the Amazons* (McGraw-Hill, New York, 1983), p. 208.

12. They reflect Gilman's delight in physical exercise and strength: she was proud of her agility on the gymnastic 'travelling rings' at the age of 65. Charlotte Perkins Gilman, *The living of Charlotte Perkins Gilman* (D. Appleton-Century, New York, 1935), p. 67.

13. The charge of over-eating seems to have been commonplace: their official history, *The Harmony society in Pennsylvania* (Wm. Penn Assoc., Philadelphia, 1937), p. 32, remarks defensively that despite 'five meals a day, they were as temperate in their eating as they were in their drinking'!

14. Wiggin wrote much of this novel while a temporary resident in a Shaker community (her own 'refuge'). She read aloud from her work (with some embarrassment): her listeners acknowledged the narrative's elopement of a pair of young lovers as a 'not infrequent . . . tragedy'. *My garden of memory, an autobiography* (Hodder and Stoughton, London, [1924], pp. 346–7.

15. Mrs Alcott's experience of community life made her very sceptical of the nearby Shaker settlement which Bronson toyed with joining (he had already adopted celibacy): she commented, 'There is servitude somewhere I have no doubt . . . wherever I turn I see the yoke on woman in some form or other.' Martha Saxton, *Louisa May: a modern biography of Louisa May Alcott* (Houghton, Mifflin, Boston, 1977), p. 144.

16. Barbara Taylor, *Eve and the new Jerusalem: socialism and feminism in the nineteenth century* (Virago, London, 1983), pp. 238–60 discusses the British communities; Jill Harsin, 'Housework and utopia: women and the Owenite socialist communities' in Ruby Rohrlich and Elaine Hoffman Baruch (eds), *Women in search of utopia, mavericks and mythmakers* (Schocken, New York, 1984), pp. 73–84, discusses the American.

17. See Marilyn Bensman, 'Frances Wright: utopian feminist' in Rohrlich and Baruch (eds), *Women*, pp. 62–9. Fanny Wright was one of the few women actually to found a community.

18. *The grand domestic revolution: a history of feminist designs for American homes, neighborhoods, and cities* (MIT Press, Cambridge, Mass, 1981), p. 4.

19. Howland failed when she tried to put these principles into real-life practice in a socialist community (Topolobampo) in Mexico, making housekeeping truly co-operative by including the men. Somehow their idealism did not encompass 'women's work'. Thomas A. Robertson, *A southwestern utopia* (Ward, Ritchie, Los Angeles, 1964), p. 109, discusses the difficulties of making 'co-operative' housekeeping truly co-operative. The problem is endemic to egalitarian societies — see note 16 on the Owenite socialists.

20. See Carol Smith-Rosenberg, *Disorderly conduct: visions of gender in Victorian America* (Alfred A. Knopf, New York, 1985), p. 120.

21. Mari Jo Buhle, *Women and American socialism, 1870–1920* (University of Illinois Press, Urbana, 1981), p. 84.

22. Ibid., p. 91.

23. Interview in *Pearson's Magazine*, February 1910, quoted in Andrew Sinclair, *The better half. The emancipation of the American woman* (Harper and Row, New York, 1965), p. 286.

24. See Madeleine Stern's introduction to *The Victoria Woodhull reader* and her *We, the women: career firsts of nineteenth century America* (Schulte, New York, 1963). James Brough, *The vixens: a biography of Victoria and Tennessee Claflin* (Simon and Schuster, New York, 1980), is longer, more factual — and condescending. The identity of the senile sage is not established in either.

25. Barbara C. Quissell, 'The new world that Eve made' in Kenneth M. Roemer (ed.), *America as utopia* (Burt Franklin, New York, 1981), p. 154.

26. Lois Banner, *Women in modern America: a brief history* (Harcourt Brace Jovanovich, New York, 1974), p. 90.

27. Women entered the professions in America earlier and in far greater numbers than in Britain. By 1910 there were 'well over 8,000 women physicians in the United States', and the first woman was admitted to the bar in 1869. W. E. and Mary M. Brownlee, *Women in the American economy: a documentary history, 1675 to 1929* (Yale University Press, New Haven, Conn., 1976), pp. 272, 288. Comparable figures for England were 2,580 women physicians by 1927, and admission of the first woman lawyer to the Bar in 1922. Charlotte (Franken) Haldane, *Motherhood and its enemies* (Chatto and Windus, London, 1927), p. 109.

28. Buhle, *Women and American socialism*, discusses awareness of prostitution, 'the Social Evil', in the first decade of the century, with Progressives, socialists and women reformers agreed on the role of low wages (pp. 253–7).

29. *Strike* became part of the literature of the American movement for continence and psychic love. With its sequel. *After the strike of a sex* [1891] it was reissued by sex reformer Dr Alice Stockham (Stockham, Chicago, 1905). See Linda Gordon, *Woman's body, woman's right: a social history of birth control in America* (Grossman, New York, 1976), and Hal D. Sears, *The sex radicals: free love in high Victorian America* (Regents Press of Kansas, Lawrence, Kansas, 1977). Miller wrote the introduction to the American edition of Dixie's *Gloriana*.

30. For a history of her involvement, see Sears, *Sex Radicals*, and Margaret S. Marsh, *Anarchist women, 1870–1920* (Temple University Press, Philadelphia, 1981).

31. William L. O'Neill, *Divorce in the Progressive era* (Yale University Press, New Haven, Conn., 1967), p. 20.

32. Quissell, 'The new world', p. 156.

33. For the full text of the original document, see *The Free Enquirer*, 2 June 1832, pp. 255–6.

34. Maren Lockwood, 'The experimental utopia in America' in Frank E. Manuel (ed.), *Utopias and utopian thought* (Souvenir Press, London, 1973), p. 198.

Bibliography of Primary Material

Griffith, Mary (1836) 'Three hundred years hence' in *Camperdown: or News from our neighborhood*, Carey, Lea and Blanchard, Philadelphia.

Chamberlain, Betsey [Tabitha] (1841) 'A new society', *The Lowell offering*, 1, pp. 191–2.

Appleton, Jane Sophia (1848) 'Sequel to "The vision of Bangor in the twentieth century" ' in *Voices from the Kenduskeag*, D. Bugbee, Bangor, Maine

Hale, Sarah Joseph (1853) *Liberia; or Mr Peyton's experiments*, Harper and Brothers, New York

Davis, Rebecca Harding (1866) 'The harmonists', *Atlantic Monthly*, vol. XVII, no. C111, pp. 529–38

Corbett, Elisabeth T. (1869) 'My visit to utopia', *Harper's New Monthly Magazine*, vol. 38, pp. 200–4

Woodhull, Victoria (1870; reprinted 1974) 'Constitution of the United States of the World' in Madeleine Stern (ed.), *The Victorian Woodhull reader*, M. and S. Press, Weston, Mass.

Cridge, Annie Denton (1870) *Man's rights; or, How would you like it? Comprising 'dreams'*, Wm Denton, Boston

Alcott, Louisa May (1873; reprinted 1915) 'Transcendental wild oats' in Clara Endicott Sears (ed.), *Bronson Alcott's Fruitlands*, Houghton, Mifflin Boston

Howland, Marie Stevens Case (1874; 1975) (reprinted in 1918 as *The Familistere*) *Papa's own girl*, Porcupine Press, Philadelphia

Phelps, Elizabeth Stuart (1874) 'A dream within a dream', *The Independent*, vol. 26, no. 1

Douglas, Amanda (1880) *Hope mills, or Between friend and sweetheart*, Lee and Shepard, Boston

Lane, Mary E. Bradley (1880–1 in *Cincinnati Commercial*; 1890, 1975) *Mizora: a prophecy*, Gregg Press, Boston

Wood, Mrs J. (1882) *Pantaletta: a romance of Sheheland*, American News Co., New York

Phelps, Elizabeth Stuart (1883) *Beyond the gates*, Houghton, Mifflin, Boston

Shelhamer, M.T. (1885) *Life and labor in the spirit world, being a description of the localities, employments, surroundings, and conditions of the spheres*, Colby and Rich, Boston

Dodd, Anna Bowman (1887; reprinted 1970) *The republic of the future*, Gregg Press, Boston

Phelps, Elizabeth Stuart (1887) *The gates between*, Houghton, Mifflin, Boston

Ford, Mary H. (1889) 'A feminine iconoclast', *The Nationalist*, pp. 252–7

Mason, Eveleen Laura Knaggs (1889) *Hiero-Salem: the vision of peace*, J.G. Cupples, Boston

Mead, Lucia True (Ames) (1889) *Memoirs of a millionaire*, Houghton, Mifflin, Boston

Woods, Katharine Pearson (1889) *Metzerott, shoemaker*, Crowell, New York

Pittock, Mrs M.A. Weeks (1890) *The God of civilization*, Eureka, Chicago

Stone, Mrs C.H. (1890) *One of 'Berrian's novels*, Welch, Fracker, New York

Bartlett, Alice Elinor [Birch Arnold] (1891) *The new aristocracy*, Bartlett Publ., New York

Brodhead, Eva Wilder McGlasson (1891) *Diana's livery*, Harper, New York

Yourall, Agnes Bond (1891) *A manless world*, Dillingham, New York

Moore, M. Louise (1892) *Al-Modad; or life scenes beyond the polar circumflex. A religio-scientific solution of the problems of present and future life*, Moore and Beauchamp, Shell Bank, Louisiana

Tinckner, Mary Agnes (1892) *San Salvador*, Houghton, Mifflin, Boston

Giles, Fayette Stratton (1893) *Shadows before, or a century onward*, Humboldt, New York

Jones, Alice Ilgenfritz and Ella Merchant [Two Women of the West] (1893) *Unveiling a parallel: a romance*, Arena, Boston

Winslow, Helen (1893) *Salome Shepard, reformer*, Arena, Boston

Knapp, Adeline (1894) *One thousand dollars a day. Studies in practical economics*, Arena, Boston

Waisbrooker, Lois N. (1894; reprinted 1985) *A sex revolution*, New Society, Philadelphia

Sherwood, Margaret Pollack [Elizabeth Hastings] (1895) *An experiment in altruism*, Macmillan, New York

Von Swartout, Janet (1895) *Heads, or The city of the gods*, Olombia Publishing, New York

Graul, Rosa (1897) 'Hilda's home', *Lucifer, the light bearer*, nos. 641–86.

Orpen, Adela (1897) *Perfection city*, D. Appleton, New York

Clarke, Frances [Zebina Forbush] (1898) *The co-opolitan; a story of the co-operative commonwealth of Idaho*, Kerr, Chicago

Mason, Eveleen Knaggs (1898) *An episode in the doings of the dualized*, E.L. Mason, Brookline, Mass.

Adolph, Mrs Anna (1899) *Arqtiq*, the author, Hanford, Calif.

Mason, Caroline Atwater (1900) *A woman of yesterday*, Doubleday, New York

Richberg, Eloise O. Randall (1900) *Reinstern*, Editor Publishing, Cincinnati

Henley, Carra Dupuy (1901) *A man from Mars*, B.R. Baumgardt, Los Angeles.

Cooley, Winifred Harper (1902) 'A dream of the twenty-first century', *Arena*, no. 28, pp. 511–16

Kinkaid, Mary Holland McNeish (1903) *Walda*, Harper, New York

Evans, Anna D. (1905) *It beats the Shakers, or A new tune*, Anglo-American Corp., London and New York

Fry, Lena Jane (1905) *Other worlds*, the author, Chicago

Rogers, Bessie Story (1905) *As it may be. A story of the future*, Richard G. Badger, The Gorham Press, Boston

Wiggin, Kate Douglas Smith (1909) *Susanna and Sue*, Houghton, Mifflin, Boston

Gilman, Charlotte Perkins (1911; reprinted 1968) *Moving the mountain*, Greenwood, Westport, Conn.

Irwin, Inez Haynes (Gillmore) (1914) *Angel Island*, Henry Holt and Sons, New York

Gilman, Charlotte Perkins (1915; reprinted 1979) *Herland*, Pantheon, New York

Fisher, Mary Ann (1916) *Among the immortals in the land of desire. A glimpse of the beyond*, Shakespeare, New York

Gilman, Charlotte Perkins (1916; reprinted 1968) *With her in Ourland*, Greenwood, Westport, Conn.

Snedeker, Caroline Dale Parke [Caroline Dale Owen] (1917) *Seth Way: a romance of the New Harmony community*, Houghton, Mifflin, Boston

Bennett, Gertrude Barrows [Francis Stevens] (1918; reprinted 1970) 'Friend Island' in Sam Moskowitz (ed.), *Under the moons of Mars*, Holt, Rinehart and Winston, New York

Bennett, Gertrude Barrows [Francis Stevens] (1919; reprinted 1952) *The heads of Cerberus*, Polaris Press, Philadelphia

Bruere, Martha S. Bensley (1919) *Mildred Carver, USA*, Macmillan, New York

3

A Crisis of the Spirit

The novels of this period contrast quite dramatically with those of the past. This goes beyond mere change from one set of single-issue eutopias to another: it involves a change of form as anti-utopias and dystopias increase and eutopias decrease. In their responses to wars ending and beginning, to revolutions and the rise of the modern totalitarian state, these novels illustrate the barometric sensitivity of the genre to social and political change. Each decade has a distinctive motif which overlaps into its neighbours. Yet in spite of this intriguing state of flux, the period from 1900 to 1950 has been 'the single most neglected period in the history of utopian literature', with the exception, of course, of those great monuments of twentieth-century dystopianism, *We*, *Brave new world* and *Nineteen eighty four*.[1] The quality and quantity of utopian writing by British women during this period makes this neglect even more regrettable.

During the 1920s, for example, anti-utopian satires flourish as they had not since the eighteenth century: where one might have expected a spate of pacifist utopias in the post-war period, what erupted was scepticism about human nature and the meaning of utopia. A trickle of anti-communist dystopias were written in response to the Russian Revolution, displaced in the 1930s by anti-fascist dystopias, mostly depicting England under Fascist rule. The few feminist novels of this entire 40-year period were also published in the mid-1930s. The wartime 1940s produced the spiritualist novels, which experience shows are standard responses to war (here patriotically anti-German, rather than politically anti-Fascist); and the post-war forties, an unfocused pessimism. In the 1950s the definitive element is nuclear holocaust. The publication curve over these 40 years adds a quantitative element to qualitative differences: the 1920s, eleven novels; the 1930s, sixteen novels; the 1940s, eleven novels; and the 1950s, six. Because of the differences so apparent between decades in this chapter, after a brief introduction to its major issues, we will examine the novels chronologically in order to retain a sense of these changes.

World War One marked a watershed in utopian thinking. During the Edwardian period only faint echoes of the Victorians' optimism survived: the experience of the war to end all wars silenced it completely. The onward march of progress foundered in its barbarism, and the eutopia was one of its casualties. An anti-utopian of the 1920s, Muriel Jaeger, prefaces her *The question mark* (1926) thus (her 'question mark' is human nature):

> I accept the Bellamy — Morris — Wells world in all essentials — with one exception; I do not and cannot accept its inhabitants. At this point my effort to realise Utopia fails. With the best will in the world, I have found myself quite unable to believe in these wise, virtuous, gentle, artistic people. They do not seem to have any relation to humanity as I know it — even by the most distant descent; they suggest, rather, Special Creation. (pp. 11–12)

Referred to by L.P. Hartley as 'a singularly disquieting uncomfortable book',[2] Jaeger's is a remarkably elastic socialist future, which, despite its many concessions to individuality, cannot accommodate increasing ennui and violence. Jaeger's viewpoint of human nature is shared by other writers, producing satires of varying intensity.

However, even more than the age of anti-utopia, this was the age of dystopia. Croft notes

> the small number of attempts at socialist utopias in these years . . . over half of those that *were* written appeared before 1935. By then the full implications of events in Germany were clear to most people on the left . . . *The utopian spirit was, for the time being, on the defensive.*[3] (original emphasis)

Most of the socialist utopias were written by men, however; the closest one comes to a socialist utopia by a woman is Mitchison's fictionalised account of her visit to Soviet Russia in *We have been warned* (1936, written 1932). Quite probably other writers, like Mitchison, regarded the social experiments in Russia during the 1920s as a eutopia in action, directed as so many of them were to creating equality for women, and freeing reproductive control through liberalisation of birth control and abortion laws. Whether of right or left, dystopian writers, fearful than human nature might be changed without 'special creation', marked how conformity and repression, the framework of the totalitarian state, were often couched in the language of utopian idealism. Storm Jameson, author of three political dystopias, looked back in 1941 on the change:

> Even our idealism has misled us. We have seen that it is easy for young men to be trained to a fine temper of devotion, and for this devotion to issue in bestiality . . . Writers have had dreams of a society in which the young were trained to a self-sacrificing obedience. The first model of this utopia is Nazi Germany: there are, there will be, others. Our grandfathers could sleep quietly on the deeply-rooted and intangible ideas of a more or less humane and liberal creed. Though they did not always practise tolerance, they invoked it at least as an ideal to be reached by going forward.[4]

One effect of this change is the disappearance of the heroic feminist role models of Chapter 1. The quiescence of feminist issues apparently substantiates the myth, conveniently soothing to anti-feminists, that the suffragettes had 'packed up the hammers, and picked up the stones, bundled up the banners and . . . returned, tired but contented, to the confines of domesticity'.[5] The heroic battle of suffrage now won, the multitude of feminist groups that had unified in its cause now went their several ways, but there were still important issues at stake. During the 1920s and 1930s, the movement remained fragmented, though not divided by the bitter ideological disputes of contemporary American feminists. These were not years of inactivity, but a time when 'romantic rebellion yielded place to necessary drudgery'. There was 'a much more complex, much trickier problem of dealing with legislation in a large number of highly specific and often ferociously complicated cases — boring, thankless, nit-picking work for the most part, entrusted to highly dedicated elite cadres'.[6] One similarity with the women's movement in the US during the same period is between their ill-fated Equal Rights Amendment (1923 — see the next chapter) and the British Sex Disqualification (Removal) Act (1919), a grand-sounding bill that proved useless in reality.[7] A more effective one (the Equal Citizenship (Blanket) Bill) disappeared without trace somewhere in the Commons in 1943.

The only work directly in the tradition of the Victorian novels, Gresswell's *When Yvonne was dictator* (1935), is indicative of the change. The title is not pejorative, but suggestive of a feminist riposte to the Methuen series, 'If I were dictator', published in 1934–5.[8] Yvonne faces quintessentially 1930s problems. She must choose between marriage and a career; and her fiancé, a physician, wants a 'proper' wife who will stay at home. (Her father, a GP, encourages her career; her old-fashioned mother opposes it.) In choosing a career rather than marriage, Yvonne faces a conflict that had not affected women in earlier eutopian novels. Her initial electioneering platform is a lowered birth rate; and she subsequently campaigns (and wins) on a 'Peace Pact'. Having become Prime Minister, she is declared Dictator by popular demand, and one of her first acts is a new marriage contract, which allows the stipulation of individual grounds for divorce (in this, nothing has changed). A women's strike against 'motherhood' leads to a 'Women's Charter' (which she supports) which demands equal pay, equal rights in marriage, equal education, and rights for unwed mothers. It is the fictional resolution of issues that involved 1930s women, and the 'Women's Charter' replicates in particular the aims of the feminist Six Point Group.[9]

Just as the business of lobbying for piecemeal change lacked the unifying and dramatic effect of a single-issue feminist movement, so too there is an almost complete absence of single-issue feminist utopian novels during this period. 'Throughout the century, feminists had been increasingly prominent in internationalism, and it is understandable that for many of them the struggle against patriarchy assumed the form of opposing Fascism and/or opposing war.'[10] Most of these writers are demonstrably internationalists: many were journalists, several with the feminist weekly *Time and Tide*. Holtby became political writer for the *News Chronicle* in the year she wrote her anti-utopia; she was also an enthusiastic proponent of the League of Nations. Jameson, as president of International PEN (an international fellowship of writers), was closely involved with exiled writers from Europe. So, too, were Naomi Mitchison and the journalist Charlotte Haldane. Many of these women had travelled to communist Russia or Nazi Germany (sometimes to both) during the inter-war years. Politically alert, their dystopias are warnings, usually depicting a Britain under a Fascist dictator.

In the absence of a single focus for feminist writers, are the categories of nature and culture still relevant? The answer is a definite 'yes', and it centres on women's right to be something other than breeding machines. The 'natural selection' which Victorian women thought *they* could control proved beyond their reach: in at least 50 per cent of these novels it becomes a function of the state. It is a complex and highly political issue. Both dystopia and anti-utopia introduce societies which dictate women's reproductive behaviour, whether their eugenic policies are designed to restrict or to enforce pregnancy. During the 1920s and 1930s, birth control became 'an issue that split the British Labour Party'.[11] In one of the novels discussed in this chapter, Mitchison's *We have been warned* (1936), the author discusses attitudes to birth control in a North of England electorate, where working-class women suffer from lack of information, and where the men are not prepared to change their prudish attitudes. Birth control clinics were set up during the 1920s, but gaining official sanction for them proved difficult.[12] Soviet Russia's immediate post-revolutionary government gave free access to birth control information and abortion: this, and their reversal of policy in the 1930s, and Nazi Germany's 'kinder, kuchen, kirche' policy for women, which closed professional and educational avenues and stressed women's 'natural' functions as mothers, are all reflected in these novels. In the few eutopias of the period (Gresswell, Ertz, both 1935), birth control also plays an important role. Over and over one is made aware of the vulnerability of women's private lives to male dictators and male governments, and in the most nightmarish of the dystopias (Burdekin, *Swastika night*, 1937), women have been stripped of all contact with culture (this is defined as exclusively male) and reduced to the sub-human. They are even kept in cages, and so defined by their natural functions that once past breeding age their already meagre rations are further cut.

In works as disparate as the anti-utopian satires by Macaulay (1919), Boswell (1926), Stevenson (1936), and the dystopias by Tillyard (1930), Brash (1933), Mitchison (1936), Burdekin (1937) and Greenwood (1944), as well as Haldane's ambiguous eutopia (1926), eugenic science and politics are prominent. What is found in these novels, eutopia, anti-utopia and dystopia alike, is reference to different attitudes to birth control. The first gives the ideal circumstance of individual women's control over their sexuality and reproduction, the second, how attempts to remove it are outwitted. The third is a dystopian *absence* of that control, whether it involves a restriction on bearing children, or a compulsion to do so.

While Yvonne campaigns and wins on the birth control issue

(and the strike against motherhood (sex?) is a powerful weapon for women to use to achieve their economic aims), in *Woman alive*, by Ertz, the same power is used by the last, the only, and so precious, woman alive to achieve world peace. Against government pressure to begin childbearing and continue the race, she holds out until she can do so in the way that *she* chooses, to ensure a eutopian future by increasing the ratio of women to men. Her daughters (*not* 'surplus women') will find sanctuary for their ideals in numbers.

Of the anti-utopias, Macaulay's satire centres on eugenic controls in a post-war Britain, Boswell (1926) sees them as a population control measure imposed in the future by powerful unions, Stevenson (1936) by an eccentric scientist in a post-catastrophe Britain, in order to create a master race. In each of these satires the attempted controls fail, and women decide their own futures.

There are similar regulations in Tillyard's *Concrete* (1930), and Brash's *Unborn tomorrow* (1933), both works which present socialised dystopias with a eugenic programme which includes euthanasia. These institutionalised controls aimed at social control and the destruction of the family are part of a wider dystopian spectrum: individual response in both cases is a dangerously low Anglo-Saxon birth rate, a symbolic refusal to breed in captivity. The women in Burdekin's *Swastika night* (1937) are equally involuntarily producing only sons, which also puts the race in peril.

Haldane's *Man's world* (1926) is a more complex work, illustrative of the difficulties that can be encountered when classifying utopias. Bibliographers and critics deal quite variously with this work: Patai calls it a 'Satire of a future scientific state';[13] Gerber, 'one of the least satirical modern utopias, [where] a genuine conflict arises between the new science and the imaginative religious man';[14] Armytage terms it 'Wells-type'; and Sargent, 'a eugenic dystopia'.[15] Yet the dust-jacket of her later (1927) *Motherhood and its enemies* describes it as 'a romance of the future . . . brimful of new and exciting ideas regarding the future of the human race', and includes sections of a review from *Labour Magazine* praising it as a 'prophecy' and 'a comprehensive survey of [modern woman's] ideals'. The other reviews cited (which include *Scientific Worker* and *Berliner Tageblatt*) carry no references to satire, and I believe that Haldane intends *Man's world* to be read as a eutopia. In her later *Motherhood and its enemies*, she castigates the role of the Church ('the cloistered virgin took precedence of the wife, the wife of the mother'), and criticises the 'marriage bar' against teachers because it limits the profession of schoolteacher to 'mannish' 'inter-sex' (lesbian) spinsters, who are (as she condemns a past Principal of Newnham College) 'in every way the wrong [people] to have charge of young and impressionable girls'.[16] *Man's world* presents entirely the same point of view, as these quotations from the novel prove:

> Only those mothers who possessed certain specific qualities were chosen as teachers for the young. For vocational motherhood was a career which had its grades like all others. (p. 71)

> It was the Church that took all the asexuals into the convents, and persecuted the 'fallen'. It was not until the mothers were completely under the sway of the priests that they were duped into bearing every-one else's burdens. (p. 77)

Although it is tempting to read *Man's world* as a satire, the evidence of *Motherhood* renders that impossible, and therefore the strict eugenic controls of the future, the division of women into the ranks of mothers, entertainers (asexual and thus non-reproducing creative artists) and neuters should be read in its light.

Mitchison's *We have been warned* concludes with a Fascist takeover in Britain. The body of her novel concerns the wife of a Labour Party politician, member for a working-class constituency in the north of England, as was Mitchison herself. The narrator travels to Russia, where she visits an abortion clinic: the description, says Mitchison, is 'straight from the diary of my visit there in 1932'.[17] Her description of this, and of the prudish attitudes of the British Labour Party (very outspokenly portrayed in the working-class constituency) led to several years delay in publishing this novel, which was rejected by three separate publishers on grounds of its explicit treatment of sexuality and birth control.[18]

Her condemnation of current political attitudes is taken even further by Burdekin, who extrapolates from Nazi attitudes to women, but in a context of polarisation of the categories of nature and culture, which theories accounting for exclusion are taken to their extreme: 'She saw that it is but a small step from the male apotheosis of women as mothers to their degradation as mere breeding animals.'[19] This 'reduction of women' is a corner-stone of Nazi ideology, which is also the subject of Greenwood's *The heart consumed* (1944), in which a plan to create a 'master race' is defeated. The subject of birth control is never treated as a personal matter in these novels, but a political concern. As such, with the examples of Russian openness turning into restriction in the mid-1930s (when abortion was illegalised, and women were encouraged by state subsidies to have large families), and of the German apotheosis of motherhood/denigration of women's participation in public life, before them, the sinister implications of totalitarian governments for women writers, whether of the right or the left, were concentrated on their attitudes to women.

1920s: the satirical decade

Satire was the prevailing tenor of the 1920s. Malcolm Bradbury comments on the period's 'remarkable revival or reinvention of comic forms in fiction': 'as if they offered an ideal means for coping with a postwar world in which disorder seems notably prevalent, value historically extracted, chaos come again, as a direct result of the war and its disorientations and dehumanizations'.[20] Aldous Huxley and Evelyn Waugh, who were foremost in this wave, later wrote satirical anti-utopias and dystopias; *Brave new world* (1932), *Ape and essence* (1948) (Huxley); 'Out of depth' (1933), *Love among the ruins* (1953) (Waugh). In several instances one can see that their satire derives from a religious belief in which original sin dictates attitudes to human nature (and which has rarely, if ever, played a role in American utopianism). Gerber defines the religious utopia as a *contradictio in adjecto*, for 'a truly religious utopia is Heaven, or an Earthly Paradise, and should not depict this world, but the next'.[21] Certainly, it is hard to square the doctrine of the Fall with utopian expectations of the plasticity of human nature. Sometimes satire hinges on a rejection of middle-class conformity, which makes them particularly docile sheep for the bureaucratic shepherds. Often it is associated with the British tendency to 'muddle through', which, whatever its resultng inequities, is reassuring in a world of uniform Alphas and Deltas. Macaulay and Burdekin see it as an endearing, if exasperating, national tendency; Burdekin's future hope of world salvation lies with the British, dominated by Nazi ideology for centuries, yet 'just as queer as ever, sloppy and casual and yet likeable' (p. 20).

Of the eleven titles by women in the 1920s, six are anti-utopias: Macaulay, *What not? A prophetic comedy*, 1919, *Orphan Island*, 1924; Hamilton, *Theodore Savage*, 1922, (reprinted in 1928 as *Lest ye die*); Boswell, *Posterity*, 1926; Jaeger, *The question mark*, 1926; and Bowhay, *Elenchus Brown, the story of an experimental utopia, compiled by a student of Battersea Polytechnic*, 1929. Holtby's *The astonishing island* (1933) and Stevenson's *The empty world* (1936), although published later, also belong with this group. Their tone is rueful laughter (sometimes tempered with exasperation) at the spectacle of imperfect nature 'in a sad and precarious world' (Macaulay, *What not?*, p. 236). Yet there is a sense of relief that in a time of rapid change and conflicting theories, the very sameness of human nature may be relied upon to provide stability and comfort.

Rose Macaulay's two anti-utopias are among the early works of an accomplished writer. Her witty satire on bureaucracy, *What not?* (1919), describes a post-war government attempting to raise the general level of intelligence through a combined programme of adult education and eugenic controls. Macaulay had been a civil servant during the war: she had worked for a time in Propaganda, and her fictional government's advertising techniques are bizarre — but believable. The eugenic programme fails when a secret marriage (of the Minister for Brains and his chief assistant) becomes public knowledge: he has sub-normal siblings and is classified as being unfit to be a parent. Macaulay cleverly inverts the marriage bar which had operated against women in the Civil Service since 1894.[22] Because of the Minister's commitment to the eugenic programme, his marriage loses *him* his job, and also destroys the Ministry. Boswell's *Posterity* (1926) also deals with eugenic controls. These are administered by the unions (who refuse to admit any *man* with more than two children), despite opposition from capitalists and the Church. However, women find quite ingenious ways to flout the ruling, as a crop of illegal maternity homes testifies.

Macaulay's *Orphan Island* (1924) is an amusing variation on the theme of the island utopia, equally critical of conformity and the bourgeoisie. Not a laboratory for social experiment, tropical Orphan Island is a gelid museum of hypocritical Victorian attitudes to class, perpetuated by descendants of a nineteenth-century shipwreck of orphans and their guardians. Its 'ruler', Miss Smith, is a parody of Queen Victoria, reliant on alcoholic 'medicine' and off-hand in the treatment of her 'heir', Albert Edward. She maintains a rigid class system ('Smith' and 'non-Smith') until her failing health (and the arrival of a sociology professor from Cambridge) provide the conditions for necessary change. Middle-class conformity takes a very strong dose of satire, as it did in *What not?*, where the upper and lower classes either ignored or subverted the eugenics laws, while the middle classes took them seriously.

Bowhay's *Elenchus Brown* (1929) and Holtby's *The astonishing island* (1933) are also satirical variations on the traditional island utopia. *Elenchus* makes gentle fun of a utopian idealist who uses his inheritance to experiment with different forms of government. His quest for the perfect political system is frustrated by the insistence of his recruited members on always acting in accordance with their own desires whatever system of government is being tried out: the lazy are lazy, and the active active, irrespective of oligarchy or anarchy. A short but charming work, it encapsulates the anti-utopian spirit prevalent during the period.

Holtby is more malicious towards her targets. Her (unnamed) island is modern Britain, 'discovered' by a naïve traveller from Tristan da Cunha, who is a parody of every earnest utopian voyager in the history of the literature. Holtby equips Mackintosh with a journalist friend, who interprets national stereotypes for him, and generally acts as his utopian guide. She ridicules English newspapers, and political, educational and religious institutions in a spirit that is relatively playful — until it comes to feminist issues. The fun that she has exploding stereotypes of 'the mother', 'the career woman', 'the old maid', is lost when Robinson Mackintosh meets a young woman pharmacist desperately miserable as a housebound wife and mother, who is a victim of the 'marriage bar' (to which, as an employee of local government, she had been liable). However, she has taken her husband away from his former wife, and so there is a sense that the punishment may fit the crime. As a balance, he also meets a rather jolly, motor-bike riding woman medical student, also a mother, but one with an outlet for her intelligence and energy.

Also predicated on earlier genre novels is Stevenson (1936); her central character is introduced reading *Erewhon*, a sure sign of authorial intent! With the world destroyed by a strange new star, the remnant saved is temporarily at the mercy of a crazy scientist who wishes them to be guinea pigs in a social experiment, which includes controlled breeding. Fortunately, his bodyguards assassinate him, and so a freer, pastoral community emerges at the conclusion, though it is not followed long enough to test its viability.

Jaeger's *Question mark* fails to fit human nature into even an unusually tolerant eutopian world where social freedom 'meant also the freedom to be the sort of fool one wanted' (p. 71). This book is indeed (as Hartley says) uncomfortable, for, when the narrator returns to his own time period (the 1920s), he can find no solace in 'muddling through': the misfits of the future fare even worse in the present than they do in the twenty-second century.

Darker still is Cicely Hamilton's *Theodore Savage* (1922; reprinted in 1928 as *Lest ye die*). This powerful novel by the author of *How the vote was won* (1909, Chapter 1) is an anti-utopia that verges on dystopia. Its underlying impulse is a cyclic view of history that completely excludes any possibility of progress. Her autobiography describes the work's inception, her reaction to an air raid in France, when she felt the 'truth of the Eden legend' and 'prohibition of the knowledge that makes us like unto gods, "lest we die!"':

> Many peoples have traditions of a vanished Golden Age: and the fire-breathing dragons familiar to legend, may they not sometimes have been a dim race-memory of machines familiar to ourselves. . . If our civilization destroys itself utterly, the memory of our achievements, handed on from one barbarian generation to another, would soon take the form of legendary giant and magician; steam, electricity, and chemical action would be wizardry.[23]

This form of anti-utopianism is ultimately more pessimistic than a dystopia (and usually gives rise to one), for even the most repressive of these usually offers some hope of a return to freedom. *Theodore Savage*'s primitive world, which denies all knowledge as the work of the devil, is barbarism camped on the ruins of civilisation, which if it rises again will do so only to fall. In this world women are despised; in a society ruled by ignorance and superstition they are the oppressed of the oppressed, the remembered daughters of a forgotten Eve. *Theodore Savage* is notable for being an early treatment of the theme of civilisation versus the barbarians, which is increasingly relevant in later decades for British women writers.

In the general run of anti-utopias, wayward human nature successfully refuses to fit into the slots prepared for it by a bureaucratic state: the dystopia takes place on a darker stage, where the state (totalitarian rather than bureaucratic) is a formidable enemy of individualism (usually personified by a few rebels).

Anti-communist dystopias of the 1920s

This is a small group of four novels, which breaks into two equal sections. The first of these concerns itself with violence transplanted from the Russian Revolution: Coron, *Ten years hence?* (1924); and

Grant, *A candle in the hills: the story of the counter revolution* (1926). The second group describes totalitarian socialist governments established in Britain in a distant future: Tillyard, *Concrete: a story of 200 years hence* (1930); and Brash [John Kendall], *Unborn tomorrow* (1933). Fears of a left-wing dictatorship are never as strong as those of one from the right. The two earlier novels suggest that the British Labour Party could, in its naïveté, put the country at the mercy of an international communist conspiracy. Some writers include favourable references to Mussolini's programme of social reform. They all display highly elitist attitudes to class and race (the racial inferiority of the Slavs is a common topic); as one might expect, their anti-materialism often has a religious basis. The two later novels provide bridging histories of European war and plague, using physical contagion as a metaphor for moral contagion (the same strain also appears in American works of the same period, though with a different outcome).

Coron's (1924) target is the British Labour Party, particularly in matters of international diplomacy. It was published during Macdonald's first (brief) Labour government, which fell on its pacifism and the wish to recognise Soviet Russia. In this rather weak, sensationalist novel, Coron's international conspirators trade on fears of a possible Fascist government, 'such as had saved Italy some time back' (p. 66). *A candle in the hills* (1926), by Scottish writer Isabel Grant, forecasts a 'Soviet government of Great Britain', with the counter-revolution led by a woman who acts as a rallying point for the Scottish clans. The Red Guards have murdered most of the royal family and the nobility, and the North as the bastion of individualism is the centre of resistance (a theme that is to recur in the dystopias of Tillyard, Brash and Jameson).[24]

Tillyard (1930) and Brash (1933) are more concerned with an established, over-regulated, materialist society than with bloody revolution. Tillyard's troubled world is 200 years in the future:

The World Revolution of the Proletariat made horrible reading. Still more horrible had been the civil wars in China and India . . . The great epidemic which followed had killed more than the wars had done. Great tracts of the world lay desolate . . . After the Great Death, ten years of madness had supervened. (pp. 110–11)

Something of the same history leads to Brash's *Unborn tomorrow* (set in 1995), a world war begun by a Russian invasion of Europe (1938), with a subsequent Great Epidemic. Both works are based on religious objections to scientific materialism. Tillyard was a Quaker, and her fictionalised namesake appears in a contemporary Quaker eutopia, Slonczewski's *Still forms on Foxfield* (1980, see p. 168). Tillyard's novel draws a dark picture of religious oppression, including in her dystopia a Christian eutopia (called Cambridge) on a Pacific island. From this saving remnant comes a convert ready to challenge the sterility of a dystopian Age of Reason, whose Minister of Reason (Manlius) is known as 'Big Brother'.

There are also obvious Christian overtones in the 'Creed of the State' from Brash's *Unborn tomorrow* (1933), worth quoting in its entirety because it encapsulates the dread of totalitarian enforcement common to all dystopias:

> We, the World Community, believe in the brotherhood of man, the abnegation of the individual to the needs of the State. We believe in equality of opportunity, in the glory of science, the service of machinery, in the beauty of sacrifice, in the limitless rights of the State, the infallible wisdom of its decrees. We believe in the power of the material, the cessation of life after death, the triumph of the physical and the temporal. (pp. 58–9)

These novels are more fully detailed expositions of the religious reactions to socialism and materialism of the late nineteenth century (although far more common in America than Britain), grafted on to fears prompted by the Russian Revolution, and often bolstered with racist prejudices.

Eutopia

So few eutopias were published by women during these two decades that there is good reason to overlook the barriers of time and take them as a group. The first, Griffiths's *Three worlds* (1922), is a slender spiritualist work, its purpose being chiefly to console those who had lost those they loved in the war: on a heavenly Jupiter they are reunited. It is a utopian form common to wartime, as the novels published during World War Two will demonstrate.

Haldane's eugenically ordered world has already been discussed to a point. For further understanding, it should be mentioned that the novel concerns the relationship of brother and sister, he rebelling against the stratified order of a materialist, rational society. Finally, the new Icarus impelled by his 'sterile mysticism', he takes a suicidal flight in his aircraft. Then, but only then, his sister decides on the vocation of motherhood. (Haldane's husband, geneticist J.B.S. Haldane, published a monograph entitled *Daedalus* (1924), in defence of the future role of science, in reply to Bertrand Russell's sceptical *Icarus* (1924).)

The remaining novels are unabashedly feminist. Two of these are by Katherine Burdekin, who also wrote the most devastating of the anti-Fascist dystopias. Her *The rebel passion* (1929) and *Proud man* (1934) contain partial eutopias. These two novels are thoughtful examinations of the suffering caused by excessive sexual stereotyping, and of the 'herd instinct' in human behaviour (both of these themes contribute to her powerful *Swastika night*). The former (pity is the 'rebel passion' which separates humans from animals) completes a survey of human history, reaching from the Middle Ages into a eutopian twenty-second century which has dispensed with marriage and divorce, and with private ownership of land: in fact, it is a medieval world of guilds and small settlements very like Morris's Nowhere, but with the addition of modern medicine and communication systems. She describes a change in human history towards the end of the twentieth century, and, in the twenty-first, birth control 'by all but the diseased and half-witted', later corrected by the sterilisation of male half-wits, condemnation of rape, and equal pay for women. After a Mongolian invasion of Europe (the League of Nations and Germany act to save civilisation), the twenty-second century brings peace and eutopia.

Proud man concerns the arrival in the modern world of a genderless individual from a eutopia in an unnamed place, populated by self-reproducing, telepathic androgynes. The novel concentrates on the effects on this autonomous, rational and detached visitor of a rigid gender division, experienced first hand through the visitor's 'Tiresias-like' experience: 'I could not be a *person*, for none were in existence, but must appear to be either a woman or a man!' (p. 65). The traveller finds life as a woman closer to peaceful coexistence with nature, observes the pride of men 'in being men', and condemns the 'herds' (mostly masculine) of modern life: 'nations, churches, fascists, communists, trade unions, the BMA, the Great White Race, the Nordic Myth, the proletariat, the bourgeoisie, the gangsters, the priesthoods of all religions' (p. 147). As Alethea (in female life) and Gifford Verona (in male life), the voice of the visitor is the voice of truth.

There are two additional feminist eutopias, both published in 1935: Gresswell (already introduced) and Susan Ertz's *Woman alive*. While the former's Yvonne is the last of the eutopian feminist Prime Ministers, Ertz's Stella is a variant on the 'last man' theme. Her 'last woman' is the survivor of a species of chemical warfare that is not lethal to men. When she is discovered alive, all men rejoice, but she refuses to co-operate in a scheme to repopulate the world until she has time to refine her own proposals.[25] In a letter written after the catastrophe (she thinks she, too, will die), she expresses the principles that she will later have the power to implement:

> War belongs to the dark ages, but has been fostered until our own day by men who saw no other way of getting money, advancement, or glory. Men! . . . We ought to have destroyed the majority of them years ago, only keeping enough to increase the population, or perhaps keep it from declining. (p. 62)

She continually refers to man as 'the fighting animal' whose aggressive instincts must be tamed (so too does Burdekin in *Proud man*, describing soldiers as 'killing males'). Once she has accepted her responsibility to continue the race, and the power to influence the future that this carries, she determines to take advantage of the scientific ability to choose the sex of her future children, declaring:

> If I marry and have children, and their children begin a new world, there will only be one man to every three or four women. I'm convinced that it's the only way. The logic men show as individuals they entirely lose in groups. With women it may be the other way round, which will be far less dangerous. (pp. 165–6)

Here, as in most of the British novels, the role of science is important only insofar as it relates to biology and genetics, and it can hold a crucial key to the peaceable future of the world.

Anti-Fascist dystopias

The anti-Fascist dystopias began to appear in 1935, and there are four of them in the next few years, all set in England, all describing rule by a Fascist dictator: Hunter [George Lancing], *Fraudulent conversion* (1935); Jameson, *In the second year* (1936); Mitchison, *We have been warned* (1936); Burdekin [Murray Constantine], *Swastika night* (1937). There is also Curtis's *Landslide* (1934), with a predominantly pacifist theme, which also describes Britain ruled by a dictator, though whether of right or left is uncertain. The trend of these novels is modified during the war by another group, set outside Britain, which is nationalistic and anti-German rather than ideologically anti-Fascist; they form the subject matter of the next section.

The anti-Fascist dystopias express fears that the economic situation and high unemployment of the depression would replicate the situation that led Germany towards Fascism, and propel Britain along the same path. The British Fascist Party under Oswald Mosley receives scant attention (only from Hunter); the perceived dictator was a different character. Jameson describes her first anti-Fascist novel, *In the second year* (1936), as being prompted by accounts of Hitler's 30 June purge of the SA (storm-troopers) 'brown shirts' in 'the night of the long knives':

> What I wanted to do was to expose why a dictator was forced, almost always, to kill the very men who fought for him when he was only a brutal adventurer. I thought I knew why, and I could imagine an English Fascism, the brutality half masked and devious, with streaks of a Methodist virtue.[26]

These novels were serious warnings of political danger. Jameson (like Mitchison) was proud of being in the Nazi 'Black Book' as a consequence of her political beliefs (active membership of the Labour Party), journalism and fiction. Jameson was also proscribed by the Russians.

These anti-Fascist novels that fictionalise the rise of a Fascist state in England differ in the time-frame of their warnings: Hunter (1935) deals with contemporary events related to Mosley's activities, which escalated in 1934; Jameson (1936) as her title indicates, introduces the second year of a Fascist dictatorship — time enough for the establishment of concentration camps and for the persecution of Jews and dissident intellectuals to have become part of the fabric of society. Mitchison's (1936) is undated, but follows a Labour victory at the polls. Burdekin (1937) has a much longer time-frame — predicated on a thesis of Nazi victory, it describes a Fascist-dominated twenty-sixth century.

Katherine Burdekin's *Swastika night* (1937), which examines a future world under Nazi domination, is particularly horrifying in its depiction of the probable status of women in that world — higher than the worm, lower than the despised Christian (Christian women are the lower than low). This Nazi world also has its creed, a lengthy affirmation of Aryan male solidarity and the godhead of Hitler, which concludes: 'And I believe in pride, in courage, in violence, in brutality, in bloodshed, in ruthlessness, and all other soldierly and heroic virtues. Heil Hitler' (p. 6). In this 'heroic' future, any woman over 16 may be raped by any man at any time, unless wearing the insignia of male ownership. Younger girls are protected only because their offspring would be puny. Sons pass from their mothers' care at 18 months, and are taken into the care of the men.

The three small lights that promise some end to this dystopia are biology, the British character and the Christian remnant. Despite the domination of Nazi culture, an Englishman, Alfred, begins to learn the truth of human history and tries to learn the even more difficult lesson of appreciating a daughter. He is given, by a dissident German knight who has no heir, a carefully guarded book that reveals suppressed truths (that the British once had an empire, that women were once loved). This he passes to his son (also Alfred), who hides the book with the Christians and, though puzzled by it, tries to accept his father's dying wish that he cherish his sister.

Curtis (1934) asks her reader to imagine a world without the League of Nations with Western Europe threatened by an outside enemy. Perhaps the unspoken assumption here is that the threat is from Eastern Europe (Russia), but the source of the threat is not the major focus, it is the dictator ('Leo Steele') who achieves power in Britain, and suspends basic human rights, including habeas corpus and the freedom of the press. The landslide of the title occurs in Europe, whose links with Britain are emphasised.

Hunter (1935) subtitles her work 'A romance of the gold standard', and focuses on a combination of economic factors and Mosley's 'black shirts' (who become, for fictional purposes, the 'purple vests').[27] Her unlikely protagonist is an unworldly professor who is given the power to coin money at will. At first reluctant to do so (not needing it himself), he gradually becomes aware of the economic and political situation. After observing unemployment on the coalfields and in London, and seeing the Fascist bullies in action, he uses his gift to do battle. He takes on a corrupted capitalist system and its press, and at the conclusion of the novel the forces of good are making some impact.[28]

Jameson's *In the second year* (1936) examines the same combination of circumstances; but, while at the conclusion of Hunter's novel, her professor is still battling against Fascism (with some success), Jameson examines a British Hitler consolidating his rule. The sequence of events that she charts are taken from German history and from current events in Britain, like Hunter's: a miner-led general strike, intervention by a Volunteer Guard, and the ascendancy of a Messianic demagogue. 'In the second year' of his power, five million dissident intellectuals, socialists and Jews are in labour camps, street violence against Jews is increasing and a gullible population is hoodwinked, collaborating or cowed, and British storm-troopers are conducting purges. Jameson was passionately concerned with international politics, knew and feared the trend of events in Germany, and her novel is intended as something more than an intellectual exercise on the face of 'British Fascism'.

Pacifism

With the fear of another war in the 1930s, pacifism becomes an important eutopian aim. Many of these writers were interested in possibilities that the League of Nations might keep the peace through international government. In 1935 Lady Rhondda, a staunch feminist, responded to an invitation from the American journal *Forum* to contribute to their series 'The world as I want it'.[29] Her priorities for change are, firstly, 'a world in which peace is ensured'; secondly, 'sufficient food, good housing, warmth and comfort, good air and light for all'; and, thirdly, no barriers of 'race nor class nor sex nor marriage' (p. 243). The 'internationalism' of feminists could not be more marked; nor could their awareness in the 1930s that forces are gathering against them, and that another war may be inevitable.

The end of the 1930s is a leaner period, however. As war came closer, hopes of peace faded, and political scenarios seemed less appropriate. The two works that come between the anti-Fascist dystopias and the wartime anti-German eutopias are Warde's play *The shelter in Bedlam* (1937) (republished 1938 as *Peace under earth: dialogues from the year 1946*), the story of a materialistic future in which life is being transferred underground as a result of war, and air-raid shelters expand to become permanent homes. Christianity has disappeared, and the dialogue is between an adult of the future trying to describe the Nativity, and a listening child. It seems an expectable response to the period, as does Newton's *My life in time* (1938), which is a theosophical-type eutopia, suffused with Egyptology and references to Revelations. which, among references to the golden lotus, contains a short description of London during wartime — 'Blood to run like spilled wine over the street' (p. 233). Against this, however, is balanced a vaguely heavenly eutopia that she has glimpsed in another dimension.

The wartime 1940s

Obviously there is pressure on writers during wartime to avoid unpatriotic and defeatist attitudes. As a result, a Germany ridiculed or overcome therefore replaces a resurgent or triumphant Fascism, although there are several novels warning against trusting the Germans and settling for anything other than unconditional surrender. When Burdekin's *Swastika night* was reissued by the Left Book Club in 1940, it was with a publishers' note, stating:

> (a) *when* it was written (1937 — that is, before the outbreak of war);
> (b) that it is 'symbolic rather than prophetic';
> (c) that the author has not changed 'his [sic] opinion that the Nazi idea is evil . . . he has changed his mind about the Nazi *power* to make the *world* evil' (p. 4) (original emphases).

The wartime novels are a blend of mysticism, patriotism and mistrust of the Germans: Jameson, *Then we shall hear singing* (1942); Sackville-West, *Grand Canyon* (1942); King-Hall, *Fly envious time* (1944); Vigers, *Atlantis rising* (1944).

Sackville-West's novel is the least optimistic of these, for it suggests an overly naïve America signing an armistice with Germany, only to be betrayed and invaded. The novel is written in two parts, and the grim predictions of the first are offset by the calm spiritual harmony of the second. Sackville-West introduces a mystic strain here: the figures winding their way down into the Grand Canyon in Part Two are revealed to be the spirits of the invasion victims of Part One. Not surprisingly, the novel was rejected by a number of publishers, including Woolf's Hogarth Press, and drew 'some bloody reviews' when it appeared.[30] (In the following year she published her biographical study of two Catholic mystics, St Teresa of Avila, and St Thérèse of Lisieux.)

Jameson's novel is also set outside Britain, in an occupied East

European country (the subtitle, 'A fantasy in C major', implies Poland). Her autobiography also includes notes on the inception of this novel:

> Suppose a German scientist had discovered a means . . . of turning the men and women of an occupied country into obedient docile animals, with healthy bodies and neither individuality, in the human sense, nor will. Would anything, any memory, survive or revive in the nation so treated?[31]

The answer is 'yes', and develops a celebration of the mystic relationship between culture and land. Something does stir and revive in the people so treated, a spiritual essence that overcomes the brutal domination of the German oppressor.

Vigers writes in the same strain. She depicts Britain as heir to the civilisation of Atlantis, the lost Earthly Paradise. Exploiting the myth of the return of King Arthur, Vigers turns Hitler's theories of race to patriotic advantage. She characterises the Aryan race as power hungry, sadistic and brutal, afraid of the supernatural, rigid and lacking initiative. The British (Atlantan) character is, of course, the obverse. The theosophical implications of these racial theories will be discussed in the following chapter: what is interesting at this juncture is how Vigers associates these with the legend of Arthur's return to create a most patriotic novel grounded in myth.

In some ways the odd novel in this group is King-Hall's novel (1944), written in three sections, comprising the 'memoirs' of women of different generations: 1937–9 (grandmother); 1977–9 (granddaughter); and 1999 (great-granddaughter). Section 1 deals with British decency (and complacency), contrasted with realistic scenes of Nazi fanaticism and hooliganism. Section 2 has a self-consciously styled eutopian future, though its equality and abrasive feminism are ironically presented; and section 3 is a brief introduction to an authorially approved eutopia, one more dependent on individualism and creativity than the scientific 'eutopia' that preceded it. This is, however, disrupted; in the second section, Germany is 'stirring', and in the third she strikes against the world federation. Like *Grand Canyon*, *Fly envious time* is a warning of German perfidiousness.

The post-war 1940s, the early 1950s

Unlike the strongly satirical period of the 1920s, the immediate post-war publications of the 1940s and 1950s did not have the same certainties to attack. Some of the novels of this period are anti-feminist, almost all are anti-utopian; their targets are politics of both left and right, psychology, bureaucracy. Although Mannin's anarcho-syndicalist *Bread and roses* (1945) is the first post-war eutopia, it was also for a long time the last. Victory in the war did not bring euphoria about the future, nor the satirical scepticism that enlivened the 1920s, although the 1960s do return to something of that mood. Instead, these novels are dystopias (often with a tiny glimmer of hope in their conclusions), or eutopias glimpsed but lost. After Mannin there are Chetwynd, *Future imperfect* and Hine, *The island forbidden to man* (both 1946); Nott, *The dry deluge* (1947); Burton, *Gone to grass* (*The roaring dove* in the US edition) (1948), Laski, *Tory heaven, or Thunder on the right* (*Toasted English* — inexplicably — in the US edition) (1948); Jameson, *The moment of truth* (1949); Frankau, *The offshore light* (1952); Richmond, *The grim tomorrow* (1953); Smith, 'The last of the Spode' (1953); Bennett, *The long way back* (1954); Wallace, *Forty years on* (1958); Laski, *The offshore island* (1959). Although the spectre of World War Two is present in the earliest of these novels, it is soon suplanted by fears of nuclear war. The most cohesive feature of this decade is not the absence of idealism, but of a sure and agreed-upon political target: while one may not expect this to emerge, clear-cut, in every period of utopian literature, its absence is notable here. Every movement to the left, it seems, is answered by a movement to the right, and even the appearance of anti-Americanism, which is so strong a feature of the 1960s, is balanced by the opposite view.

Mannin's 'utopian survey and blueprint' spells out her ideals for a post-war Britain. An anarcho-syndicalist, she offers detailed non-bureaucratic proposals for the revitalisation of industry and agriculture, including collective farming, based on co-operative work and a non-cash exchange. Her attitude to feminist issues is rather unadventurous, based on a world in which 'Utopian women are not concerned with asserting intellectual equality with men' (p. 152): she quotes from William Morris the passage from *News from Nowhere* quoted in Chapter 1 (p. 18), and her only concession to professional women is that there will be many more women doctors in Utopia. Mannin expects that economic independence, birth control and a greater respect for motherhood ('women's primary

95

creative work is the production of children', p. 153) will raise women's status in marriage, although, like Morris, she concludes that there will continue to be 'unhappiness in human relations'.

Chetwynd and Hine belong in quite a different category. Their anti-feminism is associated with the war: the first has fears that the women who enjoyed a more varied public life during wartime might spearhead a feminist revolt reducing men to effeminacy. Told from the standpoint of a moderate feminist Member of Parliament, it tells of her disapproval as younger, more radical feminists repeal male franchise ('to absolve men from the wearisome responsibilities of politics' — p. 28), repeating all the old anti-feminist arguments against men. There is a drop in the birth-rate, as everyone waits for 'experiments in transplanting embryos to be perfected'. Where role reversal was satire with a point when written by Cridge in 1871, in 1946 it reads more like the anti-feminism of a male writer than the work of a feminist. Erosion of the universal franchise (the dream of nineteenth-century reformers) is hardly calculated to provide any equable solution to any problems. Hine presents an island of women, spiteful, malicious and frustrated, whose acceptance of men signals a return to normality. She suggests that, during wartime, women who refuse to comfort warriors, and to bear their children, are not only sour old maids, but treacherously unpatriotic.

Kathleen Nott's (1947) *The dry deluge* is a far superior novel. An anti-utopia by a committed Liberal who is particularly contemptuous of B.F. Skinner's behaviourism,[32] which satirises his social theories through describing the elaborately planned underground community designed by a psychologist, Dr Nore. Partly a social experiment, partly a retreat from coming war, the experiment proves to be a failure, developing factions and strange outcrops (there are suggestions of weird cults and animal sacrifices). It is also inadequate as a refuge against the 'dry deluge' (fire bombing). The survivors are a young doctor and a lower-class girl, who acts instinctively rather than intellectually. When the modern 'ark' is destroyed, this Eve and her Adam enter bombed-out London, his alienation from the natural world subordinated to her awareness of it, to create a new, pastoral Eden on the ruins. Her behaviour is less a sign of her alienation from a desirable culture, than a judgement on how that culture has allowed itself to become alienated from basic human needs. This book, like Stevenson's, points up the futility of attempting to prefabricate human nature to suit a pattern of belief, and, like it, it closes on a small, natural community, likely to create utopia from more humble cloth.

There are three overtly political novels in the late 1940s. Laski's is anti-right wing, Kerby's anti-socialist, Jameson's anti-communist. All deal with post-war politics, and all deal with the excesses that they fear might result from the pressures of post-war reconstruction. Wherever they might start, politically, they return to a middle-of-the-road, humane liberalism as the arbiter of relations between individual and state.

Laski's novel begins with a tone of light political satire, but ends in dystopia. The central characters have been shipwrecked during the war; and, when eventually rescued (by SS 'Cathartic'), they discuss Morris's *News from Nowhere* and speculate on the new post-war world. However, the 'Tory Heaven' has repealed the Reform Bill, re-introduced the workhouse and child-labour, and classified its citizens numerically according to their political beliefs — the A's are on the far right, and all others are behind them. The unthinking young Tory narrator is initially delighted to find himself now an 'A' with all its privileges; but after boredom comes revulsion, as he finds his more liberal friends reduced to starvation (male) and prostitution (female) as a direct result of their political beliefs. Finally he defies the system by helping some of them to escape.

Kerby's *The roaring dove* carries an epigraph from G. Lowes Dickinson: 'Satire may roar; but, in England at any rate, it roars as gently as any sucking dove.' On the mythic Atlantic island of Triona is a socialist society, acknowledged to be eutopia, yet a eutopia that few wish to visit, and none may leave. The English visitor (Fabian Clarke!) assists the revolutionary leader, a dynamic young Abbott, with his abortive coup, returning to England when revolution fails, an avid Liberal. This is a well-handled satire: Kerby takes sure aim at her targets — eutopia, atheism, the boredom and exclusion of Russian society, and socialist conformity. Although her tone never touches the bitterness and emotional intensity of Laski's, ultimately both reject extremism, whether of right or left.

Jameson returns with the third of her novels here. *The moment of truth* (1949) examines the scene at a North of England airport, as a group of survivors await the last plane to the US before the Russian communist conquest. Although the narrative centres on the moral dilemma of whether to leave, or to stay and join a resistance movement, the fall of European civilisation is forecast, and the coming of a new Dark Age. At this point the questions raised by Hamilton (1922) begin to re-emerge. Here the major analysis of this is given by an elderly, cultivated European. In a long speech he identifies the barbarians with those who sacked Rome:

> And then — after a long time — perhaps a century, or two
> centuries — the corruption will begin. I don't mean of Europe
> — that will be over. I mean of the barbarians . . . there will
> be curiosity, a resurrection — life, so old, millennially old,
> and new, dangerous, a birth. (pp. 48, 49)

He also invokes the Dark Ages: 'when I think of the ninth century
I always see a child, a boy, looking up at a — how do you call it?
a may tree' (p. 49). Here we return to the theme of Hamilton; the
return of barbarism, the possibility (or impossibility) of reclaiming
lost knowledge. Jameson is certainly more optimistic about the
renewal of civilisation: for her, the may tree will bloom anew. Brians
describes a new and disturbing trend in misogynistic American
science fiction, 'neo-barbarism', in which 'the authors' sympathies
lie clearly with the barbarians . . . because they prefer the excite-
ment of barbarism to the tedium of civilization'.[33] He cites
American feminist writers (specifically, Charnas and McIntyre) who
reject it, and there are many British writers, increasingly feminist,
who examine this conflict between civilisation and barbarism. One
of the earliest British novels on the theme is Richard Jefferies's *After
London* (1885), in two parts: 'The relapse into barbarism' and 'Wild
England'.[34] Hamilton, Jameson, Bennett and Wallace place it in
the context of war (in the last two, nuclear war). In the work of
the later British women writers, it is the city that signifies civilisation,
and in whose ruins the survivors live, while the barbarians roam
the countryside; the city in American writing plays a far different
role, as the locus of destruction.

Pamela Frankau's *The offshore light* (1952) is a thoughtful and
accomplished novel dealing with nuclear issues, though not post-
holocaust. It contains a novel within a novel: an American diplomat
is writing about a eutopian island, Leron, where the discovery of
a uranium-like substance threatens its traditional and peaceful ways.
Both novels end inconclusively, as Leron fights to continue its
traditions and to maintain control of 'Leronite', thereby controlling
peace, while the great powers try to buy their way in and take over
the island and its precious element. Like American novels of the
same period, there is a strong emphasis on the need for a correct
moral framework in which to make decisions. Leron is a literary
precursor of the shifting world behind the wall of Lessing's *Memoirs
of a survivor* (1974), as well as other allegorical novels of the 1970s.

Frankau dramatises the power struggle between forces of good and evil, a struggle that is not concluded by the novel's end, but which has confronted the inhabitants of pastoral Leron with choices that they never considered making. The persona of the American diplomat is a reminder of the international situation and the cold war, and also of American responsibility and the schizophrenia resulting from the nuclear bombing of Japan. Like Leron, America has been forced to make difficult choices, and to bear the responsibility not only for themselves, but for the world.

The remaining novels of the 1950s offer a bewildering range of post-nuclear holocaust societies. Richmond's 'grim tomorrow' (1953) is a tale of (thinly disguised) German nuclear retribution, in which Earth is literally blown apart, and some survivors in an airplane land on another planet, which turns out to be England catapulted into space! True to form, they set up a pacifist eutopia on the ruins of London. This is a warning of German perfidiousness, and of the dangers of ignoring it which is remarkably similar to some of the wartime novels. The nuclear dimension gives it a contemporary twist. Smith's 'The last of the Spode' is a satirical treatment of nuclear holocaust, which depicts the upper classes trying to continue their accustomed way of life in its aftermath.

Nuclear issues are also the focus of Margot Bennett's *The long way back* (1954), set in the twenty-fifth century: 'a heavily ironic but thoughtful tale in which a reindustrialized Africa which has forgotten the nuclear wars which ended the previous civilization has reinvented the bomb'.[35] England is now a primitive land roamed by wild, superstitious tribes, whose religion is a garbled mixture of Christianity and history. An exploratory group from now civilised Africa see the mutated animals and plants, the barbaric inhabitants, and visit devastated London; and they gradually realise that this world has been destroyed by nuclear explosions. Somewhat ironically, on their discovery of the wild tribes they try to cow the natives by producing a tape recorder, and playing a tape of 'the first atomic explosion in the entire history of the world', which, they think, 'heralds a new era of peace and prosperity for United Africa' (p. 92). (Yet already they gloat on the ascendancy it will give them over the 'yellow men of America'.) After their discovery, the Africans leave England with the difficult task of convincing their world of the dangers of repeating history.[36] The message of the city, which they are unable to decipher correctly, is an almost eroded engraving on a ruined church, 'The peace of God passeth all understanding': they understandably misread the archaic 'passeth', but also (a possible portent for the future?) fail with 'peace', mistaking it for 'place'.

The two remaining works deal very differently with nuclear holocausts: Wallace is pro-American, and, like Richmond, follows her apocalypse with a eutopia; while Laski is anti-American, and hers is dystopian. Wallace, whose novel has been described as 'pervaded by a snobbish Fabian socialism', places the responsibility of a devastating surprise attack on 'liberals in Europe who insisted on their countries being cleared of US missiles'.[37] As a consequence, both the Americans and Russians subsequently deny them aid. However, all is for the best: a Christian medievalism prevails among the reduced population, although there are wandering bands of 'barbarians', composed largely of young males (this is to be a recurrent theme in later decades). Laski's play is much stronger meat, and far less optimistic. Published in 1959 (although, according to the author, written in 1954),[38] the scenario is again a post-holocaust England that has been caught in American/Soviet crossfire — but viewed very differently. England has been a passive victim, one of the smaller nations ('the offshore island') on which the super-powers have used the nuclear weapons that they have not used on each other. The survivors are 'Contaminated Persons', and the help the Americans offer is sterilisation, and the prospect of expatriation to labour camps in the US. The survivors elect to stay behind, and die with dignity. Nuclear holocaust continues to figure in the works of the following decades, but it rarely takes centre stage as it does during the 1950s. The number of novels that introduce it here show even greater concern with nuclear issues than comparable American novels.

Storm Jameson and Katherine Burdekin are the most frequent contributors to the bibliography for this period. Both were feminist writers, both strongly anti-Fascist. Of Jameson we know much, and of Burdekin, very little — although Daphne Patai's research continues to uncover such information as her authorship of *Swastika night*, concealed for nearly 50 years under a male pseudonym. Jameson, on the other hand, was a public figure — a director of *Time and Tide*, a prolific journalist and novelist, president of the English Centre of International PEN during the years of the war (1938–45). She had extensive contact with European writers in exile, and was vitally interested in European politics; and she visited Eastern Europe in an official capacity in 1945, one of the first foreigners allowed in. Her autobiography, *Journey from the north*, is a fascinating introduction to the politics of the 1930s and

1940s, as well as to her own life.

Silence follows these few novels of the early 1950s. Overall, the genre was undergoing a crisis, as critical works of the period indicate. Gerber (1955) notes 'the intense malaise in contemporary utopian writing'.[39] Kingsley Amis's *New maps of hell* (1960) foresees the primary function of science fiction (including utopian science fiction) as an early-warning device, 'a medium in which our society can criticize itself, and sharply':[40] this, of course, has always been a function of utopia, but more frequently in the past by showing us new maps of heaven. Chad Walsh (1962) also uses a revealing title: *From utopia to nightmare* examines the decrease in utopias, and the increase in dystopias.[41] Utopia, if not moribund, had, like the moon, turned its darker face. British women had been working primarily in the satirical and dystopian forms since the beginning of the 1920s. The new wave of feminism is about to gather. When it does, women writers on both sides of the Atlantic find new voices: although eutopian optimism does not entirely overwhelm the scepticism or pessimism that precedes it, nonetheless there is a lightening of tone.

Notes

1. Lyman Tower Sargent, 'The war years: British utopianism 1915–1950' in Luk de Vos (ed.), *Just the other day. Essays on the suture of the future* (EXA, Anterwerpen, 1985), p. 161. The most extensive recent analysis of 1930s socialist utopias is Andy Croft, 'Worlds without end foisted upon the future — some antecedents of *Nineteen eighty-four*' in Christopher Norris (ed.), *Inside the myth. Orwell: views from the left* (Lawrence and Wishart, London, 1984).

2. *Saturday Review*, 29 March 1926.

3. Croft, 'Worlds without end', p. 190.

4. 'A crisis of the spirit', in *The writer's situation and other essays* (Macmillan, London, 1950), pp. 138–9.

5. Dale Spender (ed.), *Time and Tide wait for no man* (Pandora, London, 1984), p. 1.

6. David Doughan, *Lobbying for liberation* (London Polytechnic, London, 1980), pp. 4–5.

7. An article in *Time and Tide*, the feminist political weekly, 26 May 1922, examines the loopholes in the Act; its declaration of no discrimination on grounds of sex or marriage were unenforceable: Spender, *Time and Tide*, pp. 129–32.

8. Sargent, 'The war years', p. 174, lists the seven (male) contributors to the series: Vernon Bartlett, Lord Dunsany, St John Erskine, Julian Huxley, James Maxton, Lord Raglan, H.R.L. Sheppard.

9. The Six Point Group, formed by Lady Rhondda in 1921, worked for women's issues. They started with six points as their target, and, if one was achieved, substituted another. The first six were: 'satisfactory legislation' on child assault, and for widows and unmarried mothers and their children, equal guardianship, equality of pay for teachers and for Civil Service employees. Spender, *Time and Tide*, p. 177.

10. Doughan, *Lobbying*, p. 11.

11. Spender, *Time and Tide*, pp. 271–2; 'Tendencies in the woman's movement' (unsigned article) discusses Dora Russell's successful bid to have birth control considered by the Executive Committee, after several years of defeat.

12. Sheila Rowbotham, *Hidden from history. Rediscovering women in history from the seventeenth century to the present* (Random House, New York, 1974) pp. 149–58, discusses the conflict in the Labour Party, including the anti-eugenic and (later) anti-Fascist aspects of male opposition.

13. 'British and American utopias by women (1836–1979): an annotated bibliography part 1', *Alternative Futures*, vol. 4, nos. 2–3 (Spring/Summer 1981), p. 196.

14. Richard Gerber, *Utopian fantasy: a study of English utopian fiction since the end of the nineteenth century* (Routledge and Kegan Paul, London, 1955), p. 60.

15. W.H.G. Armytage, *Yesterday's tomorrows* (Routledge and Kegan Paul, London, 1968), p. 151; Lyman Tower Sargent, *British and American utopian literature 1516–1975: an annotated bibliography*, 1st edn (G.K. Hall, Boston, 1979), p. 92.

16. pp. 56, 149. Jeffrey's *The spinster and her enemies: feminism and sexuality 1880–1930* (Pandora, London, 1985) inverts Haldane's title, and her attitudes.

17. *You may well ask: a memoir 1920–1940* (Victor Gollancz, London, 1979). Charlotte Haldane was married to Naomi Mitchison's brother, J.B.S. Haldane. Charlotte was childless; Naomi had six children.

18. Ibid., pp. 173–8.

19. Daphne Patai, introduction to *Swastika night*, p. xi.

20. *Possibilities. Essays on the state of the novel* (Oxford University Press, Oxford, 1973), p. 144.

21. Gerber, *Utopian fantasy*, p. 58.

22. Lee Holcombe, *Ladies at work: middle class working women in England and Wales, 1850–1914* (Archon Press, Hamden, Conn, 1973), p. 193, notes that the marriage bar was modified during the inter-war years, but not abolished until 1946.

23. (Mary) Cicely Hamilton, *Life errant* (J.M. Dent, London, 1935), p. 149. J.M. Miller's *Canticle for Leibowitz* is the closest modern equivalent to Hamilton's.

24. Grant wrote a number of Scottish histories, and the 'candle' of her title is a reference to Cameron of Lochiel, Bonnie Prince Charlie's supporter, 'the light of the north'.

25. I.F. Clarke, *Voices prophesying war 1763–1984* (Oxford University Press, London, 1966), p. 173, describes Stella as 'a redemptive Aphrodite', though I should think that Aphrodite would hardly have been in Ertz's mind; Minerva, perhaps.

26. Storm Jameson, *Journey from the north* (2 vols, Collins and Harvill,

London, 1969), vol. 1, p. 335.

27. Gerber comments on the appeal of Fascism and Nazism to the British sense of humour before World War Two, satirising 'some absurd megalomaniac together with an abundance of uniformly coloured shirts': *Utopian fantasy*, p. 74. Croft, while conceding that 'the uniform fetishes' were 'easy targets for the satirists', remarks that 'none of these novels however lost sight for a moment of the seriousness of their subject matter': 'Worlds without end', pp. 204–5.

28. His press baron appears to be a thinly veiled portrait of Lord Rothermere, whose *Daily Mail* newspaper supported Mosley's campaign in 1934.

29. She was the only woman, and the only Briton, asked to contribute to this series, which is a briefer version of the 'If I were dictator' monographs of the same period.

30. Victoria Glendinning, *Vita: the life of V. Sackville-West* (Weidenfeld and Nicolson, London, 1983), p. 326. Virginia Woolf, Vita's former lover, constant friend, had suicided in the preceding year.

31. *Journey*, vol. 2, p. 82.

32. In her later *The good want power. An essay in the psychological possibilities of liberalism* (Jonathan Cape, London, 1977), she attacks his approach in 'Scapesheep and miracle-workers' and 'Latter-day Thoreau'. Her anti-utopia anticipated Skinner's *Walden two* by one year.

33. Paul Brians, *Nuclear holocausts: atomic war in fiction, 1895–1984* (Kent State University Press, Kent, Ohio, 1987), p. 75.

34. John Fowles, in the introduction to a recent edition of *After London* (Oxford University Press, Oxford, 1980), quotes William Morris's reaction to this novel:

> I have no more faith than a grain of mustard seed in the future history of 'civilization', which I *know* now is doomed to destruction, probably before very long: . . . it consoles me to think of barbarism once more flooding the world, and real feelings and passions, however rudimentary, taking the place of our wretched hypocrisies. (p. viii)

35. Brians, *Nuclear holocausts*, p. 130.

36. Bennett also published *The intelligent woman's guide to radiation* (1964).

37. Brians, *Nuclear holocausts*, p. 334.

38. Ibid., p. 241. Brians notes that 'the story was aired in a shortened version by BBC radio'.

39. *Utopian fantasy*, p. 76.

40. *New maps of hell. A survey of science fiction* (Harcourt, Brace and Co., New York, 1960), p. 155.

41. (Geoffrey Bles, London, 1962).

Bibliography of Primary Material

Note: * denotes works cited in other bibliographies, but not located or read.

Macaulay, Rose (1919) *What not? A prophetic comedy*, Constable, London
Griffiths, Isabel (1922) *Three worlds*, Arthur H. Stockwell, London

Hamilton, (Mary) Cicely (1922; reprinted in revised form as *Lest ye die*, 1928), *Theodore Savage, or, a story of the past or the future*, Leonard Parsons, London

Coron, Hannah (1924) *Ten years hence?*, J.M. Ouseley, London

Macaulay, Rose (1924) *Orphan Island*, Wm Collins, London

Boswell, Diane (1926) *Posterity*, Jonathan Cape, London

Grant, Isabel F. (1926) *A candle in the hills: the story of the counter revolution*, Hodder and Stoughton, London

Haldane, Charlotte (Franken) (1926) *Man's world*, Chatto and Windus, London

Jaeger, Muriel (1926) *The question mark*, Hogarth, London

Bowhay, Bertha Louisa (1929) *Elenchus Brown, the story of an experimental utopia, compiled by a student of Battersea Polytechnic*, H.R. Allenson, London

Burdekin, Katharine [Kay Burdekin] (1929) *The rebel passion*, Wm Morrow, New York

Tillyard, Aelfrida Catharine Wetenhall (1930) *Concrete: a story of 200 years hence*, Hutchinson, London

*Tillyard, Aelfrida Catharine Wetenhall (1932) *The approaching storm*, Hutchinson, London

Brash, Margaret M. [John Kendall] (1933) *Unborn tomorrow*, Wm Collins, London

Holtby, Winifred (1933) *The astonishing island, being the experiences undergone by Robinson Mackintosh from Tristan de Cunha during an accidental visit to unknown territory in the year of Grace MCMXXX — ?*, Lovat Dickson, London

*Williams-Ellis, Annabel (1933) *To tell the truth*, Jonathan Cape, London

Burdekin, Katherine [Murray Constantine] (1934) *Proud man*, Boriswood, London

Curtis, Monica (1934) *Landslide*, Victor Gollancz, London

Conquest, Joan (1935) *With the lid off*, T. Werner Laurie, London

Ertz, Susan (1935; serialised in *The Delineator*, as 'One woman alive', 1936) *Woman alive*, D. Appleton-Century, New York

Gresswell, Elsie Kay (1935) *When Yvonne was dictator*, John Heritage, London

Hunter, Bluebell Matilda [George Lancing] (1935) *Fraudulent conversion, a romance of the gold standard*, Stanley Paul, London

Rhondda, Margaret Haig (1935) 'The world as I want it', *Forum*, 93 (February)

Cunningham, Beall (1936) *The wide, white page*, Hutchinson, London

Jameson, (Margaret) Storm (1936) *In the second year*, Cassell, London

Mitchison, Naomi (1936) *We have been warned*, Vanguard, New York

Stevenson, Dorothy Emily (1936) *The empty world; a romance of the future*, (US edition, *The world in spell*), Herbert Jenkins, London

*Wootton, Barbara (1936) *London's burning*, George Allen and Unwin, London

Burdekin, Katharine [Murray Constantine] (1937; reprinted 1985) *Swastika night*, Lawrence and Wishart, London

Warde, Beatrice [Paul Beaujon] (1937) *The shelter in Bedlam*, reprinted as *Peace under earth: dialogues from the year 1946*, privately printed, London

Newton, Bertha (1938) *My life in time*, C.W. Daniel, London

Jameson, (Margaret) Storm (1942) *Then we shall hear singing. A fantasy in C Major*, Cassell, London

Sackville-West,Vita (1942) *Grand Canyon*, Michael Joseph, London

Greenwood, Julia Courtney [Francis Askham] (1944) *The heart consumed*, John Lane, The Bodley Head, London

King-Hall, Lou (1944) *Fly envious time*, Peter Davies, London

Vigers, Daphne (1944) *Atlantis rising*, Andrew Dakers, London

Mannin, Ethel (1945) *Bread and roses: an utopian survey and blueprint*, Macdonald, London

Chetwynd, Bridget (1946) *Future imperfect*, Hutchinson, London

Hine, Muriel (1946) *The island forbidden to man,* Hodder and Stoughton, London

Nott, Kathleen (1947) *The dry deluge*, Hogarth, London

Burton, Alice Elizabeth [Susan Kerby] (1948) *Gone to grass* (US edition, *The roaring dove*), Hutchinson, London

Laski, Marghanita (1948) *Tory heaven, or Thunder on the right* (US edition, *Toasted English*), The Cresset Press, London

Jameson, (Margaret) Storm (1949) *The moment of truth*, Macmillan, London

Frankau, Pamela (1952) *The offshore light*, Wm Heinemann, London

Richmond, Mary (1953) *The grim tomorrow*, Wright and Brown, London

Smith, Evelyn (1953) 'The last of the Spode', *Fantasy and Science Fiction*, June

Bennett, Margot (1954) *The long way back*, The Bodley Head, London

Wallace, Doreen (1958) *Forty years on*, Collins, London

Laski, Marghanita (1959) *The offshore island: a play in three acts*, Cresset, London

4

A Widening World,
a Narrowing Sphere

The conflicts of feminism and a sequence of changing decades are ingredients as important in this chapter as in the previous one, yet, when they are assembled and a growing sense of internationalism is added to them, the results are quite different. The American 1920s as an era saw the publication of some feminist, some spiritualist eutopias; the later 1930s, of feminist eutopias and anti-socialist dystopias. Silence during the war years is broken at the end of the 1940s and in the 1950s by a surge in publication, either anti-socialist or questioing the future role of nuclear power. This is similar to the publication figures for British writers of the same period, except that comparative publication rates for American novels are more consistent during the period.

Overall, the earlier American optimism is tempered, significantly shifting from depiction of an imminent, domestic, communitarian setting to a future America often affected by a world-wide cataclysm (war or natural calamity) that begins in Europe, and acts as the clearing-house for an age of peace. While not always linked directly with a Day of Judgement theme, the religious element of many of these works (which is frequently theosophist) easily incorporates this passing of the Old World as a necessary precursor to the new. A view of society as beyond immediate transformation suggests a diminution of optimism about the possibility of reform; yet optimism remains, the intermediate dystopias are transcended, and America emerges as eutopia.

One strong impression is of anxiety about America's role in international affairs, a direct result of its participation in World War One. Yet the mood is not isolationist. The (temporary) dystopian consequences of involvement are displaced on to geological disasters (earthquakes, new Ice Ages), just as the British anti-socialists displaced Russian derived 'plagues', but the political consequences are absent, and they remain so until after World War Two. A collaborating pair of novelists of this group describes the connection between the moral and the physical world thus: 'Evil, when it outweighs good, causes an overbalance and then we have catastrophes, such as earthquakes, storms and epidemics' (Morris/ Speer, *No borderland*, (1938), pp. 25–6).

The 'narrowing sphere' of this chapter's title is, of course, the sphere of women. Showalter calls the 1920s the 'awkward age' of feminism, 'a period of retreat and postponement'.[1] Although now able to vote, American women found themselves hard pressed to use their political influence in a public context. Feminism in America, as in Britain, was without a unifying issue. Furthermore, a strong anti-feminist backlash developed, and feminists faced relentless enemies, as, for example, in the dissemination of the infamous 'Spider Web' chart. External challenge was harder to meet because of internal conflict: women's organisations were riven by fissures over their aims as the culture and nature debate became significant in the US. All of these were contributing factors to the loss of that fine impulse to take charge that is so obvious in the eutopias of Chapter 2.

The divisive point for feminist organisations was where to take their stand on women's role in society. Hard-core feminists supported the first, stillborn Equal Rights Amendment (ERA), which was introduced into the House and the Senate in 1923. Their more moderate opponents, who had been active in support of pro- tective legislation for women and children in industry, and for public health measures which sought to protect the health of mothers and babies, saw Equal Rights as their enemy.[2] If it became law, they feared the loss of all that they had achieved. These opposing views introduced new tensions into the American feminist movement. The lines of argument were drawn on the biological difference, or similarity, of women and men. Moderate feminists felt that they had to argue for women as mothers; radical feminists argued for them as human beings. Thus, women's association with nature, children and the home continued to be foremost for conservative feminists: they stressed 'biology as destiny'. Radicals, on the other hand, insisting on equality, maintained that women would not be disadvantaged if the ERA were passed. The battle was bitter, the only victors their reactionary opponents.

The 'Spider Web' chart, the work of conservative anti-feminists, purported to reveal a conspiracy 'to disarm the nation and promote a Bolshevist takeover', linking such subversive organisations as the Parent–Teacher Association, pacifist organisations, and both moderate and radical feminist organisations.[3] Those who gave it credence considered even the protective child labour laws were 'destroying the family'. We can hear the voice of these opponents in the dystopias of the period.

In some of them we find this negative association of reformism, pacifism, socialism and feminism: Dell, in *The silent voice* (1925), describes a socialist society in America where effeminate men are ruled by mannish 'large-bosomed, coarse-featured, broad-framed females' (p. 12), whose demand for equality has turned them into pseudo-males, and it is not a pretty sight. One remembers Bellamy's identification of socialism with 'sexual novelties': the sexual novelty here, however, is not promiscuity but is the un-feminine 'New Woman'. In the eutopias that accompany these dystopias, the women are delicate, romantic and if they have power in society it is because of their age, or their inherited position. Works such as these reinforce the stereotypes of the 'unnatural-ness' of women's participation in 'culture', and their 'natural' difference to men.

However, attitudes in the 1920s were conditioned by something more than a fear of socialism. There was a new sexual freedom, offensive to conservatives and feminists alike. Charlotte Perkins Gilman condemned it scathingly in 1923:

> Now that [women] have in large measure reached their goal of 'equality with men' — not real equality in social development but equality in immediate conditions — it is sickening to see so many of them using their freedom in a mere imitation of masculine vices.[4]

In 'the decade of the 1920s — when Freud and the Flapper reigned',[5] the strong-minded, independent, and often single feminist became anathema to many — hence the satiric portraits of her 'unnatural' mannishness. Freud's theory of femininity operates from a clear presumption of natural difference, and an early letter perpetuates nineteenth-century anti-feminist propaganda concerning women's identification with nature, their exclusion from the world of culture:

> It is really a stillborn thought to send women into the struggle for existence exactly as a man . . . Nature has determined woman's destiny through beauty, charm, and sweetness.

> Law and custom have much to give women that has been
> withheld from them, but the position of women will surely
> be what it is: in youth an adored darling and in mature years
> a loved wife.[6]

It is a sad irony that at a time when the 'feminine mystique' was
grafted over the feminism of an earlier period, and marriage was
touted as every 'normal' woman's ambition, some of the precious
freedoms already wrenched from 'law and custom' were eroded by
'marriage bars' similar to those operating in Britain. These
increased alarmingly during the Depression.[7]

The history of feminism's internal conflict and external enmity
is reflected in the almost total disappearance of feminist eutopian
novels during this period. Those few with a feminist consciousness
are, as Kessler so rightly points out, 'twinkling candles [which] glimmer between the slats of a bushel basket stretching across four
decades'.[8] The strong feminist heroes of Gilman (1915, 1916),
Bennett (1918) and Bruere (1919) (see Chapter 2), clustered in the
years immediately preceding suffrage, disappear almost completely
in succeeding decades. It seems appropriate that the only woman
writer with two novels included in this chapter is Ayn Rand, whose
female characters exemplify the principles of the feminine mystique, their circumstances and achievements notwithstanding. Dagny
Taggart, central to Rand's *Atlas shrugged* (1957), is a woman
engineer, ruthless, intelligent, wealthy — and stunningly beautiful.
Once Dagny leaves the rapidly decaying socialised US of the novel,
and enters its eutopia (which Rand entitles 'A utopia of greed'),
she meets her master, and strikes a bargain with him (fraught with
sexual implications) to work as his housemaid for 50 cents a day;
and so she fumblingly mends his shirts, and gains 'sensual satisfac-
tion' from cooking his breakfast. She may regain some strength
when they return 'to the world', but the conclusion of the novel
has them side by side, Dagny listening to and watching *him*. The
40 years between Gilman's Ellador and Rand's Dagny can be
summed up in their women engineers of the future.

However, there are some 'twinkling candles' in the darkness,
and their placement is most interesting. Elaine Showalter notes that
historians regard the year 1925 as a turning-point (downturning)
for American feminism.[9] It hardly seems coincidental that this is
the beginning of the 'silent decade', the point at which women's
utopian writing, whether conservative or radical, peters out for
almost ten years; or that, when it resumes, it is with novels that

question utopian alternatives, rather then presenting achieved societies. Very few of the women writers discussed in this chapter were actively involved in the feminist movement. Cleghorn (1924) is one of these: a feminist, a socialist and a Quaker, in her eutopia, women join in suicide pacts that put an end to racism, poverty and war. For each lynching, each death in war, a woman takes her own life; and individuals in slums or in prison are accompanied by a woman who volunteers to share their misery. It is 'a great illumination of illogical and immeasurable sisterly love' (p. 67). Reminiscent of Waisbrooker's (1894) (see Chapter 2) feminist prescription for ending war, Cleghorn's is one of the few pacifist works of this period, and her autobiography mentions publishers' unwillingness to accept pacifist novels during the 1920s.[10] Her set of four eutopian tales was published in *Atlantic Monthly*. (In the foreword to the second edition (1928, as *Lest ye die*) of her *Theodore Savage*, Hamilton notes that, when the novel was first issued (1922), American publishers refused it, because there was 'a full reaction against any and everything that dealt with war'.

How short is the list of works that contain even elements of feminist consciousness: Cleghorn (1924); Pettersen (1924); Kirk (1931); Spotswood (1935); Sterne (1937); and Short (1949). Pettersen (1924) concerns exotic 'Nusians' who bring a comparatively feminist (though also theosophist — the only work to combine the two) message from Venus. Their message of women's moral superiority is familiar, but comes in a package that would have astounded earlier feminists (skin-tight silver suits, 1-inch eyelashes, and round eyes lacking whites), as would their rejection of marriage. Kirk's *A woman's utopia* (1931), like *Venus*, advocates sexual freedom for women: she mentions trial marriages, serial marriages, and easier annulment.

A novel outstanding in its consideration of the difficult question of career or marriage for a young woman is Spotswood's *The unpredictable adventure* (1935), a satirical novel of her quest through philosophies and 'utopias', which concludes with her placing work and sex above marriage and family. A quite different 'quest' novel is Sterne's *Some plant olive trees* (1937), a communitarian novel which examines a young woman's quest through philosophies and historical utopias to understand herself and the values of utopian idealism. Short (1949), like Pettersen, depicts an all-woman eutopian society on Venus (but without the sensationalist elements). Feminist and pacifist, she discusses the need to apply the moral principles of feminism to ensure that nuclear energy is used for peace, not war.

These works are few, however, and are outnumbered by those which are specifically anti-feminist. Sometimes this animus against feminism arises from the novelist's religious convictions (Kayser, Dell), and sometimes from a secular anti-socialism (Rand, Caldwell). There is no parallel to the fears of British women writers that women might be a particularly oppressed class in a totalitarian state: the identification of feminism with left-wing totalitarianism leads to quite the reverse conclusion — i.e. that women in power are a sign of political disorder. Not surprisingly, the comparative ideal worlds often paired with the anti-socialist dystopia are traditional, stratified societies, territorially aggressive, and often with an Aryan racist bias. In many ways, these 'eutopias' are similar to the parallel dystopias of British women. The bright voices of American women before and after them are, in the main, silent.

What has happened to more liberally inclined writers? Perhaps, like Cleghorn, they either had trouble finding publishers, or did not write because they viewed the New Deal as a practical experiment in socialism (rather as British writers considered Soviet Russia): Cleghorn wrote in 1936: 'With this humaner turn of mind . . . should it be long, I ask myself, before Socialism . . . comes into practical power?'[11] Not only did American writers have this hope, but they were not forced on to the defensive by the propinquity of European politics. Although the model of European-conceived destruction does recur in the late 1930s, it is never anti-Fascist. The silence of feminist writers continues to remain elusive, although one may speculate on the reasons. Perhaps the firmest conclusion that can be reached is that the obvious anxiety of many of the conservative writers is a mirror of the unspoken anxiety of many of the silent radicals and reformers, who, if they could not write with optimism, chose not to write at all.

However disappointing in subject (and often style) these novels may be, they do chart the tensions of the period. One can perceive the rise and fall of movements through their preoccupations: there is meaning in silence as well as words. As flux continues to be an important characteristic, we will once more adopt the chronological approach developed in the previous chapter, attempting to find reasons for obvious imbalances in the publishing history of the genre, and to examine within a domestic and an international context the changes that occur.

The twenties

It seems clear from reading the novels of this decade that Americans came out of World War One suffering from shell-shock — not because of enormous casualty rates (to Americans it was no pyrrhic victory), but because of the mere fact of their involvement. This led them to question the consequences of embroilment in the causes of the Old World, and, observably for women writers more than men, to jolt their eutopias from the achievable present into the future. The novels of the twenties are: Johnston, *Sweet rocket* (1920); Kayser, *The aerial flight to the realm of peace* (1922); Scrymsour, *The perfect world* (1922); Thompson, *Idealia, a utopian dream, or Resthaven* (1923); Cleghorn, 'Utopia interpreted' (1924); Pettersen, *Venus* (1924); Dell, *The silent voice* (1925); and Gazella, *The blessing of Azar* (1928). Most of these were 'one novel' writers. For Johnston, who was not, a utopia was a radical departure from her usual historical novels: 'This development was doubtless linked to the shock of the World War and the widespread conviction that only through far-reaching changes in human nature could world cataclysm be avoided.'[12] The result is a mystic utopia set in another dimension.

All contain successful eutopias, mostly reached after a clearing-house that would have been unthinkable and unnecessary for pre-war American writers. All but one make reference to the war. Kayser offers an alternative planet, which maintains peace through a 'Tribunal of Arbitration', and from which the narrator refuses ('Never! NEVER!! *NEVER!!!*') to return to Earth. Scrymsour's *Perfect world* is on Jupiter, reached by a spaceship, which pulls away from Earth as it is destroyed by cataclysm, fire and earthquake. One of the seeds of Cleghorn's future world is a threatened Ice Age and a 'monstrous inferno' of earthquakes in Alaska, that draws sightseers 'as they'd once gone to see the devastated war-areas in France' (p. 56).

The most fully worked-out sequence of events is in Dell (1925), whose American dystopia ('New America') and eutopia ('True America') of the future develop after 'the death of the finest Aryans in world war one' (p. 38): there are subsequent invasions of Europe and America. Earthquakes, the result of explosives and chemicals used in twentieth-century wars, 'have almost de-populated the world' (p. 227).

Pettersen's eutopia is an evolutionarily superior Venus: the human girl (Mary), who is the hope of the future, is the only one of the main characters who has not been involved in the war. Only Thompson's novel has no reference to war or peace, introducing a serene community devoted to culture and rational living.

Of the eight novels published between 1920 and 1929, seven appear in the first half of the decade. All eight have some religious basis; the Quaker Cleghorn's is the most socialist.[13] During this time the theosophical novels first appear. Theosophy began in America in 1875 and reached its peak in the 1920s. A 'synthesis of the idea of evolution with religious concepts chiefly from Hinduism and Buddhism', it had obvious eutopian appeal, and many of the early generation of theosophists were active supporters of the Nationalists.[14] Reincarnation, astral travel, Egyptology, numerology, the cabbala, and elements of Indian occultism combine to make this most eclectic of creeds. Part of theosophist teaching concerns the 'seven root races' of evolutionary development: 'Selfborn', Hyperborean, Lemurian, Atlantan and Aryan are the five races that have so far emerged. (We have seen how Vigers (1944) countered German racial theories by comparing Aryan with Atlantan.) From its inception on the east coast, the theosophical centre of gravity moved to California, and 'the next evolutionary Round, with attendant religious advance, [was] projected for the Pacific'.[15] Theosophical ideas are to be found in Pettersen (1924) (re-incarnation, astral travel, the 'Spiral of Eternal Life'); Dell (1925) (the 'root-races', which supplement her offensive contrast of Aryan purity with black and 'mongrelised' races, although approving of past Atlantan mixing with the Mayans); and Gazella (1928) (Kabbalah, references to the 'theosophic school in Paradise', Egyptology). These three novels, written at the height of theosophical influence, are the most concentrated group; other novels with the same theme are scattered through the following decades.

The other novels have a variety of more orthodox Christian belief. Johnston's *Sweet rocket* (1920) has elements of Franciscan mysticism: spiritual interconnection between human beings is extended to the natural world, to Father Sun, King Wind, Queen Rain. As a post-war plea for peace and harmony its spiritual alternative world is persuasively described. In *The aerial flight to the realm of peace* (1922) Kayser describes a utopian world of 'Divine Laws and Universal Brotherhood', it is 'a glimpse of Heaven' (p. 53) where there are still separate nations, but a universal language to promote understanding.

The population of Scrymsour's *The perfect world* (1922) is

descended from an Adam and Eve 'who have not sinned' (p. 234), although they practise conventional marriage and reproduction. It is clear that this 'perfect world' is not Heaven, for there are allowances for falls from grace: if any of the people should feel strong, negative passions, for instance, they are isolated until 'cured' (ibid.). Moreover, it has a class system, and the society itself is utopian in the sense not of its equality, but of the common acceptance of strict divisions and hierarchies.

Cleghorn's contribution also concerns the peaceful unification of the world's population through the removal of barriers between nation, sex, race, age and religion. The Ice Age and the anti-war women 'Death Sharers' are two means to this eutopian end; and fruitful collaboration between art and science and a nomadic way of life for youth are others, promoting knowledge, co-operation and international understanding. A valuable member of the group that meets to discuss the threat of a new Ice Age, 'an ignorant old woman, worn by a life of labor in the fields', is: 'the representative of the Dukhobors [who] astonished everybody by her pose and calm . . . Perhaps this was only because, like all habitual mystics, she lived in the presence of cosmic thoughts' (p. 59).

Taken all in all, the overriding theme here is religion as a means to peace. Whether theosophical, Quaker or Franciscan mysticism, a more spiritualised life is seen as the way to increase chances of international understanding. These writers are deeply interested in the issue of war — how and where it may originate, its consequences, and how and where it may be resolved.

The thirties

The 'silent decade' that followed was not completely silent, though 1925 does mark an abrupt cessation of the preceding flurry of publication. It was broken only by two short novels: *Ultimo* (1930) by Ruth Vassos, and Mrs Kirk' *A woman's utopia* (1931). *Ultimo* is a spare, effective novel (enhanced by the modernist illustrations of her husband, John), which depicts the suffering of an unnamed male in an ant-like, underground world. Nature, refusing subjection, retaliates with a new Ice Age (a familiar theme from the 1920s with a more modern twist). *Ultimo* is dedicated to D.H. L[awrence], 'WHO LOVED THE SUN', and its stifling, mechanistic world, where mating and breeding is also mechanistic and impersonal, is the antithesis of Lawrence's naturalism. The narrator complains of 'this very perfectness' and, from sheer boredom, volunteers for an experimental projectile to another planet, thus (ironically) seeking a technological escape from an over-mechanised world. In a later book, *Humanities* (1935), Vassos wrote: 'Were the mechanistic development used to promote welfare for the many rather than to make profits for the few, the situation would be reversed, and, instead of being enslaved by the machine, we would be freed.'[16] The world of *Ultimo* describes this helpless enslavement, intensified by its divorce from nature. Here, in this allegory of a soulless world, the worker, when no longer able to work, is simply 'removed', as in Robert Frost's 'Departmental' (1936), an ant world where 'One crossing with hurried tread/The body of one of their dead/Isn't given a moment's arrest — /Seems not even impressed'. Vassos's sympathy for the worker in industrialised society makes her the only one of these writers to respond directly to the Depression and to the increasing alienation of the individual in a mass society.

Mrs Kirk's *A woman's utopia* (1931) is, according to her introduction, a reply to Hauptmann's *The island of the great mother* (1925). Although by an American author, this has a London setting, and shares the preoccupations of earlier British utopias (parliamentary women, marriage).[17] Kirk makes some radical proposals connected with marriage, and also proposes a women-only House of Lords, although her separatism is based on rather tenuous grounds: 'The natural division of the human race is man and woman. Women and men together are no good' (p. 32).[18] As she also advocates limitation of the franchise to property holders (shortly after the universal franchise became law) and praises Mussolini's rural irrigation and electrification schemes, she is rather difficult to 'place' — particularly as the 'women geniuses' of whom she approves are, surprisingly, Queen Elizabeth, and the biblical characters Judith and Jael.

The five novels published between 1935 and 1940 fall into two distinct groups. Spotswood (1935) is an idiosyncratic, satirical, feminist *bildungsroman*; Sterne (1937), while not so radical, is a pacifist, anti-racist, quest novel which raises serious questions about the nature and value of utopia. The three anti-socialist novels of the later 1930s are all published in 1938. De Forest provides an anti-communist, anti-semitic *Armageddon*; Morris/Speer forecast Atlantan renewal through theosophy; Rand's *Anthem* (also, like Kirk's novel, published in Britain) contrasts the oppression of socialism with the liberation of the ego through her objectivist philosophy. All three of these dystopias are specific in mentioning the moral evil of communism, though only De Forest names Russia as its source.

Regarding, firstly, the two quest novels, Spotswood and Sterne: while neither depicts a fully realised utopia, both writers examine utopian idealism with an awareness more common to British writers of the same period, though their conclusions do not lead to an anti-utopian position. Both novelists ask questions about what constitutes utopia for women: their answers differ, but each of their central characters undertakes an intellectual journey of self-discovery (Spotswood's hero is called Tellectina). Her *The unpredictable adventure: a comedy of woman's independence* (1935) and Short's *A visitor from Venus* (1949) are the only radically feminist novels during these entire four decades. This adventure takes place in an allegorical landscape, where Tellectina encounters an astonishing number of contemporary thinkers and writers, who speak to her, and whom she tests against her experience (they include Bertrand Russell, Havelock Ellis, Dorothy Parker and James Branch Cabell).[19] Tellectina is accompanied along much of her way by her 'sister' (alter-ego) Femina, who brings endless trouble; she is emotional, sensual and utterly uninterested in ideas.

> Equality? What do I want with equality? I can get all the things I want without equality. Am I not a woman? Do I not know ways — subtle ways . . . What I want is marriage and a husband to protect me and lean on, a home and security, and — and a baby! (p. 330)

(Freud appears in *The unpredictable adventure* only in an aside, when Tellectina, sickened by Femina's obsession with sex, wonders whether he was right (p. 213).) Together they join the free-love colony, 'New Chimera', and co-habit with one man: initially he maintains a spiritual union with Tellectina, declaring his admiration for her mind, while Femina sulks in the corner (p. 113). Later events take a more conventional turn, and Femina bears his child. (Increasing conventionality destroys the colony.)

However, Tellectina continues to search for the answer to her questions about life. She introduces the words of sex reformers Bertrand Russell and Havelock Ellis on women's need for erotic liberation to a most disapproving audience, and is rebuked by Femina who counsels discretion. This conflict, between the independent Tellectina and the feminine mystique of Femina, is resolved, at least for Tellectina, with the help of their aunt,

Sophistica. She accepts Sophistica's advice that women should take sex less seriously, and work (and birth control) more seriously, and dedicates herself to creative writing. 'Writing books takes the place of both husbands and children if one cares enough about the books — but they don't take the place of the lovers' (p. 441).

Although unusually outspoken on birth control, Spotswood, anticipating some later feminist writers, sees it only as an interim measure: 'women as a race will never be able to accomplish any great and enduring work in the world until babies are conceived and born in test tubes in the chemical laboratories' (p. 436). (Clyde's similar recommendation (though without condoning heterosexual lovers) was made in the previous year: see Chapter 1, note 12.) In rejecting the truisms of Freud (chaste girlhood, noble wifehood), Spotswood places herself in the company of feminists; her emphasis on sexuality, particularly in her association with Havelock Ellis, distances her. Certainly she exemplifies that adoption of 'masculine' vices so abhorrent to Gilman (it is striking that so many of Spotswood's exemplary thinkers are male, rather than female). Her satire has a certain bounce and freshness, but illustrates Kessler's criticism of one aspect of this period, that 'although sexuality receives positive treatment, its excess centrality suggests Freudian influence'.[20]

Sterne is also a feminist, though less outspoken. Her central character is a young girl, married to a utopian idealist. Charles is a fictionalised version of a founder of the historic Vine and Olive colony of Napoleonic exiles at Demopolis, Alabama, 1817.[21] Sterne's selective use of this community reveals her purpose in writing this novel: her opposition to racism is conveyed through the attitudes of slave-holders and references to Alabama's statehood debate, her pacifism through conflict between the militarist and visionary elements of the small colony. Nina leaves the colony because she resents her husband's idealism, and undertakes a symbolic journey through Mobile, Huntsville and Washington, DC. This experience of people and ideas gradually leads her to accept the necessity for utopian 'dreamers', although she is too pragmatic fully to understand them. (Sterne associates practicality with women, and also with native-born Americans.) One important voice in the novel is that of the ageing (and discredited) visionary, L'Enfant, original planner of Washington, who tells her: 'It is well known women have never planned a Utopia' (p. 289). Yet Nina concludes that utopian visionaries are essential to our humanity: the world that the materialists would have she glimpses, and this teaches her the value of high ideals. In the conventional ending, Nina returns to the utopian colony, now seriously undermined: her commitment to her husband's ideals of liberty, equality, fraternity is also the author's commitment. Their contemporary relevance for Sterne is pacifist in the face of an increasing possibility of another world war, and anti-racist.[22]

Of the 1938 anti-socialist novels, *Armageddon* combines fear of the coming war and reaction against communism with anti-semitism and a literal interpretation of the predictions of Revelations. A villainous Russian Jew, Ivan Sikorski, is the false Messiah (anti-Christ). The book has little redeeming merit, but is a fascinating repository of the contemporary fears.

The theosophical *No borderland* concerns the discovery in South America of Lamach, a city of descendants of the Atlantans. Egyptian temples, astral travel and reincarnation form the substance of the theosophical elements. Here, as in Pettersen's *Venus*, recall of past lives is an important means of education. The novel concludes with newspaper 'reports' of sightings of domed buildings in California, surrounded at night by a mysterious white light — a probable reference to the theosophical community at Point Loma, noted for the 'immense domes' of its buildings.[23] The American connection is stressed by the authors' claim that every third person in the US is an 'Atlantean incarnate' (p. 143).

A far different work is Ayn Rand's dystopian *Anthem*, a shorter and far better handled narrative than her better-known polemical novels, *The fountainhead* (1943) and *Atlas shrugged* (1957). Written in 1937, *Anthem* was not published in the US until 1946, when (in the wake of *The fountainhead*) it had 18 printings. Perhaps *Anthem* would have found an American market sooner if she had proposed a religious eutopian alternative to collectivism, but Rand considered religion 'the first enemy of the ability to think'.[24]

Anthem, whose brevity is one of its strengths, is set in a future America, after war and fire ('the Dawn of the Great Rebirth') have destroyed civilisation. Here, as in Hamilton's *Theodore Savage* (1922, 1928), is a future where knowledge is suppressed. When Rand's Equality 7–2521 rediscovers electricity he is told:

> The Candle is a great boon to mankind, as approved by all men. Therefore it cannot be destroyed by the whim of one . . . This would wreck the Plans of the World Council . . . and without the Plans of the World Council the sun cannot rise. It took fifty years to secure the approval of all the

Councils for the Candle, and to decide upon the number needed, and to re-fit the Plans so as to make candles instead of torches. (p. 82)

His refusal to accept this decision brands him as a heretic, and he is marked for death. (When Equality escapes from this totalitarian state, he takes the name of Prometheus.) There are similarities between *Anthem* and fellow-Russian Zamiatin's *We* (1922): both describe totalitarian societies in which individuality is crushed, and names replaced by numbers. Branden notes the major difference — that Zamiatin's society is 'brilliantly mechanized and industrialized', while Rand's is intellectually impoverished and technologically backward, illustrative of her belief that collectivism quashes intellect and initiative.[25] This equation of science with progress places her in the pre-1950 mainstream of utopian fiction by American women. There is remarkable cohesion (until the nuclear debate and the ecological movement) in this view that scientific progress is not only a good in itself, but that it can only occur as the outcome of individualism, whether religious or secular, and as such is a mark of the 'elect'.

Anthem is in many ways the standard American anti-socialist dystopia which lacks a religious underpinning, but Rand introduces one sophisticated literary device that separates it from that rather banal group: her society has banned the first person singular pronoun. While this makes the first-person narrative initially cumbersome to read, it is a constant reminder of the restriction that she wishes to convey, and vividly reinforces the loss of individualism that is the heart of her criticism of socialism. *Anthem* takes the form of so many successful dystopias, the secret diary; her Equality 7–2521 writes:

It is a sin to write this. It is a sin to think words no others think and to put them down upon a paper no others are to see. It is base and evil. It is as if we were speaking alone to no ears but our own. And we know well that there is no transgression blacker than to do or think alone. We have broken the laws. The laws say that men may not write unless the Council of Vocations bid them so. May we be forgiven! (p. 11)[26]

The extreme naïvety of the prose style more than adequately conveys Rand's thesis of the restricting effect of collectivism. Once

Equality 7–2521 has escaped (with Liberty 5–3000), the language mirrors the rupture of the social bond, and the birth of the Ego: 'I am done with this creed of corruption. I am done with the monster of "We", the word of serfdom, of plunder, of misery, falsehood and shame' (p. 112). However, the first task of the new Prometheus is to build an electrified fence around his new home, 'a barrier my brothers will never be able to cross' (p. 117). Rand leaves no room between totalitarian repression in the name of co-operation, and the self-imprisonment of the ego triumphant. While the new Prometheus pores over books from the 'Unmentionable Times' (the twentieth century), prior to claiming the forbidden word, 'I', Liberty 5–3000 (now Gaea, mother of the earth and the gods) is locked into her own prison — of narcissism:

> No words of ours could take the Golden One away from the big glass which was not glass. They stood before it and they looked and looked upon their own body. When the sun sank beyond the mountains, the Golden One fell asleep on the floor, amidst jewels, and bottles of crystal, and flowers of silk. (p. 105)

Anthem is a more skilfully written dystopia than others of the period; yet its skill does not disguise a philosophy that is anti-feminist, anti-humane, and concludes with the major characters breaking the mind-forged manacles of the state only to adopt the self-forged manacles of the ego.

The wartime forties

It is not surprising to find that the number of utopias declines during the war, or that those written express a guarded optimism, and a renewed emphasis on spirituality as refuge and salvation. The two published then are: Dardanelle's *World without raiment* (1943), and McElhiney's *Into the dawn* (1945). They offer the hope of peace after destruction — Dardanelle, a return to nature, a return that nature herself forces (though more beneficently than in *Ultimo*) through the disintegration of all artificially made objects. Subtitled 'A Fantasy', it tells of the coming of a new star, whose rays leave the Earth without houses, clothing, or any manufactured objects. (The obvious analogy to this is de Bury (1904)). One character wonders whether 'the stone and cement and wood that we stole from the ground and the forest hasn't taken a fool notion to return to the ground' (p. 175). It has. Due to the foreknowledge granted a minority, plans have been made to prepare for a pastoral future when 'the sunshine will bake our bread and dry our bricks' (p. 260): this somewhat Lawrentian eutopia of a revitalisation through contact with nature concludes with the lion lying down with the lamb, heralding the arrival of a 'world without sin' (p. 260).

McElhiney's *Into the dawn* opens with a woman pilot crashing near a Pacific island during the war. Here she is acquainted with a litany of theosophist belief — a 'Brotherhood of Great Souls', remnants of a Lemurian city, experiments on the astral plane, the Pacific as source of the new race — and a Master to explain their significance. McElhiney quotes liberally from Blatavsky's *The voice of Isis* to reinforce her point; she also forecasts the Second Coming of Christ in 1949, and the birth of a theosophical new age.

Late forties and fifties

The three novels published in 1949 belong in spirit to the seven 1950s novels. In a diversity of narrative approaches, they resound with echoes of the war and the cold war: Short, *A visitor from Venus* (1949); McCarthy, *The oasis* (1949); Sutton, *White city* (1949); Barber, *Hunt for heaven* (1950); Merril, *Shadow on the hearth* (1950); Caldwell, *The devil's advocate* (1952); Brackett, *The long tomorrow* (1955); Maddux, *The green kingdom* (1957); Moore, *Doomsday morning* (1957); Norris, *Through a glass darkly* (1957); Rand, *Atlas shrugged* (1957).

Some of these novels are anti-socialist, some face new issues of science and technology, particularly the nuclear question, which were also appearing in British novels. American reaction is stronger, however, and covers a wider spectrum of responses. Short and Sutton offer positive examples of nuclear power in the service of peace, both stressing the moral guardianship that will be needed to control it. Merril describes the horrible impact of nuclear war on a suburban family as they deal with the problem of survival. Brackett debates with more complexity, concluding that knowledge gained cannot be suppressed; Moore rejects this. Brackett and Moore are particularly interesting because they are the first to question the role of science and technology, especially nuclear technology. Thoughtful works such as these entirely replace the earlier, stereotypical attitudes to science.

The first of these novels to address the problem of nuclear energy is Short, in *A visitor from Venus*, which is also the only feminist work during this period. *A visitor from Venus* has a woman pilot who makes an emergency landing during the war (in North America), but the eutopia subsequently revealed to her differs from McElhiney's. Finding shelter, she watches on a television screen what she assumes is a play like Wells's 'The war of the worlds'.[27] However, it is the reunion on Venus of Zua (a physicist) who has visited Earth on an atomic-powered ship of her own design, with her friend Veh. The substance of their conversation does indeed resemble a 'Herlander's view of Ourland':[28] both Gilman and Short present the reactions of eutopian women from all-female societies to the wartime 'real world.' The listening Roberta is reminded of her own fears since Hiroshima and Nagasaki as the Venusian women discuss the destruction of the entire planet that might result from nuclear power in the hands of the unevolved human race; it has happened with other worlds. Zua asks her friend: 'How can we get a message to Earth that they must stop their self-destroying activities, and turn to arts of unselfishness and sisterly affection, or else disappear?' (p. 29). The peaceful use of the atom on Venus offers an alternative, *if* women will spread the message of 'unselfishness and sisterly attitudes', and undertake the 'world-wide education of their children to prevent future conflicts' (p. 31).

As well as the horror of war, the incredulous listener on Venus hears from her Earth-travelling friend of 'man': 'In all languages it means the same, and that is "the boss". On Earth it is "he" the boss, and "she" the bossed! . . . Another name is "man-ag-her.' And believe me he does!' (p. 13). As for 'woe-man': 'They have a name on Earth for sorrow. They prefix that name to man, and that gives them woman!' (p. 14).

The evolution of life on Venus has gone far beyond that on Earth — beyond the war of the sexes and the divisions of nation or race, beyond the necessity for law and government, which have been replaced by the conscience of the individual. Zua despairs of establishing contact with Earth until it has shown itself taking at least some steps in this direction.

Like Short, Sutton in *White city* presents a positive view of nuclear energy, but within a controlling religious framework that is possibly theosophical (it uses a symbolism of colours and auras, aspects of the pure 'white light').[29] These novels have little else in common, for while Sutton's foreword states that, once radioactivity has been controlled, uranium holds the key to unlimited combustive power (which is also the message of Short), the controlling moral force is not feminism, but esoteric theosophy. Reincarnation and thought transference figure here, and echoes of the war in the story of a German attempt to occupy the white city.

The three novels of the 1950s that deal with similar problems are by accomplished science fiction writers: Judith Merril (1950), Leigh Brackett (1955) and C.L. Moore (1957). Judith Merril's *Shadow on the hearth* (1950) concerns a suburban woman and her children trying to cope with the contamination of nuclear radiation and the breakdown of services as the US is involved in (and wins) a nuclear war. 'The battleground is the neighborhood; the war throws its blighting shadow across the domestic hearth.'[30] It also emphasises the dangers of mob-action in time of trouble, and the housewife figure acts as a common-sense individual, refusing to be caught up in hysteria. Her husband's long-drawn-out (and eventually successful) attempt to return home, although not foremost in the novel, sketches tangentially some of the horrors of the world outside. Only minimally a tract against nuclear war, the novel is much more a psychological study of several characters under stress, and fighting an invisible enemy: radiation.

Brackett's future world is post-nuclear holocaust. In reaction, the survivors have renounced all innovation, and turned their backs on urban life:

> No city, no town, no community of more than one thousand people or two hundred buildings to the square mile shall be built or permitted to exist anywhere in the United States of America. Constitution of the United States Thirtieth Amendment. (Epigraph to *The long tomorrow*.)

They adopt the religious principles and the simple life of the Mennonites ('they were the only ones who could still tie their own shoelaces') in order to prevent another 'Destruction'. The difference between this novel and Hamilton's *Theodore Savage* or Bennett's *The long way back* is that 'the Destruction' is followed by a deliberate rejection of science and technology within an organised framework of continuing government. The survivors do not live a primitive tribal existence; they are settled and agricultural, and have not fallen back to barbarism, merely to an earlier, simpler America. Yet in a forbidden city scientists have built a nuclear reactor. There is no simple choice between the two worlds, however:

While the God-fearing majority is patently wrong in its reactions to changing social conditions, its basic values — caution about technological excess, respect for the spiritual aspects of humankind — are self-evidently right. At the same time, we sense the importance of the scientists' dream, but realize that their zeal and single-mindedness have imposed an inhumane regimentation upon the citizens of Bartorstown.[31]

Two young boys (the modern Huckleberry Finn and Jim) find Bartorstown, and, despite all of their fears, choose to accept the dangers of knowledge rather than return to ignorance, however familiar and secure.

Moore also depicts a future America, but not after nuclear war. In her dystopia sophisticated technology is used by unscrupulous politicians for monitoring, persuasion and surveillance. The conflict between the individual and the state ends in a successful 'Second American Revolution' which sabotages all existing electronic devices. As planes fall from the sky, and communications networks sputter out, they look forward to 'a new world . . . a harsh world, full of sweat and bloodshed and uncertainty. But a real world, breathing and alive' (p. 215).

Moore and Brackett both look to the American past, but their conclusions are quite different. Moore rejects the dominance of technology in favour of a more difficult but 'natural' society; Brackett examines the suppression of knowledge to which this attitude might lead.

The second, more political, group is anti-communist: McCarthy, Barber, Caldwell, Rand. Despite the commonality of their theme, they are an oddly assorted group — the liberal, witty, satirical McCarthy and the arch-conservative, prolix, stylistically wooden Caldwell and Rand. In the earlier novels McCarthy and Barber use communitarian settings as a background. McCarthy's *Oasis* (later republished as *A source of embarrassment*) is described by its author as 'the only one of my books that aimed at the moral reform of its targets'.[32] 'The title, she has said, comes from Arthur Koestler, who suggested the possibilities of establishing oases — small libertarian groups that would try "to change the world on a small scale".'[33] This oasis falters through several crises, which highlight the inadequacy of its members' ideals. The third, and most serious, occurs when faced with working-class trespassers. Idealists, dreaming of America as a 'vessel waiting to be filled' with the poor and oppressed of Europe (p. 121), and of their own roles in a new socialist state, they panic at the appearance of a family of uncouth picnickers in their own eutopia within eutopia. It is 'the invocation within themselves, at the smallest threat to their property and their appetites, of the most primitive emotions'.[34] After this shock, the community quickly disperses.

Barber also introduces a utopian community that fails. Unusually for the period, hers is a return to a popular type of the late nineteenth century, a fictionalised Christian community set in the late nineteenth century, a response to the Haymarket riots. When it fails (intransigent members, failing crops), its founder on his deathbed sends his daughter out into the world, with the familiar 'the kingdom of God is within you'. Among these other novels it is anachronistic, although familiarly anti-socialist. Another apparent anachronism is Norris (1957), which combines 'single-tax' theory with that Victorian staple, the heavenly life as eutopia. It includes the same movement from the spirit world to Earth, and proposes much the same form of interference from across the barrier of death, and the process of education of the living.

A more down-to-earth, although non-fictional, work of the same period introduces the Llano Co-operative colony in Louisiana. Loutrel (1957) considers the role of the small community as part of a national network, and the work is an attempt to publicise the Llano colonies, and to raise public, and government, support for them.

Both of the remaining two novels depict a dystopian future America, enslaved to an ideology, and conclude with a return to sanity. Both, like *Anthem*, depict a socialised America as shabby, inefficient, rundown and flaccid, eutopia only for the mediocre. Both use strong-minded individuals critical of socialism who undermine the system from within to accelerate this decay implicit under collectivism — Caldwell, the Minutemen, Rand, the members of her hidden valley community, the 'utopia of greed'. Caldwell also returns to the stereotype of the twenties, the mannish 'feminist' women who will take power under socialism, although hers are even more sinister: lesbians.

The other novel of this period is Maddux's *The green kingdom*. It is engaging and poignant, rich in symbolic description of a 'lost world' within the Rocky Mountains: human nature and its potential are measured in this paradisal 'Green Kingdom'. Here, those with inner resources find them strengthened, while those with humane and dignified values find them confirmed. The subjective nature of eutopia is hinted at in the evocative prose with which

Maddux heralds its finding:

> You are deaf. You have always been deaf. You have never
> heard anything. I take away your deafness. I point to a harp.
> I place your hands upon the strings. You move your hands
> across the harp.
>   That is how the Green Kingdom looks. (p. 163)

Those who wish for a 'utopia of greed' find the kingdom to be a
hell in which their desires recoil upon them. Here the dreams of
the heart are granted, although in unexpected ways. The author
(dust-jacket) calls this work a parable, which she began to write
during the war, and in the arid country of the west. The antithesis
of both, the green kingdom, is Eden.

Sargent remarked on the critical neglect of this period in British
utopian fiction. American fiction is equally neglected, although it
is easier to see why. The previous chapter included strong and
politically aware works by accomplished writers, but the same can
not be said for the US. (Sinclair Lewis's *It can't happen here* (1935)
is one of the few relevant to the contemporary situation.) American
response to international issues indicative of their 'widening world'
is defensive rather than immediately political, and the absence of
utopian futures for women reflects their embattled and narrowing
sphere. Zua is the only mid-century Ellador. Seen through her eyes,
the ills of Earth are clear and the cure for them all is to be found
in her eutopian home; but the novella (43 pp.) is frustratingly short.
We do not know the relationship of the two women of Venus whom
the earthwoman observes. Mother/daughter? Lovers? Platonic
friends? Yet this briefly glimpsed world of serenity and peace is the
most fully realised of the feminist utopian visions in this chapter.

Within these 40 years of change, it is significant that Ayn Rand,
a Russian immigrant, should be the only writer who published more
than one genre novel and who is also most representative of this
period, just as Charlotte Perkins Gilman was of hers. Rand's stri-
dent individualism and her anti-socialism (though not her atheism)
are typical of the reactionary mood of the time. Her female character
in *Anthem*, the 'Golden One', is a passive character, seen only
through the eyes of her lover. Dagny Taggart, of *Atlas shrugged*,
woman of steel, is as trapped by the feminine mystique as any suburban housewife of the 1950s. Throughout all the change, through
reactions to involvement in two world wars, the first bringing con-
fusion and anxiety which take the fictional form of natural disaster,

the second opening a new debate on science and nuclear power, American optimism and individualism undergo several metamorphoses. Sometimes this optimism barely masks a querulousness about America's international role; rarely does it dare to forecast a eutopian future for her women, a deficiency that is to be more than compensated for in the 1970s.

Notes

1. Elaine Showalter (ed.), *These modern women: autobiographical essays from the twenties* (Feminist Press, Old Westbury, New York, 1978), pp. 26–7.

2. J. Stanley Lemons, *The woman citizen: social feminism in the 1920s* (University of Illinois Press, Urbana, 1973), p. 191. (See generally for a comprehensive analysis of feminism and legislation during this period. For truly depressing reading I recommend Lemons's history of the Sheppard-Towner Act.)

3. Ibid., p. 215.

4. *His religion and hers: a study of the faith of our fathers and the work of our mothers* (1923, reprinted 1976, Hyperion Press, Westfort, Conn.), p. 54.

5. Carol Farley Kessler (ed.), *Daring to dream. Utopian stories by United States women, 1836–1919* (Pandora Press, Boston, Mass., 1984), p. 15.

6. Freud, letter of 5 November 1883, quoted in Friedan, from Ernest Jones, *The life and work of Sigmund Freud* (Basic Books, New York, 1953), vol. 1, pp. 176ff.

7. A survey of 1,500 cities in 1930–1 found that 63 per cent dismissed women teachers on their marriage, and 77 per cent hired only single women: Winifred D. Wandersee Bolin, 'American women and the twentieth century work force: the depression experience' in Mary Kelley (ed.), *Woman's being, woman's place: female identity and vocation in American history* (G.K. Hall, Boston, 1979), p. 306.

8. Kessler, *Daring to dream*, p. 15.

9. Showalter, *These modern women*, p. 9.

10. Sarah N. Cleghorn, *Threescore: the autobiography of Sarah N. Cleghorn* (Harrison Smith and Robert Haas, New York, 1936), p. 217.

11. Ibid., pp. 300–1.

12. Edward T. James (ed.), *Notable American women*, 3 vols (Harvard University Press, Cambridge, Mass., 1971), vol. 2, p. 283.

13. In 1924, the year that her eutopia was published, she co-founded Manumit, a socialist Quaker school.

14. Bruce Campbell, *Ancient wisdom revived* (University of California Press, Berkeley, 1980), p. 61. For the connection between Nationalists and theosophy, see Sylvia E. Bowman in Bowman (ed.), *Edward Bellamy abroad: an American prophet's influence* (Twayne, New York, 1962), Chapter 14.

15. Jill Roe, 'Theosophy and the ascendancy' in Jim Davidson (ed.), *The Sydney-Melbourne book* (Allen and Unwin, Sydney, 1986), p. 210.

16. Ruth and John Vassos, *Humanities* (E.P. Dutton, New York, 1935), p. 71.

17. Kirk has 35 novels listed in the National Union Catalogue. *A woman's utopia* is the only one of her works published exclusively in Britain. Written under the pseudonym of 'A Daughter of Eve' (the title of one of her earlier works, 1889), she was 89 when it was published (b. 1842).

18. In a test case in 1922, Lady Rhondda and other peeresses claimed entry to the House of Lords, on the basis of the Sex Disqualification (Removal) Act, 1919. They lost, and women were not admitted to the Lords until after World War Two.

19. She is much influenced by Cabell's style, and adopts a series of appallingly precious anagrams — i.e. the 'Gatherulic Iron' (ironic laughter) with which she learns to face the world. Her publishers referred to the novel as a 'feminine *Jurgen*'.

20. Kessler, *Daring to dream*, p. 14.

21. Nan Albinski, 'The vine and olive colony', *Journal of General Education*, vol. 37, no. 3 (1985), pp. 203–17, more fully examines the relationship between the novel and the historical community.

22. *Contemporary authors* lists Sterne's membership in the American Civil Liberties Union, the Women's International League for Peace and Freedom, and the National Association for the Advancement of Colored People. She is a native Alabaman.

23. Paul Kagan, *New world utopias. A photographic history of the search for community* (Penguin, Harmondsworth, Middlesex, 1975), p. 51.

24. Barbara Branden, *The passion of Ayn Rand* (Doubleday, New York, 1986), p. 165.

25. Ibid., p. 143.

26. Ursula Le Guin dispenses with the possessive pronoun in *The dispossessed* (1974), with a very different purpose: to emphasise the positive aspects of community on anarchist Anarres; Marge Piercy, *Woman on the edge of time* (1976), removes gender distinctions by using 'per' (person's) in place of 'his' or 'hers'. See Chapter 6.

27. Short's obituary in the 1969 issue of the yearbook *Screen world* (Greenberg, New York) describes her as 'an early film comedienne' who 'retired from films to work at Lockheed'; *Who was who on the screen* lists 54 films in which she appeared during 1913–38.

28. Kessler, *Daring to dream*, p. 15.

29. Paralee Sweeten Sutton's introduction dedicates this novel to the memory of Mike Sweeten (d. 1935) and his dream of science for peace. He appears in the narrative as a character from the past.

30. *Nuclear holocausts*: atomic war in fiction, 1895–1984 (Kent State University Press, Kent, Ohio, 1987), p. 41. Brians notes that the novel was made into a television drama entitled *Atomic attack*, ABC, 1954, p. 259.

31. Rosemarie Arbur, 'Leigh Brackett: no long goodbye is long enough' in Tom Staicar (ed.), *The feminine eye: science fiction and the women who write it* (Frederick Ungar, New York, 1982), p. 8.

32. Doris Grumbach, *The company she kept* (Coward-McCann, New York, 1967) p. 147.

33. Ibid., p. 130.

34. Ibid., p. 140.

Bibliography of primary material

Johnston, Mary Ann (1920) *Sweet rocket*, Constable, London

Kayser, Martha Cabanne (1922) *The aerial flight to the realm of peace*, Lincoln Press, St Louis

Scrymsour, Ella (1922) *The perfect world: a romance of strange people and strange places*, Frederick A. Stokes Co., New York

Thompson, Harriet Alfarata (1923) *Idealia, a utopian dream, or Resthaven*, J. Wallace Thompson, New York

Cleghorn, Sarah Norcliffe (1924) 'Utopia interpreted', *Atlantic Monthly*, vol. 134, no. 56, July–Dec., pp. 216–24

Pettersen, Rena Oldfield (1924) *Venus*, Dorrance, Philadelphia

Dell, Berenice V. (1925) *The silent voice*, Four Seas, Boston

Gazella, Edith V. (1928) *The blessing of Azar. A tale of dreams and truth*, Christopher Publishing, Boston

Vassos, Ruth (1930) *Ultimo: an imaginative narration of life under the Earth*, E.P. Dutton, New York

Kirk, Mrs Ellen Warner (Olney) [A daughter of Eve] (1931) *A woman's utopia*, Ernest Benn, London

Spotswood, Claire Myers (1935) *The unpredictable adventure: a comedy of woman's independence*, Doubleday, New York

Sterne, Emma Gelders (1937) *Some plant olive trees*, Dodd, Mead, New York

De Forest, Eleanor (1938) *Armageddon: a tale of the AntiChrist*, Erdman, Grand Rapids, Michigan

Morris, Martha Marlowe and Laura B. Speer (1938) *No borderland*, Mathis, Van Nort, Dallas

Rand, Ayn (1937 & 1946 p. 115) *Anthem*, Caxton, Idaho

Dardanelle, Louise (1943) *World without raiment. A fantasy*, Valiant, New York

McElhiney, Gaile Churchill (1945) *Into the dawn*, Del Vorss, Los Angeles

Joseph, Marie Gertrude Holmes (1946) *Balance the universe*, Hobson, New York

McCarthy, Mary (1949) *The oasis*, Random House, New York

Short, Gertrude (1949) *A visitor from Venus*, William Frederick Press, New York

Sutton, Paralee Sweeten (1949) *White city*, Palopress, Palo Alto, Calif.

Barber, Elsie (1950) *Hunt for heaven*, Macmillan, New York

Merril, Judith (1950) *Shadow on the hearth*, Doubleday, New York

Caldwell, Taylor (1952) *The devil's advocate*, Crown, New York

Brackett, Leigh (1955) *The long tomorrow*, Doubleday, New York

Loutrel, Anna Gregson (1957) *A constitution for the brotherhood of man*, Greenwich Book Publishers, New York

Maddux, Rachel (1957) *The green kingdom*, Simon and Schuster, New York

Moore, C.L. (1957) *Doomsday morning*, Doubleday, New York

Norris, Kathleen (Thompson) (1957) *Through a glass darkly*, Doubleday, New York

Rand, Ayn (1957) *Atlas shrugged*, Random House, New York

5

Living in the Ruins

After the silence of British writers in the 1950s, succeeding decades come to life with satire, allegory and ambiguity as their significant response to utopia and to society. At first the anti-utopia predominates, as it did in the 1920s. In the 1970s, the polarities of eutopia and dystopia return, but most often they are fragmentary, not the subject of an entire work. American writers of the same period also tend to a multiplicity of worlds, but theirs are more fully detailed, more directly relatable to contemporary life, even if, paradoxically, more likely to include other planets and alien races. Benford's comment on British science fiction, although made in the context of a discussion of male writers, applies equally to women:

> There is a contrary flavor to British sf, of disconnectedness from experience, as though the future is more approachable through dreaming than through extrapolation of the present. Travel by metaphors, they seem to say, not by the icons of gadgetry, or even science.[1]

While the strong political realist tradition is not completely overwhelmed, the work of the two major writers of this period, Doris Lessing and Angela Carter, and of many others, relies on just such metaphorical shifts.

The shadow of the nuclear holocaust is transformed into one of these metaphors: in providing an explanation of change, nuclear war or accident functions as the *deus ex machina* of utopian fiction. However, it is the clearing-house neither for a new and better society, nor for one demonstrably worse. British writers, less optimistic than their American contemporaries, see ahead a period of social change, a time in which the familiar world will be altered.

130

It is largely immaterial whether this is caused by nuclear accident or war, or by a more ambiguous breakdown of the social system; it is what lies beyond that matters. They describe the transition by remarkably similar names, whether referring to the pressures of over-population, radiation leaks or war: Mitchison (1962) to 'the crisis of Aggression'; Brooke-Rose (1964) to 'the Displacement'; Lessing (1969) to 'the Catastrophe'. What is remarkably consistent is the sense of a coming major dislocation; not the political turmoil that so determined the writing of the 1930s, but one whose consequences rather than mode is important. The novels that do not include some crisis point of social breakdown, nuclear accident or war (however briefly mentioned) are few: Mitchison (1962); Kettle (1969); and Spark (1974). Rather surprisingly, the post-holocaust societies are more often the setting of satires than of nightmare states of mutation and death. While American writers give clearer warnings about the horrors of nuclear radiation or ecological disaster, British writers, although no less aware of their dangers, keep the consequences in the background. These metaphorical shifts produce attitudes to reality that slide between the more literal positives and negatives of American fiction.

This period is particularly rich in anti-utopias, whose settings are rarely those of the national politics and bureaucracy so popular in the 1920s, being instead the conduct of international relations, and in particular America's growing role as a world power. British response to the cold war is later than, and different from, the (understandably partisan, conservative) American response. It is an outsider's view, concentrated as much on satirising style as political substance, although with some of the outsider's fear of being caught up in the side-effects.

Overlapping this type of anti-utopian satire is the more ambiguous, allegorical society, sometimes desirable, sometimes not. Lessing describes her movement into the world of space fiction in terms of a general movement: 'Novelists everywhere are breaking the bonds of the realistic novel because what we all see around us becomes daily wilder, more fantastic, incredible' (*Shikasta*, p. ix). Lessing's involvement with 'space fiction' is far from typical, however: from the futuristic epilogue to *The four-gated city* (1969), through *The memoirs of a survivor* (1974) to her five-volume novel sequence, *Canopus in Argos* (1979–83), she has pursued a wide-ranging series of eutopias and dystopias. Although fragmentary, they are connected by Lessing's moral vision, which sets them into a consistent perspective. The work of Angela Carter, whose dystopias are also fragmentary, allegorised way-stations visited by her central characters, has not undergone such a shift as that of Lessing. Carter's fiction has always been more wayward: 'a witty, elaborate, many-sided and passionate attack on 'reality' (i.e. the traditional consensus) and hence of course on realism';[2] Carter's epigraph to *Heroes and villains* (1969) is Leslie Fiedler's 'The Gothic mode is essentially a form of parody, a way of assailing clichés by exaggerating them to the limit of grotesqueness.' Some of the clichés that she assails are utopian — the rational society, the Noble Savage, matriarchal as well as patriarchal communities. Despite the dissimilarities of their writing, both Carter and Lessing attack the commonplaces of unthinking, mass reactions.

Now, with the 1980s, a new group of women writers is appearing, and adding a new form to the genre. Science fiction has never been as widely published, read or academically acceptable in Britain as in the US, and has generally been a male preserve: serious women writers of science fiction in the 1970s generally published with American, rather than with domestic, publishers. The science fiction balance is currently being redressed, however. The Women's Press science fiction series offers a publication venue for new British writers, and their recent anthology of science fiction stories, *Despatches from the frontiers of the female mind* (1985), includes an encouraging 13 stories (out of 17) by British women. The earlier predominance of American women writers is shown in both: the editors' introduction to the anthology lists only one British writer among the ten best-known and established feminist writers of science fiction. She is Naomi Mitchison, also the only British writer to be reprinted in their re-issue of earlier feminist science fiction classics. British author Josephine Saxton, who has mostly published in America (and many of whose stories are set there) is also publishing and republishing with the Women's Press, and smaller feminist presses (e.g. Onlywomen) are publishing science fiction. Although there has been a delay in British women's entry into the genre, particularly when compared with American women's busy and successful decades, an upswing in this area seems likely to continue for some time, particularly as it offers such rich possibilities for a feminist critique of society. Dale Spender has reminded us that *There's always been a women's movement this century*,[3] but its re-emergence as an influential public movement came a little later in Britain than in the US. Fairbairns's frightening dystopia, *Benefits* (1979), is the first of the single-issue feminist novels to appear in Britain, a decade after American writers had begun examining feminist issues intensively in science fiction (although Carter had already satirised one aspect of the American movement in *The passion of new Eve*, 1977).

Once again we return to the nature/culture debate. The identification with culture and with the city that underwrote Victorian women's utopias (Chapter 1), and that influenced their defence of civilisation against the barbarian (whether politically or culturally defined) (Chapter 3), becomes even stronger in this period. Awareness of the frailty of civilisation, its vulnerability to the weight, even oppressiveness, of political systems or to the particular threat of the nuclear age, is pervasive. The title of this chapter is a reflection of such novels as Lessing's epilogue to *The four-gated city*, her *Memoirs*, and *Shikasta*, Carter's *Heroes and villains* and some of the recent science fiction stories, notably Forbes's 'London fields' (in her anthology *The Needle on full*, 1985). Women writers increasingly foresee the destruction of the cities, with groups of survivors (sometimes groups composed solely of women) living in the ruins, scavenging the left-overs. The tower blocks of London's East End, those crumbling, phallic ghettos built for the working class in the 1950s and 1960s, are sometimes depicted as warehouses of useful materials, sometimes physically dangerous to the women who live in their shadow and either cannibalise or demolish them. Their takeover is an emerging metaphor for feminist hopes of revitalising the world that they know, which, significantly, they do not abandon for the countryside. Alike in their shared commitment to equality and the elimination of power structures in decision-making, in other ways these co-operatives squatting in the ruins of capitalist society could not be more different from the pastoral eutopias of the American feminists. American women identify the city with alienation, the misuse of power, violence — and men; they identify the natural world with women. British women identify the city, however decayed, as the source of civilisation: the natural world is the preserve of wandering tribes of barbarians, either composed of, or dominated by, men.

The division between the two is primarily a distinction between the values ascribed to urban life; it is also a further sign of the greater secularisation of British writers. There is the same split in British feminism that was so disruptive of American feminism during the 1920s and 1930s, and which can be seen in the difference between their contemporary utopias: androgynous or separatist. The same split in Britain is referred to by Lynne Segal as the 'final and fundamental rift between feminists at the end of the 1970s', based also on 'opposing attitudes to heterosexuality and to the significance of male violence'.[4] Evidence of this can be seen in some of the recent science fiction, which, like American separatist works, describes societies of women that may be driven to kill encroaching males in order to preserve their eutopias (see Chapter 6). The difference between the two national groups is the absence of the spiritual matriarchal associations so appealing to American separatist writers whose women celebrate female rituals, and joyfully claim the pastoral world.

Several writers of the 1970s have satirised this separatism. Carter's *The passion of new Eve* (1977) parodies a matriarchal society in the American desert (though putting it to a witty, feminist narrative purpose), and through a black American woman ridicules the idea of female as well as male gods ('there's a great deal of redundancy in the spirit world' — p. 175). Carter expresses this even more forcefully in her *The Sadeian woman*:

> If women allow themselves to be consoled for their culturally determined lack of access to the modes of intellectual debate by the invocation of hypothetical great goddesses, they are simply flattering themselves into submission (a technique often used on them by men) . . . Mother goddesses are just as silly a notion as father gods. If a revival of the myths of these cults gives women satisfaction, it does so at the price of obscuring the real conditions of life. This is why they were invented in the first place.[5]

The tone is hardly less scornful than Clapperton's (1888) sneer at the 'childish theology' of the Oneidans.

In Fairbairns's *Benefits* (1979), a women's community squatting in a tower block is bound by these matriarchal ties. It stays marginal to the political battles which are being fought outside, and is eventually cleared out, although the younger generation of women who have been nurtured there emerge as strong political bargainers when eutopia is finally achieved. Saxton's *The travails of Jane Saint* (1980) includes in its allegorical landscape an all-devouring womb that holds its contented prisoners like children, *and* a strange group of nineteenth-century Marxist revisionists who wish to rewrite the history of the world as a history of women only, which is dismissed as 'a trick'.

> 'Well, so far, we haven't had much parthogenesis, right? If there had never been males there would have been no human world at all, the way I see it.'

'Sound like they weren't after women's liberation but Armageddon.' (pp. 86–7)

The society in Forbes's 'London fields' (in her anthology *The needle on full*, 1985) does indeed perpetuate itself by parthogenesis; it is a gift of nature (as it is in Gilman's *Herland*), but a rarity in British women's utopias. Absent are the mystic associations of motherhood in earlier American novels, or mystic associations of sisterhood in recent novels, with all the spiritual networks connecting women and nature. There are none of the paranormal abilities found in American separatist utopias; when invoked in a similar recent story (Ireland, 'Long shift' in Green and Lefanu's anthology, 1985), they are exercised within the city (and, in the story, demolish a tower block!). Without the spiritual link with nature, though Forbes's novella has much in common with American separatist utopias, the title shows that in its setting it is vastly different from theirs. Thus, for example, Gearhart's 'Hill women' repel attacks from the men in the cities, the only place where they are potent — see Chapter 6. British writers associate male violence with barbarianism, and, in threatening women, it also threatens the values of civilisation.

The complete identification of women with nature continues to be a dystopian fear, rather than a eutopian dream. The reduction of women to 'breeding machines' for the state (Fairbairns) occurs here not as the result of an ideology (as in Burdekin, 1937 — see Chapter 3), but as the outcome of economic decline (which includes the dismantling of the welfare state) which makes Britain the most vulnerable nation in Europe, and ready to sacrifice its women to scientific experiment in order to gain national status. This programme is not halted for political reasons, but because government experiments with chemical contraceptives had produced monsters. The other writer who discusses planned eugenic programmes (Mitchison, 1975) also shows a failed science subverting political planning. If the city still has its place, there is evidently little room in it for even the most controlled use of science and technology. Attitudes towards science are at their most divergent between the two cultures during this period. Yet in the utopian fiction of women there is not the 'technophobia' ascribed by Benford to British science fiction.[6] Science and technology are not sinister, for the simple reason that they do not work properly, whether they are laughably inadequate (anti-utopia) or disastrously inadequate (dystopia). As well as Fairbairns's and Mitchison's novels, that of Duke (1967) wrings a great deal of amusement from a technologically sophisticated so-called eutopia in which nothing functions, while Bennett's (1970) omniscient, computerised 'Big Brother' is easily outwitted by individuals with a modicum of imagination. In Ireland's 'Long shift' (Green and Lefanu, 1985), we learn in the first paragraphs that the presence of a (working) 'Electra Cruiser' does not signal technological marvels: Bee Baxter is soon having trouble with its 'parkbox' and administers 'the much-satirised remedy for the unreliability of this latest showpiece of anti-theft, anti-vandal technology: a swift kick to the controls' (p. 48). 'A swift kick to the controls' deftly sums up the prescription for dealing with science throughout this period.

The metaphorical function of nuclear accident or war has already been introduced: it is hardly surprising that the peaceful use of nuclear energy has no proponents in these novels. Both Sully (1960) and Hewson (1965) introduce post-nuclear holocaust societies apparently for the specific purpose of satirising religion, the first through a messianic sect, the second targeting the 'best of all possible worlds' notion of the 'divine plan'. Brooke-Rose (1964) makes a selective radiation sickness the key to the role reversal of the (susceptible) whites and the (immune) blacks. Nuclear war is briefly mentioned in Dakers and Duke (both 1964), and nuclear accident is the catalyst of Anna Kavan's (encroaching) *Ice* (1967), but in each of these novels the focus is on subsequent events. Carter's *Heroes and villains* (1969) is one of the only two to describe the effects on landscape and (some) people of nuclear war. The bizarre effect on flora and fauna and the presence of the mutant 'Out People' heighten the sense of the 'otherness' in her modern Gothic, transforming mundane society into a fantastic landscape. The epilogue to Lessing's *The four-gated city* (1969) is vague about the 'catastrophe' that causes a massive shift in the Earth's population away from affected England and America. It is less vague about radiation sickness and some mutation, from which she extracts hope for the future, a new generation of children with paranormal powers. In Fairbairns's (Green and Lefanu, 1985) story, 'Relics', the Greenham Common women are hustled into shelters by soldiers at the start of a nuclear attack, snap-frozen, and revive to a very different male world. Bennett (1970) uses a fall of acid rain as a social turning-point, but simply, again, as a source of change.

The prevailing tone of these decades is best summed up as a wry pessimism. In the sixties and early seventies, women novelists take a variety of approaches, many of them satirical, most of them marked by a good-natured rather than a corrosive wit. Malcolm

Bradbury characterises the post-war period as one of:

> an enormous retreat from the kind of revolutionary politics
> that had been around in the 1930s. This was the time when
> people were writing books with titles like *The god that failed*
> . . . a liberal position seemed to me the dominant mood.[7]

This response to extremism is noticeable in these novelists' general
avoidance of the abrasions of domestic politics. The tendency to
enjoy some 'innocent' fun at the expense of the Americans, particularly in their new role as superpower, finds an outlet in a variety of targets, from American tourism and politics to the satirisa-
tion of feminist matriarchies. The political dystopias, traditionally
a British form, is continued only in Dakers (1964) (anti-socialist);
Kettle (1969) (anti-feminist); and Fairbairns (1979) feminist.
Because there are no strictly divided themes but a high proportion
of authors with two or more bibliographic entries, we will look first
at these more prolific writers, examining the continuity or overlap
of their themes, and then at the single-entry writers. The feminist
science fiction writers of the 1980s will be considered together in
the concluding section.

Mitchison's two science fiction novels (1962, 1975), written when
in her sixties and seventies, are the fruits of her 'love–hate' relationship with science.[8] In the introduction to *Solution three* (1975),
she comments that she was 'brought up to biology' (p. 6) and it
was a lifelong interest. These two late works show both sides of that
interest: in the first, genetic experiments are successful and
liberating; in the second, restricting and oppressive.

The spacewoman narrator of *Memoirs* is Mary, a biologist/
geneticist who specialises in communicating with alien cultures. She
finally manages to bear an interspecies child after mating with an
alien, a precarious business indeed, and unusual in British science
fiction, as is the 'female hero' of the novel. (The role of the alien
generally will be discussed in Chapter 6.)

Solution three (1975) is much less optimistic about science, particularly the biological engineering used to solve over-population
which has brought on the 'terrible crisis of Aggression' (p. 7) The
first two solutions are a world scientific council, and the controlled
use of cloned cells, gestated *in utero*, to regulate reproduction. The
third is official sanction of homosexuality as the normal means of
sexual expression. Heterosexuality is regarded as deviant; natural
reproduction shameful. Cloning combines the genes of the perfect

pair, 'He' a negro male from North America, 'She' a blue-eyed blonde from the Shetland Islands. The sudden appearance of disease in genetically altered grains causes concern, but the discovery of some untouched, hardy strains and the emergence of two hetero-sexual 'deviants' among the first generation clones offers hope for a return to nature. As in most contemporary American feminist science fiction novels (e.g. Wilhelm, 1974 — see Chapter 6), clon-ing is a workable response to crisis but not acceptable as a perma-nent method of reproduction.

Duke's two novels, *Claret, sandwiches and sin* (1964) and *This business of Bomfog* (1967), are witty, political anti-utopian satires. The first is set in a post-nuclear holocaust future (1979) 'eutopian' world in which science has eliminated problems but not changed human nature: this is conventional, anti-utopian wisdom. (The nuclear wars have affected Africa and South America.) The subse-quent international balance is maintained by a group of retired pro-fessional women, who monitor world leaders for signs of territorial ambition, and arrange to assassinate the offenders. There is sly humour in the idea of world peace being maintained by a secret anarchist cell of respectable older women (all widows, aged between 80 and 100 years) whose revolutionary ideal, derived from Thomas Paine, is that 'government even at its best state is but a necessary evil'.[9] (Their regular meetings are ostensibly for 'claret and sand-wiches'.) The novel concludes on an ironic note when their leader receives the Nobel Peace Prize, although she does adopt more peaceful methods by sending fruit doctored with a hallucinogen to the President of the US to curb his aggressive instincts. Brians describes this satire as 'written in response to the Kennedy assassina-tion':[10] if true, her wit is hardly a sensitive response.

The second of her novels, *This business of Bomfog*, set in 1989, has a more explicitly American genesis:

> In a sense, if you spell it out, Brotherhood-of-Man-Fatherhood-of-God is rather too '67 a concept to appeal to people nowadays . . . Originally the doctrine of Bomfog was evolved in the States. In the 'sixties, when Senator Rockefeller was running for the governorship of California he electioneered on the platform of Bomfog. (p. 6)

Here she has a natural target. Not only does the slogan exemplify smug patriarchy, but the acronym is the very synthesis of bumb-ling and obscurantism. Appropriately, the (British) government department which bears this title, ostensibly dedicated to 'the termination of wars . . . in the teeth of enormous opposition from Atomic Industry, the Arms Industry and the various Mercenary Soldiers' Trade Unions' (p. 7), spends its time coddling visiting VIPs, and diverting them from any real political bargaining. In an internal joke, the 'author' of her earlier work, Maxim Donne, is now a fictional character, and in consequence of the novel's success co-opted to work for 'Bomfog'. The earlier novel is credited with influencing history:

> *Claret, Sandwiches and Sin* was a work of remarkable political insight. Besides the book had an impact . . . The idea of an 1890-type anarchism almost certainly triggered off the assassinations which freed the world from a generation of troublesome politicians. (p. 6)

One running joke is the political doublespeak of the novel; another is the continual breakdown of the technological marvels of the future — misdirected travel by suction tube, bumbling automatic feeding devices, constantly punctured 'inflatable' cars. *Claret* described the successes of medical science, particularly in cybernetics, in the wake of the nuclear war: the inefficiency of *Bomfog* is a far more British response to science.

Popular novelist Daphne Du Maurier, in *Rule Britannia* (1972), also mines a vein of anti-Americanism. Britain's withdrawal from Europe and alliance with America produces USUK, and USUK produces an intrusive 'protective' military presence and wholesale Americanisation. The development of a 'tribal' sense of British patriotism results in disruption and American withdrawal. The secondary intention of the Americans (to make Britain a kind of historical Disneyland) suggests that Du Maurier is transforming an invasion of American tourists into a military invasion to make her point. It is worth noting that the leader of her resistance movement is also an old (80-year-old) woman, who uses her considerable wit and sense to mastermind non-violent aggression.

In *Adam and Eve and Newbury* (1970), Bennett also writes anti-utopian satire. This is a lighter-hearted Orwell, with an escape hatch. Set in 1984, in a bureaucratic, conformist, computerised Britain (personal surveillance, institutionalised violence to channel aggression), the system can be subverted by those with intelligence and initiative. This the three dissidents of the title succeed in doing, although Newbury goes too far, causing the 'cruds' to riot (like the savage in *Brave new world*), and so is exiled to a Mars being settled by criminals and social misfits (more shades of *Brave new world*).

Carter's glittering fantasies belong with this tradition of satire but they are set in exotic, jewelled, bizarre landscapes, with equally bizarre characters and a coruscating narrative style. Jackson refers to Carter's work as part of a genre of 'subversive Gothic' which uses the fantastic 'to subvert *patriarchal* society — the symbolic order of modern culture'.[11] Carter's *Heroes and villains* (1969) and *The passion of new Eve* (1977) upend the symbolic order brilliantly: *bildungsroman* respectively of a female and a male, the two novels dovetail, showing how Carter kneads and slices the sexes into equality, adding power here, removing it there. *Heroes* is a post-nuclear holocaust novel with a female hero, Marianne, who leaves one group of survivors (the orderly, settled hierarchical world of the Professors) where she has grown up, for another (the nomadic, instinctive, violent world of the Barbarians). However, Carter's Barbarians are a little different from those of other writers: they may be primitive, but they are not ignorant. Jewel, their leader, quotes from Tennyson to Marianne at their first meeting: 'It's the same everywhere you look, it's red in tooth and claw' (p. 18). The enclave of the fathers (the Professors) is the world of Reason, ordered and cold: Jewel and the barbarians are ignoble savages; or, in Freudian terms, the Professors' world is that of the superego (Marianne, there, lives in a tower). And Jewel? Carter says of him:

> Well, there's a bit that's very important in that novel, when they're walking across the beach, and Marianne says to him, 'You're a phallic and diabolic version of female beauties of former periods', and of course that's what he is, though in fact he doesn't want to be — he's id.[12]

Having escaped the arid reasoning of the world of the fathers, however, Marianne, no submissive maiden, survives to conquer the world of the irrational. Having married Jewel, she gradually turns from victim to predator, surmounts rape and degradation, and takes his place as leader, prepared 'to be the tiger lady and rule them with a rod of iron' (p. 175).

> [The Barbarians] may play at being violent but Marianne grows, precisely through her female experiences, into a force far more effective than they, more pragmatic and less bound by ritual and superstition. In the end, both male-dominated

worlds look like different aspects of the same nursery.[13]

Marianne transcends the Gothic, post-holocaust world of the exotic and irrational jungle, keeping her sense of herself. Through the boredom of the world of the fathers, the danger and insecurity of life with the Barbarians, she tests her independence. Landon describes Marianne as 'an Eve to whom patriarchal mythology has nothing to say', as indeed she is.[14]

The 'Eve' of Carter's later (1977) novel has different lessons to learn: the 'new Eve' is a male Evelyn. The novel opens in London, where Evelyn is serviced by an anonymous female pickup while he watches the films of 'Tristessa', a screen goddess, one of those 'female beauties of former periods'. When finally he meets Tristessa he learns that 'she' is a transvestite. No matter. He has by then been changed from the male Evelyn to the female Eve. In the interim he has travelled in America, and been a prisoner in an underground matriarchal society where he is forced to undergo a sex-change operation. (The women hope to impregnate him with his own sperm, thus producing a unique self-fertilised foetus; this is autoparthogenesis with a vengeance!) He escapes, as 'Eve', only to be trapped in a patriarchal community as one of the seven wives of the polygamous Zero.

The hopeless blurring of gender distinctions in this novel is continued at its end, when 'Eve', having learnt something about the common *human* nature of us all, goes through a symbolic re-birth which ends by the sea, where 'Eve' meets 'Tiresias-Mother', and is offered, on a bed of dry ice (but refuses), 'the set of genitals which had belonged to Evelyn' (p. 187). Where Marianne of *Heroes* learns to assume power, the obnoxious Evelyn learns to relinquish it. To return to Carter's discussion of *Heroes*:

> But you see, one of the things I love about Charlotte Brontë, about Jane Eyre, is that she won't *look* at Rochester until she's castrated him, he doesn't stand a chance. In fact she hasn't castrated him, she's given him a vasectomy — it's obvious that she retains the sexual use of him, therefore it's a peculiarly feminine and applaudable version. And also she's very nice to him, she can afford to be, this is where she can start behaving like a human being.[15] (original emphasis)

These protagonists of Carter's two novels have both achieved the ability to behave like human beings through their contact with symbolic communities of rational fathers, irrational barbarians and castrating mothers. Both occur against backgrounds of disintegration. *Heroes* follows nuclear war, *Eve* the social disruption of 1970s America. Carter expressed the opinion that 'some bits [of *Eve*], notably the science fiction matriarchy in the desert, were perhaps not concretely enough imagined (it should, she said, have revealed a proper economic and social structure)'.[16] However, the absence of these structures in no way limits the accessibility of the mythologies of both matriarchy and patriarchy which she rejects.

Anna Kavan's *Ice* (1967) invokes nuclear accident, the precursor of dislocation in government and national boundaries, increasing militarism, and the slow spread of a new Ice Age. In this doomed world, hostility thrives, for 'by making war we asserted the fact that we were alive and opposed the icy death creeping over the globe' (p. 138). The ice in the novel is a metaphor for the disorientation and alienation of the modern world. 'In *Ice*, the narrator's deflection into many selves is symptomatic of a universal chaos that Kavan perceived, with the narrator taking his cue from his depersonalized, derealized surroundings.'[17] Her dystopia includes both the personal and the social and political world: her work is often likened to Kafka's and surely is never more so than in the surreal landscape and changing forms of *Ice*, in which all the familiar signposts of life disappear.

Dakers's (1964) is a more conventional dystopia. Although her future society is the outgrowth of a nuclear disaster, the consequence that matters is the development of a materialist left-wing society. (Dakers describes this as anarchist, but its over-regulation reads more like state socialism.) Here, science rules, Christians are outlawed to the Hebrides: these are the staples of the religiously inspired anti-socialist dystopia from Cobbe (1877) onward. The female narrator, preparing herself for state-sanctioned euthanasia in order to escape her empty life, discovers that she has a soul, and Francis Thompson's 'The Hound of Heaven' becomes her focus of conversion and revolt.

The repression of Christians takes on a literal form in Harrison's *The catacombs* (1962): as the title indicates, they are forced into hiding underground, while above ground people live in a series of Communes. Eventually, there is a *rapprochement* between the two, and between (presumably) Church and state. The role of religion in a post-holocaust society in Sully, *Skrine* (1960), and Hewson, *A view of the island: a post-atomic fairy tale* (1965), is the subject of satire rather than sympathy. In the former there is the same return to primitivism as in Hamilton's *Theodore Savage*, and with violent consequences. Ross's novel, as the sub-title indicates, is much lighter in tone. By fitting nuclear war into a 'divine plan', the author makes a great deal of fun of the religious expectations of a group of upper-class survivors (and non-survivors), including one of the meek who is now to inherit the Earth, but considers it hardly worth having, given its state.

One aspect of the 'unnaturalness' of Dakers's future society is a woman Prime Minister. For determined anti-feminism, however, it would be hard to outdo Kettle's *The day of the women* (1969), where woman at the helm of government is not merely symptom, but the whole disease. Her Diana (in maternal rather than virgin huntress aspect) leads an increasingly Fascist government dominated by women: like Hitler, in power she becomes paranoid, eventually relying on a sinister astrologer. In her state, married women are penalised, sons are removed for separate education, and stud farms are darkly hinted at. The lurid cover promises them, but they do not materialise, except in discussions of selective breeding 'as women no longer want to bind themselves in marriage' (p. 132). Diana's developing megalomania leads to some political assassinations, and the novel ends with an 'accidental' death for her old friend Eve, a more balanced and 'natural' woman who has tried to offset some of the worst excesses of the regime. The novel concludes with the Fascist Diana addressing a mass rally of women from the balcony of an empty Buckingham Palace (the Royal Family have gone to Australia). Only a decade before the election of the first British woman Prime Minister, there is literary and political irony in the appearance of Kettle's novel.

It is a relief to turn to two feminist dystopias of a temporarily triumphant patriarchy, *Benefits* (1979) and *The beehive* (1980), the most political of the radical feminist novels to be published in Britain. Fairbairns depicts the possible future role of women, excluded from any participation in culture, reduced to the status of breeders. The cover of *Benefits* cites Fay Weldon's description of the author as 'a female H.G. Well's, but Orwell was clearly a reference for Fairbairns, as her structural framework indicates. The second part of the novel begins:'Nineteen eighty-four came and went, but the discussion continued: had Orwell been right?' (p. 37), and parts two and three, 90 per cent of the substance of the novel, are set in 1984–2000, and post-2000.

The future that Fairbairns projects from contemporary politics is the formation of a 'Family Party' dedicated to the preservation of women's traditional roles. In true doublespeak the 'benefits' of the title (paid to all mothers of children under 16, the only social security payment that the government does not cancel) are conditional on several factors: women's withdrawal from the labour market (although home piece-work is permitted, reintroducing the sweatshop); their association with a male-headed family; their voluntary participation in a programme of fertility control.

> And the dying welfare state brought its own newspeak as well: governments' failure to link child benefit, unemployment pay and so on to the cost of living was *the fight against inflation*; putting children on half-time schooling was referred to as *giving parents a free hand*; closing hospitals and dumping dying patients on the doorsteps of unwarned and distant relatives was *community care*; and a new political movement that saw remedies to the whole predicament, if only the nation's women would buckle down to traditional role and biological destiny, was known quite simply as FAMILY. (p. 39)

The later 'PoW' ('Protection of Women') Act forbids feminist meetings and public expression of sexism ('defined as hatred of women in their natural role') and declares lesbianism illegal (pp. 145–6).

Fairbairns's impoverished future Britain is the third world of the rich European community. However, its high rate of literacy, political stability and subservient female population make it a perfect experimental laboratory. The trial use of a contraceptive in the drinking water (access to the antidote is restricted to those women judged ideologically sound) falters when the expected super-race of children are born monsters.

O'Donnell's *The beehive* has an equally horrifying scenario. Women are divided into two social classes, workers and wives/mothers. In her future Britain, as in Fairbairns's, the motive springs for this change have been economic decline and high male unemployment, pressure to return to traditional religious values, and male resentment and fear of women. The brightest of 10-year-old girls are chosen to be workers; their education then depersonalises them — they use only surnames and dress in uniformly drab grey. They are segregated from men outside working hours, and kept under surveillance. A successful, non-violent revolution of these invisible, robotised workers takes place before the government can put into effect a massive programme of compulsory artificial insemination. O'Donnell focuses on the same contemporary issues as Fairbairns, and forecasts the same repression, based on the identification of women with nature and their biologically inferior role, and as a consequence their exclusion from culture and power.

Fairbairns's novel is dominated by the political repression of women through the appeal of the conservative Family Party with its innocuous slogans, and its 're-education' of the recalcitrant (single mothers, lesbians). Its central theme of control of women's reproductive systems and the eutopian conclusion of the novel, when women are still not able to conceive and face a future when it may never be possible, give them the kind of power held by Ertz's Stella (in *Woman alive*, 1935 — see Chapter 3). These are the latest of the truly political British dystopias: the erosion of individual freedom that they describe continues to be a matter of concern, and their novels follow on an individualist tradition that has been central to British dystopianism.

Brooke-Rose's earlier anti-racist *Out* (1964) deals not with the divisions of gender, but of colour. In a world divided (Sino-America, Afro-Eurasia, Seatoarea) an unspecified disaster ('the Displacement') identified with radiation sickness, to which whites, but not blacks, are susceptible, has reversed race relations. It is a world in which, as white tells black:

> You used to be Us and we used to be Them, to you, but now it's the other way about. Why? We tried our best. Oh, we brought you syphilis and identity and dissatisfaction and other diseases of civilization. But medicine too . . . And we couldn't bring you radiation leukaemia or chemical mutations, because we absorbed all the chemicals ourselves . . . We were whited sepulchres and never came to terms with our dark interior, which you wear healthily upon your sleeves. (p. 83)

This role reversal depicts British and Americans in Afro-Eurasia, 'the colourless', subject to all the familiar stereotypes of racism (shiftless, lazy, unreliable, irresponsible, unteachable). Eutopia is, of course, in the eye of the beholder, and for their coloured rulers it is eutopia; for the deposed colonial masters, dystopia.

Cooper's *Mandrake* (1964) is a fantasy which plays with the notion of a mystic relationship with the soil. It describes the result when a British Prime Minister, Mandrake, tries to impose stability by first encouraging, then forcing, people to return to live at the place of their birth. The novel ends in disaster as the earth responds with a build-up of psychic energy that backfires in a series of natural disasters.

Muriel Spark's *The abbess of Crewe* (1974) has a more easily identifiable (and American) genesis: Nixon's Watergate. Its parodic counterpart is a Benedictine abbey, where the nuns are 'perpetually plotting in their bugged convent'.[18] The enclosed world of the abbey as a eutopia is a notion knocked into a cocked hat: this microcosm of the world outside (its classlessness lauded by the aristocratic abbess in a masterpiece of hypocrisy) is no *hortus enclosus*, but a rigid totalitarian state firmly ruled by the abbess, where even the trees in the avenue of meditation are bugged. A satire on the kind of female world envisaged in Scott's *Millenium Hall*, the abbey combines the traditionally strict regulations of the Benedictine order (which the abbess, defying Rome, will not relax) with a complex electronic surveillance scheme. The combination of past and present in a satirical framework evokes the similar combination of old and new in many of the contemporaneous American tribal/technological eutopias.

For a period of over ten years, beginning with the appendix of her *The four-gated city* (1969), Doris Lessing's contributions have dominated the utopian genre. Forsaking social realism for a deepening comitment to what she terms 'space fiction', through a sequence of novels she has written futuristic parables which depict social breakdown and change. She has been influenced (and not least in the elliptical structure of these novels) by the Eastern philosophy of Sufism: 'the beginnings of a way of looking at things which unfolds as you go on. . . . What you start off with is shedding prejudices and preconceptions.'[19] The dedication to *City* is a Sufi 'teaching story' from Idries Shah's *The way of the Sufi*; its epigraph on the changes in nature from Rachel Carson's *The edge of the sea*. Flux on a physical and metaphysical level permeates Lessing's utopian fiction. Neither her eutopian nor her dystopian societies remain fixed for long: from *The four-gated city* (1969) to *The sentimental agents in the Volyen Empire* (1983) they introduce social breakdown, even nuclear disaster, as crisis points in a long view of (cosmic) history, whose outcome may, in the long term, be a better world. Change is the only certainty of her fictional universe.

This phase of Lessing's work has not always met with critical approval. Not all reviewers have reacted to the new element in her work as favourably as fellow novelist Margaret Drabble, who sees her as a modern Cassandra, and writes (of the epilogue to *City*):

The point is that we never see [the final breakdown of Britain] as the speculation of a writer sunk in mysticism, turning her back upon the world. Nor are any of her suggestions, alas, inherently implausible . . . Like Cassandra, she is probably right and like Cassandra there is a risk that she will be ignored.[20]

There are critics who, like Lorna Sage, see the utopian novels as a development from her earlier work rather than as an aberrant break.[21] She has also received serious critical attention as a utopian/science fiction writer, particularly in America. In critical American anthologies of women's speculative fiction, she is often the only British writer included.[22] In many ways Lessing recapitulates themes current to British writers (social breakdown, the loss of culture). However, she adds something new — the moral dimension of Sufism, and a cosmology all her own. Yet in her alternative to realism there is, as Drabble remarks, the constant reminder of the political issues examined less ambiguously in her earlier work.

The epilogue to *City* and *The memoirs of a survivor* (1974) are the first of her works that can be called utopian. *City* has Europe and America destroyed, either by nuclear or bacterial accident or war; the means is immaterial. The outcome is survival in overcrowded, plague-ridden refugee camps in Africa and Asia, overcrowded and diseased (refugee camps figure in some of Lessing's subsequent novels as a hell on Earth). Children are being born, some genetically affected by the 'Catastrophe', others with a high IQ and the gift of prescience and a group consciousness so that the novel concludes with cautious hope.

In *The memoirs of a survivor* (1974), against the breakdown of society, she offers a spiritual alternative, as ambiguous in its outcome as the onset of the initial decline:

We knew that all public services had stopped to the south and to the east, and that this state of affairs was spreading our way. We knew that everyone had left that part of the country, except for bands of people, mostly youngsters, who lived on what they could find: crops left ungathered in the fields, animals that had escaped slaughter before everything had broken down. These bands, or gangs, had not, to begin with, been particularly violent or harmful to the few people who had refused to leave . . . Then, as food became more scarce . . . the gangs became dangerous, and when they passed through the suburbs of our city, people ran inside and stayed out of their way. (pp. 12–13)

This disintegration is not explained in terms of politics, nor is politics its cure. The cities are deserted, and the figures of the barbarians, moving ever northward, are familiar ones: the last and most frightening wave is of children, violent and cannibalistic. An alternative world behind the wall of the narrator's besieged flat, which holds fragments of the past, provides a way to escape. Into this the survivor and her charges go at the conclusion of the novel:

> the one person I had been looking for all this time was there: there she was. No, I am not able to say clearly what she was like. She was beautiful: it is a word that will do . . . Both walked quickly behind that One who went ahead showing them the way out of this collapsed little world into another order of world altogether. (p. 190)[23]

Lorna Sage identifies this 'enigmatic figure' with Lessing's 'future Muse' and with Lessing herself: 'She stepped out of the mirror-world of meta-fiction with her wanderlust and her epic ambitions unscathed: this time, as a fully paid-up alien, into the outer space of a new series.'[24] For her characters it means leaving behind a spiritually bankrupt world, and moving into one that has no certainties to offer, only half-glimpsed truths, ambiguities. For Lessing, it means the transference of both; the next decade was the decade of *Canopus*, another place of dystopian refugee camps and barbarians, but also one of visions of harmony and peace.

Lessing's first major novel sequence, *Children of violence*, was published over a span of 17 years (1952–69); the five novels of *Canopus* over five (1979–83). Such concentration might suggest a continuous narrative, but *Canopus* is far from that. Each novel of the series is a different fragment of Lessing's cosmos, and introduces new problems. Her eutopian ideal, embodied in the planet Canopus, is spiritual harmony. Clare, in her paper on Lessing and feminist science fiction, has remarked how the discussion of gender relations, although not excluded, is not central to *Canopus*. 'The project of the Canopean sequence is to represent the apocalypse,' she says, and quotes from Lessing's 1975 essay in which she defines what is central to her vision, and what is peripheral:[25]

it is already clear that the whole world is being shaken into a new pattern by the cataclysms we are living through; probably by the time we are through, if we do get through at all, the aims of Women's Liberation will look very small and quaint.[26]

However, just as her feminism is subsumed into a global concern for the future, so apocalypse is subsumed into universal metamorphosis. Sometimes this is manifested in spatial arrangements that signify concordance between people and their environment, are subject to change, but are rarely lost. Sometimes this occurs with her characters, which results in a blurring of gender lines. Not only are their names not gender-specific, but Canopean ability to 'discard bodies at will' (*Sirian experiments*, p. 186) carries this blurring even further. In *Planet eight*, 'the representative' is a collective consciousness, whose members have transferred identities regardless of their gender. This is the freedom Lessing sought and found in 'space fiction'. Not all of her characters have such fluctuating identities, but she carries the symbols of change into the natural and artistic environment of her novels. Architectural and spatial harmony is a controlling metaphor for the cosmic harmony of Canopus; its disruption the sign of disorder, and of the hatred and violence of evil Shammat, the enemy of Canopus.

The early, eutopian settlement of earth (Rohanda) is depicted in the first chapters of the first novel of the sequence, *Shikasta*. The 'Natives' are instructed in the art of building cities, each 'a perfect artefact, with nothing in it uncontrolled: considered, with its inhabitants, as a functioning whole' (p. 26).

> What the Natives were being taught was the science of maintaining contact at all times with Canopus: of keeping contact with their Mother, their Maintainer, their Friend, and what they called God, the Divine. If they kept the stones aligned and moving as the forces moved and waxed and waned, and if the cities were kept up according to the laws of Necessity, then they might expect . . . to become men. (pp. 25–6)

However, Shammat succeeds in breaking the Rohandan/Canopean 'lock', and, with communication severed, the cities fall into decay. The post 'Fall' earth, now called Shikasta, enters human history with its suffering and war. At the close of the novel Shammat, a parasite that feeds off other worlds, degenerates (a process accelerated by the 'poisonous' emanations from Shikasta), and its influence wanes. As a result, the cities of Shikasta are revived again, peace returns, and a cosmic pattern is re-established through a process of mutual agreement of the 'right' way: 'there is no need to argue and argue and discuss and disagree and confer and accuse and fight and then kill. All that is over, it is finished, it is dead' (p. 346). New cities arise, one 'a circle, with scallopped edges', others 'a triangle, a square, another circle, a hexagon', a six-pointed star. ('There were no plans. No architect. Yet it grew up symmetrical'.) 'The people talk about the old towns and cities as if they are *hell*' (p. 361, original emphasis). As Shammat's influence wanes, the new cities replace the refugee camps which had dotted the earth. 'In both instances the polarity between natural/civilised is overridden, so that ideas emerge in which some fundamental differences, through which meaning is commonly constructed, no longer exist.'[27]

Lessing discusses the spatial dimensions of her utopias in the preface to *The Sirian experiments* (1981):

> I would not be at all surprised to find out that this earth had been used for the purposes of experiment by more advanced creatures . . . that the dimensions of buildings affect us in ways we don't guess and that there might have been a science in the past which we have forgotten . . . that artefacts of all kinds might have had (perhaps do have) functions we do not suspect. (p. viii)

In the second volume of the series, the lovely, fabular *The marriages between zones three, four and five* (1980), the merger of this set of associations is continued. The landscape, dwellings and social values of each of the three zones are quite different, and the marriages of the novel are not merely combinations of individuals, but of the values of each. The pavilion of the marriage of zones three and four, made to a design that was 'ordered', is laid out with the same care and meaning as the cities of Rohanda:

> the vaulting roofs, the sides open to the sky, and to the gardens, the fountains in special numerical arrangements. Thus it becomes a mandala. Not only the place for the regeneration of Al·Ith and Ben Ata, but the centre, the focus of the *self*, where the zones cross.[28] (original emphasis)

Each of the other novels of the *Canopus* series poses a different problem, a different series of shifts from order to disorder. *The Sirian experiments* (1981) presents the conflict between Canopus and Shammat on a series of planets, including Earth, and the education of the aggrandisingly colonial planet Sirius to an awareness of its effect on others. *The making of the representative for planet eight* (1982) is a parable concerning a planet, lovely, tropical, that unwillingly builds a wall under the instructions of Canopus. Lessing stresses the themes of interdependence and influence once again: the people of Planet eight had been destined for a more highly evolved society on Rohanda (Shikasta), but Shammat's interference necessitates delay, and as a consequence they must face an Ice Age. Yet even from this suffering something is learnt, a spiritual merging that makes their former way of life appear simpleminded. Yet it has been remembered as a golden age: 'how fluid it was, how adaptable, houses and streets and towns changed as plants do, turning towards or away from light' (p. 94). Their new homes are thick, blind, constructed to withstand the snow.

The sentimental agents in the Volyen Empire (vol. 5) is more overtly political than the earlier sequence novels. Its alternative title could well be taken from Lessing's 1985 Massey Lectures, *Prisons we choose to live inside*. Both discuss the political ideologies and mass movements which blinker us. In the final lecture, 'Laboratories of social change' (Lessing's term for the last two and a half centuries), she warns that:

> in order to learn from them one needs a certain distance, detachment; and it is precisely this detachment that makes possible, I believe, a step forward in social consciousness. One learns nothing, about anything, ever, when in a state of boiling ferment, or partisan enthusiasm.[29]

The sentimental agents deals with the purging of this partisan enthusiasm, and the restoration of detachment and order. There is an analogy between the horror and overcrowding of refugee camps in Lessing's fiction, and the prisons of the mind: in her final novel of the series, the disordered, dystopian architectural shape is ideology, its language and restrictions.

The Sufi method of teaching by means of parables, shifting allusions and allegory, reflecting the ambiguity of life and experience, underlies the shifting vision of Lessing's world. The moral conflict between good and evil does, however, have its absolutes. Ignorance, hate and war lead to suffering and massive dislocations of population in *Shikasta* (the refugee camps are a particular horror). In *The Sirian experiments* there are 'scientific' camps (again, on a Shammat-influenced Shikasta) where one race inhumanely uses another (considered sub-human) for medical experiments (pp. 221–3). There is also a long view of history in which civilisations rise and are swept away by barbarian hordes, from whom rise new civilisations. There is in these novels a constant sense of flux and a Sufi delight in paradox, but with them, as Drabble commented of *City*, harsh reminders of human history. *Canopus in Argos* does not forecast an apocalyptic future, but it weaves past and present into its documents of cosmic change. In the preface to the third Canopus novel, *The Sirian experiments*, Lessing rejects 'cosmologies and tidy systems of thought', 'we live in dreadful and marvellous times where the certainties of yesterday dissolve as we live' (p. vii). Although her novel sequence may include reincarnating Canopeans and non-human looking aliens, its fragmentary eutopias and dystopias expand these uncertainties into an open-ended view of human choice.

While brevity and lack of 'sufficient material for analysis' raise some definitional problems with the utopian short story,[30] the appearance of four separate anthologies (at least) in the 1980s, marking the first signs of a definite move into the realms of feminist science fiction, is too significant to ignore. These anthologies — *Despatches*; Forbes's *The needle on full*; Saxton's, *The power of time*; — appearing in 1985, and Saxton's *The travails of Jane Saint* (1980) — may be precursors of longer feminist works. It is equally likely that they are simply a different form of the modern tendency to the depiction of fragmented utopias, whatever narrative form is adopted. Carter has remarked on the partial nature of her desert matriarchy in *The passion of new Eve* that it should have 'revealed a proper economic and social structure'.[31] Yet her satire works very well without it, just as the communities in her *Heroes and villains* do. Many of these stories create their future societies through the presentation of one salient feature that differs wildly from our own world, and it is this feature that sets the society apart, whatever the unnamed element of organisation might be: the eutopian or dystopian elements being so distilled are sufficient to convey authorial intention.

Both the fragmentary nature of the stories and their overall pessimism have been the subject of a review of *Despatches* and an editorial reply in *Foundation*. Reviewer Avedon Carol comments that the collection 'seems much less hopeful than American feminist anthologies have been', but that may be because the stories are unrounded and lacking depth.[32] Jenny Wolmark has replied that 'they are neither wholly pessimistic nor wholly optimistic. They are entirely open-ended and this is where their radicalism lies.'[33] This judgement seems more accurate: although the collection does not include anything remotely similar to the optimistic visionary eutopias of the American feminists, neither are they 'wholly pessimistic'. (Paradoxically, the most frightening story in the collection, 'Morality meat', is by an American, Alice [Raccoona] Sheldon.) Two of the stories, those by Fairbairns and Ireland, are far less threatening: the first extends into a post-nuclear holocaust Greenham Common, but concludes with the triumphant shout of women's laughter; and the second ends with the possible death of one woman, but her society, which she has helped to save, seems a secure and happy one.

This story, 'Long shift', concerns the work of a 'kinotelergist' in the City Women's Industrial Co-op., part of a future world (apparently without men), who uses the power of her mind to locate structural faults in and demolish old buildings. Seriously injured, if not killed, by the effort a difficult job requires, her social setting is defined as one in which technology is still fallible, but also as one that is peaceable enough for mother/child picnics to be routine. In Forbes's story (at 74 pages in length, more properly a novella) the phallic tower block is also a source of destruction, but one that redounds upon men. 'London fields' is about the relationships of a society of women, survivors of a plague that has produced mutant sons, from which the last man has now gone. These women live in London, the city at last theirs: although 'empty, looted, and often nearly completely destroyed', the city still holds its fascination:

> The loss of vitality of London, the hustle and bustle of millions that made it such a glittering metropolis, but pride that it was theirs at last. No longer would men control it and its wealth, and maybe one day there would be time to repair the old buildings and let life flow back into its ancient streets. (p. 91)

The city is full of memories of the violence of men, which increased in their last days. The women have a peaceable community, co-operative and consensual, until the arrival of a tribe of young men, said to be the 'test-tube' babies of a scientific 'father', determined to reclaim London. In a conclusion similar to the American separatist novels, the new barbarians are killed by one woman, scarred by the violence of the last days of the men, who had discovered a cache of machine guns hidden in a tower block. Forbes is the only British writer to suggest that women and men cannot co-exist: earlier writers, such as Corbett (1889) and Ertz (1936) had created eutopias in which a majority of women was needed to maintain peace. Forbes is the first one to be rid of men entirely.

A lighter view of war and peace is Fairbairns's story 'Relics' (*Despatches*), rather surprisingly, in that its central characters are the women of Greenham Common. Fairbairns depicts them being hustled into air-raid shelters at the time of a nuclear attack: ' "We'll need you for after," say the soldiers. "Why d'you think we've kept you handy?" ' (p. 181). This is an ominous tone, but, once the women awake from their frozen sleep, it is to quite a different world: weapons are exiled to the moon, the men are reproducing themselves (any bodily cavity will do, they say, and so they use their heads), and women have become mythological creatures. However, the men, it seems, have gone from one extreme to another: they reject sexual intercourse ('it would be an act of conquest' — 'penetration, invasion, war'). Obviously they have adopted the ideology of feminism, but warped it into a patriarchal rigidity, with which the warmth and naturalness of Fairbairns's women starkly contrast; and the story ends on a healthy gust of female laughter. The world without women, it seems, has lacked the ability to laugh at itself.

The *Despatches* volume does contain several outright dystopias, McNeill's 'The awakening' is a vilely polluted world of controlled breeding and constant surveillance (set in Australia); Jones's 'The intersection' tells of the visit of a traveller from a technological, controlled eutopia to a wild, natural reserve still populated by 'indigs' (the indigenous population). Both writers created over-controlled, technological societies alienated from nature, a theme rarely found in British women's writing.

The writer who has recently approached the question of utopia in the widest variety of forms is Josephine Saxton. Her collection of short stories *The power of time* (1985) includes an early satire on end-of-the-world fantasies, 'Living wild' (1971). Her protagonist concludes from a series of domestic breakdowns that the world has ended, and takes (literally) to the hills. Later, rather sheepishly, she discovers her error — but stays out on her own, anyway. In *The travails of Jane Saint and other stories* (1980) is her 'Gordon's women' (1976), the tale of the master of a quarter of a planet whose (real) women are kept busy creating the robotised dolls it pleases him to destroy, but who eventually confront him with the real situation, and start to teach him that he must deal with human beings, not dolls. 'The Pollyana enzyme' (1980) tells of a mysterious virus that is slowly destroying all life, but has such a pleasant effect on human nature that the last days are marvels of universal love and understanding. A bunch of anarchists lynch the only man immune, unwilling to lose this happy love (and death) and return to a 'normal' world should an antidote be found.

The satirical eye for the conventions of utopia and dystopia in her *Jane Saint* has been commented on already. Saxton speaks of a literal eutopia only in her novel *Queen of the states* (1986), in itself a satire on the 'mental-patient-taken-up-by-aliens' school of fiction (and, also, I strongly suspect, of Piercy's *Woman on the edge of time* — see Chapter 6). Her Magdalen, who insists that she is the rightful queen of America, harangues a crowd of night people from the steps of the Guggenheim Museum at 1.30 a.m., outlining her plan to ban capital punishment, clean up pollution, and eradicate sexism in all its forms: 'Irish embraced Puerto Rican and black embraced cripple and cop embraced drug addict and woman and man and all knds embraced and threw down guns, knives, coshes in an obscene pile on the steps' (p. 119). And then the police cars arrive with sirens wailing to arrest the instigator of the riot. As the latest, most consistent, contributor to the British women's utopian tradition, Saxton covers the range of fantasy and satire, has a set of utopian ideals and a healthy scepticism about their reception.

Looking back over this period, the outstanding writer of utopian fiction is, of course, Doris Lessing. Few of the science fiction writers of the 1980s seem ready to follow in the wake of her *Canopus* series: although they may share her sense of coming apocalypse, the deviation occurs most markedly in terms of her overriding sense of a universal moral conflict, and (in the minor trend at least) theirs of a separation between the violent natures of men and the peaceable natures of women. Satire and an awareness of contemporary politics, particularly as it affects women, seem likely at this point to carry the day. Forecasting the developments in utopian fiction is notoriously uncertain, however: just when the most 'reliable' pronouncements seem to have been made, overtaking events deprive them of their meaning. Perhaps the only sure pronouncement that can be made is that satire and scepticism will continue to be the main focal points of British utopian fiction, that attitudes to eutopia will remain guarded and ambivalent, and that the secular, cultural values identified with the city will continue to be paramount. While this implies a sceptical attitude to visionary idealism, it also asks for a constant, vigilant watch on the political realities, however sordid, in which utopia is grounded.

Notes

1. Gregory Benford, 'In the wave's wake', *Foundation*, 30 (1984), p. 8.
2. Lorna Sage, 'Female fictions: the women novelists' in Malcolm Bradbury and David Palmer (eds), *The contemporary English novel* (Holmes and Meier, New York, 1980), p. 86.
3. Pandora, London, 1983.
4. *Is the future female? Troubled thoughts on contemporary feminism* (Virago, London, 1987), p. 65.
5. Virago, London, 1979, p. 5.
6. Benford, 'In the wave's wake', p. 5–19.
7. Interview in Heide Ziegler and Christopher Bigsby (eds), *The radical imagination and the liberal tradition* (Junction, London, 1982), pp. 63–4.
8. See Chapter 3, note 17. *Solution three* is dedicated 'To Jim Watson who first suggested this horrid idea'; on p. 15 the early biologists Watson and Mitchison are credited with their pioneering work. Mitchison's 'Jim Watson' must be British geneticist James Watson, one of the discoverers of the function of DNA.
9. Duke published under the punning pseudonym 'Maxim Donne'. *Contemporary authors* gives an interesting biography: medical psychotherapist, silversmith, holds title Baroness de Hartog.
10. Paul Brians, *Nuclear holocausts: atomic war in fiction, 1895–1984* (Kent State University Press, Kent, Ohio, 1987), p. 186. The author is listed as Maxim Donne, not Madelaine Duke.
11. Rosemary Jackson, *Fantasy: the literature of subversion* (Methuen, London, 1981), p. 104.
12. Lorna Sage, 'The savage sideshow: a profile of Angela Carter', *The New Review*, vol. 4, nos. 39–40 (June/July 1977), p. 56.
13. David Punter, *The literature of terror: a history of Gothic fictions from 1765 to the present day* (Longman, London, 1980), pp. 397–8.
14. Brooks Landon, 'Eve at the end of the world: sexuality and the reversal of expectations in novels by Joanna Russ, Angela Carter, and Thomas Berger' in Donald Palumbo (ed.), *Erotic universe: sexuality and fantastic literature* (Greenwood, Westport, Conn., 1986), p. 70.
15. Sage, 'The savage sideshow', p. 56
16. Ibid.
17. Janet Byrne, 'Moving toward entropy: Anna Kavan's science fiction mentality', *Extrapolation*, vol. 23, no. 1 (Spring 1982), p. 6. Brian Aldiss's introduction to the American edition (1970) discusses the analogy with Kavan's heroin addiction, of which she died in 1968: 'The ice was moving faster than I knew' (p. xi).
18. Nina Auerbach, *Communities of women: an idea in fiction* (Harvard University Press, Cambridge, Mass., 1978), p. 180.

19. Interview, in Ziegler and Bigsby (eds), *The radical imagination*, p. 202.

20. 'Doris Lessing: Cassandra in a world under siege' in Claire Sprague and Virginia Tiger (eds), *Critical essays on Doris Lessing* (G.K. Hall, Boston, 1986), p. 191. This includes Gore Vidal's review of *Shikasta*, in which he damns the 'woolliness of latter-day Sufism' (pp. 200–4), and John Leonard's even more contemptuous review of *Planet eight* (pp. 202–9).

21. Doris Lessing has said that her two 'Jane Somers' novels were published pseudonymously 'to settle scores with reviewers who had disliked her *Canopus* quintet' (Jonathan Yardley, 'Lessing is more: an "unknown" author and the success syndrome' in Sprague and Tiger (eds), *Critical essays*, p. 215'.

22. There are essays on Lessing by Lee Cullen Khanna in Marleen S. Barr and Nicholas D. Smith (eds), *Women and utopia: critical interpretations* (University Press of America, Lanham, Md., 1983); Ruby Rohrlich and Elaine Hoffman Baruch (eds), *Women in search of utopia. Mavericks and mythmakers* (Schocken Books, New York, 1984); and by Sandra Lott in Jane B. Weedman (ed.), *Women worldwalkers: new dimensions of science fiction and fantasy* (Texas Tech Press, Lubbock, Texas, 1985).

23. David Gladwell, who directed the film of *Memoirs*, understandably avoided any attempt to portray this scene; he described it as 'rather like the end of 2001!'. '*Memoirs* was made of this' in Jenny Taylor (ed.), *Notebooks/memoirs/archives: reading and rereading Doris Lessing* (Routledge and Kegan Paul, London, 1982), p. 239.

24. *Doris Lessing* (Methuen, London, 1983), p. 77.

25. Mariette Clare, *Doris Lessing and women's appropriation of science fiction* (Centre for Contemporary Cultural Studies, University of Birmingham, UK, 1984), p. 16.

26. Doris Lessing, *A small personal voice* (Vintage, New York 1975), p. 25.

27. Clare, *Doris Lessing*, p. 33.

28. Marsha Rowe, 'If you mate a Swan and Gander, who will ride?' in Jenny Taylor (ed.), *Notebooks/memoirs/archives*, p. 202.

29. Canadian Broadcasting Corporation Enterprises, Toronto, 1986, p. 69. See also Barr and Smith (eds), *Women and utopia* — Lee Cullen Khanna, 'Truth and art in women's worlds', pp. 121–33, and Thomas White 'Opposing necessity and truth', p. 134–47.

30. Lyman Tower Sargent, *British and American utopian literature 1516–1975: an annotated bibliography*, 1st edn (G.K. Hall, Boston, Mass, 1979), p. xvi.

31. Quoted in Sage, 'The savage sideshow', p. 56.

32. *Foundation*, 35 (1985), p. 99.

33. 'Science fiction and feminism', *Foundation*, 37 (1986), p. 51.

Bibliography of Primary Material

Sully, Kathleen M. (1960) *Skrine*, Peter Davies, London

Harrison, Helga (1962) *The catacombs*, Chatto and Windus, London

Leach, Decima (1962) *The Garthians*, Arthur H. Stockwell, Ilfracombe, Devon

Mitchison, Naomi (1962) *Memoirs of a spacewoman*, Victor Gollancz, London

Brooke-Rose, Christine (1964) *Out*, Michael Joseph, London

Cooper, Susan (1964) *Mandrake*, Hodder and Stoughton, London

Dakers, Elaine [Jane Lane] (1964) *A state of mind*, Frederick Muller, London

Duke, Madelaine [Maxim Donne] (1964) *Claret, sandwiches and sin: a cartoon*, Heinemann, London

Hewson, Irene Dale [Jean Ross] (1965) *A view of the island: a post-atomic fairy tale*, Hutchinson, London

Duke, Madelaine (1967) *This business of Bomfog: a cartoon*, Heinemann, London

Kavan, Anna (1967; reprinted 1970) *Ice*, Doubleday, New York

Carter, Angela (1969) *Heroes and villains*, Heinemann, London

Kettle, Pamela (1969) *The day of the women*, Leslie Frewin, London

Lessing, Doris (1969) *The four-gated city*, Alfred A. Knopf, New York

Bennett, Diana (1970) *Adam and Eve and Newbury*, Hodder and Stoughton, London

Du Maurier, Daphne (1972) *Rule Britannia*, Victor Gollancz, London

Lessing, Doris (1974; reprinted 1976) *The memoirs of a survivor*, Picador, London

Spark, Muriel (1974) *The abbess of Crewe*, Viking, New York

Mitchison, Naomi (1975) *Solution three*, Warner, New York

Carter, Angela (1977) *The passion of new Eve*, Harcourt, Brace, Jovanovich, London

Fairbairns, Zoe (1979) *Benefits*, Virago, London

Lessing, Doris (1979–83) *Canopus in Argos: archives*, 5 vols

—— (1979) *Re: Colonised planet 5, Shikasta*, Jonathan Cape, London

—— (1980) *The marriages between zones three, four and five*, Jonathan Cape, London

—— (1981) *The Sirian experiments*, Alfred A. Knopf, New York

—— (1982) *The making of the representative for planet eight*, Alfred A. Knopf, New York

—— (1983) *The sentimental agents in the Volyen Empire*, Jonathan Cape, London

O'Donnell, Margaret (1980) *The beehive*, Eyre Methuen, London

Forbes, Carolyn (1985) *The needle on full*, Onlywomen, London

Green, Jen, and Sarah Lefanu (eds) (1985) *Despatches from the frontiers of the female mind*, Women's Press, London

Saxton, Josephine (1980); reprinted 1986) *The travails of Jane Saint and other stories*, Virgin Books; reprinted by the Women's Press, London

—— (1985) *The power of time*, Chatto and Windus, London

—— (1986) *Queen of the states*, Women's Press, London

6

'When it Changed'

In 1972 Joanna Russ published an award-winning (1973 Nebula) short story with the apt title 'When it changed'; a (male) (Russian) space mission from Earth lands on Whileaway, a women-only planet whose men have been killed in a plague thirty generations earlier. The Earthmen wish to colonise Whileaway, and 'when one culture has the big guns and the other has none, there is a certain predictability about the outcome' (p. 10). The women have no desire to change their happy and peaceful world, their marriage partners, lovers and children, to become 'things to laugh at sometimes because they are so exotic, quaint but not impressive, charming but not useful' (p. 11). 'Our ancestors' journals are one long cry of pain and I suppose I ought to be glad now but one can't throw away six centuries' (p. 11).

Russ's title is significant and timely. Utopia also changed around this time, lifted from the dystopian path in which it seemed to be set by the arrival of feminist writers, some from the neighbouring genre of science fiction, who bring an infusion of optimism not equalled since the utopian golden age of the late nineteenth century. In numbers and in tone, they reflect the rise of feminism as the most important social movement of the 1970s, and their idealistic eutopias are radically different from the continued dystopian pessimism of male writers.[1] Feminist writers also give dystopian warnings: frequently they offer the reader (in single or multiple works) both eutopia and dystopia, so that each nightmare world is accompanied by its opposite. Russ captures the essential nature of the new eutopias in her definition:

> Classless, without government, ecologically minded with a
> strong feeling for the natural world, quasi-tribal in feeling and

quasi-family in structure, the societies of these stories are
sexually permissive . . . the point of the permissiveness is not
to break taboos but to separate sexuality from questions of
ownership, reproduction and social structure.[2]

Different though these realised societies may be from those of
earlier feminist utopists, they do continue in the same tradition.
The small community, with room for individuality to develop
without being crushed in an alienated mass, is the archetypal pattern
now as then. The classlessness and lack of government is like the
apolitical egalitarianism of the late nineteenth century, though
sensibilities have changed, and the term 'anarchist' is applied to
them in a non-pejorative way. Their ecological awareness is a reflection of earlier ease with the natural world, given new urgency by
the modern environmental movement. Community as family is also
recognisable, for American women's ideal societies have usually
been small in scale, and have often taken on some of the roles of
the family. The main differences are the tribal elements, sexual
permissiveness, and a changed attitude to orthodox religion.

The quasi-tribal elements, incorporated from pre-technological
societies (particularly native Indian), promote social cohesion and
an informal network of generally admissible behaviour and agreed-
upon taboos: even where utopia is an entire planet, it is composed
of a number of small communities, which makes such an ethos
workable. Sexual openness is a new development, one unthinkable
to earlier writers, but in these modern eutopias eroticism is accepted
naturally, including homosexual as well as heterosexual love. Legal
marriage is on balance not part of these worlds: a climate of general
aversion to law is hardly likely to promote legal interference in the
most private of relationships, which are the responsibility of the
individual, rather than the community. This sexual permissiveness
is part of a continuing, and trenchant, attack on the double standard
of morality, which still exists in dystopia. In eutopia, a single
standard prevails: it is not identical with the code of the nineteenth
century, but is nevertheless impelled by the same principles of
honesty and integrity.

These changes might be expected, but not so the change in the
view of religion. As the motive power for inspirational change in
the nineteenth century, orthodox Christianity played a vital role.
It has been replaced by a variety of spiritual and mystic beliefs,
usually pantheistic, sometimes derived from the pre-technological
matriarchal religions. These are not theocratic. They often support

the tribal and naturalistic worlds of the eutopias, and are contrasted with orthodox religion, now increasingly identified with hierarchical, male-dominated power structures, most recently through the influence of the Moral Majority.

Critical attention to the new novels has been strong, as has interest in earlier utopias, and the last decade has seen a volume of work by feminist scholars of utopia, notably Barr, Kessler, Khanna, Patai and Pearson.[3] The concept of female heroism is particularly important in defining models for women's action, and in a line of continuity extends from the utopias immediately preceding suffrage (Irwin, Gilman, Bruere, Bennett). If the interregnum of 1920–60 were ignored, and we could read straight on from 1919 to the 1960s, this development of a tradition of feminist utopias would be even sharper. Although the pre-suffrage writers might find it hard to accept the easier sexuality of these modern eutopias, and the rejection of technology in some of the pastoral societies, they would easily recognise these autonomous women, whether physicists and pilots or hunters and healers, as the natural successors of their own women.

A new awareness of politics has entered the dystopias, which differ in every detail from the eutopias. Rigidly hierarchical, totalitarian, militaristic, sexually repressive, patriarchal, set in cities alienated from the natural world, they typify a typically modern American attitude, that civilisation is the new barbarism. Women in these dystopias are defined solely by their biology, as belonging to subjugated nature. While women's eutopias vary enormously, their dystopias are virtually interchangeable. The imaginative creation of an ideal society offers more leeway than the aspects of a detested reality; but eutopia is not merely more open-ended by its nature. These dystopias are characterised by their rigidity, their narrowness and repression. The combination of power most distrusted is the alliance of the military/industrial complex with a fundamentalist patriarchy. The aggression of the arms race, the insensitivity of industry to any but commercial values, come together in frightening nightmares of how American society may be evolving. It is as part of this picture that religion assumes its dystopian overtones, discernible in dystopias of the 1970s (for example, Wilhelm (1974) and Le Guin (1978)), but even more prominent in the 1980s:

> That women are especially vulnerable to reactionary
> movements rooted in religious fundamentalism, much of

which justifies female oppression as ordained by God, is not a new insight. American political history is filled with examples, the recent involvement of the religious right against the Equal Rights Amendment and in favor of an amendment to make abortion unconstitutional being only their most recent manifestations. The religious right seeks to control the behavior of women in the realm of personal relations, especially those related to marriage and child-bearing. Here female autonomy is attacked as immoral to justify efforts to make it illegal.[4]

While religion should not displace other features of dystopia, its shift from eutopia to dystopia and increasing prominence there in reaction to a contemporary situation still in process is one of the most radical changes of this period.

Surprisingly, given the dominance in the dystopias of militarism and pollution (nuclear or otherwise), devastation through either nuclear war or accident plays a minor role in eutopia or dystopia. Charnas (1974) describes the world after 'the Wasting', a post-holocaust dystopia run by men when survivors leave their shelters; Sargent (1986), in an unusual scenario, depicts women building post-holocaust cities, exiling to the wilderness the men whose violence had caused the war. Slonczewski's (1980) Quakers have left Earth before the nuclear wars of 2024; the very different societies of Wilhelm (1974) and Singer (1980) follow leaks from nuclear reactors and widespread pollution. The one eutopia that confronts the problem of accidental irradiation from nuclear plants is Thompson's *Conscience place* (1984), with its unlikely setting of a colony of 'The People', mutants who, with the aid of prosthetic devices to overcome some of their physical disabilities, live a richly sharing, communal life. The lack of gender differentiation, the rituals that bind them as a group, the emphasis on individuality and creativity are identical with the social mechanisms of other eutopias: but not so the shattering conclusion, its destruction by the scientists (the 'Fathers'), who cut it short in order to create a different kind of social laboratory, one where they are treated like animals.

Writers of science fiction are now more actively engaged with utopian fiction, and, although the two genres do not always overlap, many of sf's best-known writers — Ursula Le Guin, Kate Wilhelm, Pamela Sargent, Zenna Henderson, Marion Zimmer Bradley, and, of course, Joanna Russ — have written utopias. Science fiction has expanded the horizons of utopia: although not always earthbound, earlier works by women rarely included off-world societies, time and space travel, or aliens. Sf too has changed, however, as 'New Wave' writers, including Russ, have humanised and feminised a genre mostly written by males for a male readership. Women were writing science fiction before the change; 1950s novels by C.L. Moore, Leigh Brackett and Judith Merril are included in Chapter 4. Like Marion Zimmer Bradley, however, they generally wrote about male protagonists (Bradley created — in her words — 'spunky women', but it was not until 1970 that she felt free to use a female protagonist).[5] Ursula Le Guin parodies how it was:

It was like this. 'Oh, Professor Higgins,' cooed the slender, vivacious Laura, 'but do tell me how does the antipastomatter denudifier work?' Then Professor Higgins, with a kindly absent-minded smile, explains how it works for about six pages, garble garble garble.[6]

New Wave and feminist writing put an end to much of this, and we can now expect Laura to invent her own version of the anti-pastomatter denudifier. For science fiction (if not utopia) in the 1960s, 'the female hero was born':

Men were finally portrayed not only as strong but as capable of fear, weakness, and insecurity. Women were allowed not only to be emotional, but to be strong and flexible, to know their own minds, to control their own destinies. Both women and men were finally being portrayed as whole human beings.[7]

Since then, many women writers have welcomed science fiction's freedom from the conventions of realism to construct role models of strong, autonomous women and of their societies.[8] Independent, intelligent and active, they may be physicist, pilot, engineer, diplomat or warrior.

These female heroes may come from either a single or a two-sex, 'androgynous' society. Whatever the range of their variation in social setting, their location in time and space, whether alien or human, pastoral or technological, the line which ultimately divides these eutopias into two groups is their attitude to men: inclusion or exclusion? In the separatist eutopias the identification of women with nature is a liberating force, because the values ascribed to woman and nature are positive. The androgynous eutopias are less exclusive, seeing both women and men as equally involved in the worlds of nature *and* culture. The difference in the literature is an extension of the division in American feminism, similar to that of the American 1920s and 1930s, and one that has also affected the feminist movement in Britain. However, feminist identification of women with nature, of culture with 'man-made', is far more pervasive in America. Susan Griffin's *Pornography and silence*, for instance, is sub-titled 'culture's revenge against nature', and, although she is concerned with the repression of men in minority groups as well as women, in her definition woman '*is* nature'.[9] This insistence on gender difference shifts the notion of the alien, or 'other', so commonly ascribed to women in dystopias, to men; in Neeper (1975) the only acceptable males are aliens.

The number of separatist societies, though still a minority, continues to grow (Russ, 1972, 1975; Bradley, 1976, 1983; Charnas, 1978; Sheldon [Tiptree], 1978; Gearhart, 1979; Young, 1979; Singer, 1980; Forrest, 1984; Slonczewski, 1986). There are also several novels of societies in which women are in authority over men: Bradley, 1978, Carr, 1979, Dodderidge, 1979, and Sargent, 1986. These societies are far from being carbon copies of a single model, as they range from small rural communities (i.e. Singer and Gearhart) to planets inhabited solely by women (Forrest, 1984; Slonczewski, 1986) or which women control (Carr, 1979; Sargent, 1986), but they have much in common. Sisterhood and sexuality have now replaced motherhood as the dominant bonds between women, and the work of feminist scholars on pre-technological matriarchal societies (including the Amazons) has expanded the historical base from which these writers work. They are generally more wary of technology than the androgynous societies (Russ and Sheldon are notable exceptions) and sustain a spiritualised relationship with nature. The polarisation of the sexes has never been as strong, and although few of these separatist writers are as outspoken as Gearhart, whose women (*The wanderground*, 1979) conclude that 'women and men cannot yet, may not ever, love one another without violence; they are no longer of the same species' (p. 115), there are many who implicitly agree. Lucky indeed is the male intruder in one of these societies who (like the males who find Herland) is allowed to stay, or even to leave unharmed.

The question of violence in relation to men is a disturbing feature of some of these works, and it is paradoxical, given the strength of their commitment to life. Gearhart's women are engaged in a battle for their lives with men from the city, and are unwilling even to negotiate with the 'gentles', men who say that they share their values. Sheldon's women, and Forrest's, destroy the astronauts whom they rescue; Singer's, the men who discover their society. Sheldon's 'Houston, Houston' is reminiscent of *Herland* except for this violence. The contradiction that peace can only be preserved through violence is confronted mainly through descriptions of the far greater violence of men. Several of the novels with off-world settings, those of Carr (not single-sex, but role-reversal) and Slonczewski, confront this contradiction, and describe societies in which women outwit would-be invaders from militaristic, male-dominated societies. Slonczewski, a Quaker, persuasively argues the case for successful non-violent resistance. Despite the suffering that they must endure, and the temptation to use force themselves, thus becoming that which they despise, the women of *A door into ocean* hold fast to their principles. Their 'victory' over the brutal colonisers who would destroy their way of life is eclipsed by their victory over the temptation to use their own, and greater, powers: in this lies their strength, and, with this strength, they accept a man into their planet.

The consequences of violence are also discussed in Sargent's recent *The shore of women* (1986), in which the women gain ascendancy after nuclear war, and keep the men in subjection because of their 'propensity for violence that was both genetic and hormonal' (p. 90). The female hero of this novel, Birana, after living in the wilderness, and meeting men both violent and gentle, comes to understand how a situation once tenable has now grown stagnant: the women in her cities have grown too fond of their power to relinquish it, although Birana's experience has influence on others who may instigate change. These two recent works, Slonczewski's and Sargent's, enter into dialogue with the earlier novels, one presenting a truly eutopian society of women, the other a eutopia now flawed.

Gender differences are deliberately minimised in the androgynous societies. These stress the commonality of human experience, and associate both sexes with the natural world. Invariably, this leads them to correct the sexual division of labour by exchanging traditional roles, so that men are seen as teachers, artists, healers, women (familiar with the 'hard' sciences) as physicists and engineers. There are no distinctions of dress or of degree of sexual activity, and some technological societies (notably Staton, 1975, and Piercy, 1976) introduce exogenetic reproduction to remove the last difference between the sexes. Of paramount importance to the androgynous writers is the need to foster in each sex the good qualities traditionally ascribed to the other, to value in women their strength and intellectual capacity, in men their sensitivity and imagination. Analogous with this redressing of stereotypes, the androgynous societies seek a balance between nature and culture. Increasing awareness of what the unlimited pursuit of 'progress' and technological 'advancement' implies generally leads not to blanket rejection, but to selective choice in terms of each aspect of use. The balance between science, technology and nature is maintained by carefully thought-out community planning, so that scarce resources may be used where they will most benefit society, and with least damage to the ecology. This does not necessarily mean avoiding all energy-intensive work, but measuring it on a carefully thought-out scale of values. In their minutest details, eutopias such as these question the most basic assumptions about the decision-making processes of society, and show the damage that the passivity of some, the special interests of others, may inflict if the community or nation does not function as an organic whole.

An innovative aspect of these modern novels is the frequent inclusion of both eutopia and dystopia in one narrative, or in a series of works by one writer. More detailed than the fragmentary societies of the British writers, their multiplicity makes for some startlingly effective works, particularly where alternative societies are compared within one novel. In the literary sense, this overcomes one of the perennial problems of the utopia — its stasis. The movement of a central character between eutopia and dystopia adds narrative tension, increased when the existence of eutopia is threatened (as it is in most of these dual-society novels). As well as this salutary literary purpose, it doubles the impact of the writer's message. The juxtaposition of eutopia and dystopia highlights their foundations in our own society, and reinforces warnings of the need for change. While most American utopias see eutopia as much closer than in the long evolutionary view more popular with the British, the immediacy of many of these recent novels is particularly striking; their writers urge the need to make the right decisions *now* on social issues, to avert a dystopian future. In the words of one time-traveller from the future, speaking to a woman of today: 'Yours is crux-time. Alternate universes co-exist. Probabilities clash and possibilities wink out forever' (Piercy, *Woman on the edge of time*, p. 77). The sense of standing at a crossroad is as strong as with the British Victorians, but without assuming that all roads will lead to the same progressive point.

With such an extensive bibliography to discuss, it is unfortunately impossible to discuss these novels other than thematically; and, rather than return to the formulation used in the earlier chapters, Russ's categories are far more sensitive to the modern temper. The implications of classlessness and lack of government, affinities with the natural world, quasi-tribe and quasi-family, and sexual permissiveness will be examined. The subject of work, always important in American utopias, will be included in the second section, and the role of the Amazon in the third.

Classlessness and lack of government

The organisation of these dystopias is authoritarian, while of these eutopias it is anarchist.

> Anarchy as a political term does not imply placing value on disorder; rather it means that no one governs others . . . The anarchist ideal is: power for everyone; power over no one . . . The feminist utopian ideal is a decentralized, cooperative anarchy in which everyone has power over his or her own life. There are no laws and no taboos, except for cultural consensus against interference in another's life.[10]

Anarchism, a horrifying concept for most late nineteenth-century feminists, is the antithesis of the rigid organisation of modern dystopias. It is politically closest to a complete absence of government, and as such preserves the right of the individual as part of a community. Stripped of the associations of black-clad bomb-throwers it held for turn-of-the-century Americans, it has become the main political element in modern feminist utopias, whether the term 'anarchy' is articulated or silent. The male astronauts in Sheldon's 'Houston, Houston', who are rescued from a time warp by an all-woman spaceship crew from a future Earth, can only conclude of life on a woman-only Earth that it is 'almost ungoverned' (p. 203). Meanwhile, the female astronauts discuss the bewildering relationships of the men:

> These people had a very rigid authority code. You remember your history, they peck-ordered everything . . . That's called

dominance — submission structure, one of them gave orders and the others did whatever they were told, we don't know quite why. Perhaps they were frightened. (p. 180)

These eutopias strenuously reject dominance/submission, pecking orders and authority codes. This is only practical in a society small enough to accommodate the voice of the individual, and even then it costs valuable time and energy to reach consensus, yet these writers present communal decision-making as the only way to overcome the problem of power.

Some face these difficulties openly, particularly Piercy (1976) and Slonczewski (1980). In *Woman on the edge of time*, the woman of the future (Luciente) speaks to the woman of the present (Connie):

> 'There's no final authority, Connie,' Luciente said. 'There's got to be. Who finally says yes or no?' 'We argue till we close to agree. We just continue. Oh, it's disgusting sometimes. It bottoms you.' 'After a big political fight, we guest each other,' the man said. 'The winners have to feed the losers and give presents.' (pp. 153–4)

There is a built-in flexibility in this future of small communities, where alternative societies offer the individuals who cannot fit in the possibility of finding a group more acceptable to *them*. While moving to seek a compatible group might seem a high price, it is preferable to compulsion, and there are no laws to penalise the potentially disruptive deviant. Slonczewski's *Still forms on Foxfield* sees the same process in the traditional Quaker meeting: ' "So everyone has to agree on the 'real truth' before taking action?" "That's right." "You must have long meetings." "Too long," Clifford groaned' (p. 147). By comparison, the much larger society on Earth contemporaneous with Foxfield offers an equal chance to participate, but it is impractical in a world federation, and would erode one's time so much that nothing else would be done.

Quaker principles of non-violent resistance and the same quite agonising difficulties of reaching agreement are examined in detail in Slonczewski's recent *A door into ocean* (1986), and by the Quakers in Le Guin's 'The eye of the heron' (1978). Her *The dispossessed* (1974) ('an ambiguous utopia'), set in part on an anarchist planet, Anarres, also examines the problems of anarchist individualism: how does one balance individual rights against social need? how is difference accommodated? — questions that are more pressing on an entire planet, and one, moreover, where resources are scarce, than in the smaller communities described by other writers. Here too there is an examination of the vigilance that it takes to preserve such an open society. Although 'ambiguously' utopian to those under such pressures within Anarres, when observed from the perspective of sister planet Urras (which is like Earth), they are more easily defined.

In place of the orthodox Christian religious framework of the past which kept the balance between individual and community, modern authors substitute a variety of ethical systems. Le Guin (1974), Staton (1975) and Holland (1976) are the only writers to name their societies 'anarchist', but across a wide spectrum of eutopias the same lack of organisation is repeated. The Quaker societies of Slonczewski (1980) and Le Guin (1978) (a minority); the 'tribal societies' (nomadic or settled) of Piercy, Russ, Singer, Gearhart *et al.*; the planets of women, or of two sexes — all practise the same methods of breaking down power structures, and preventing the establishment of hierarchies.

Violence and laws (and law-breaking) are associated with male rule. Ursula Le Guin considers ' "the female principle" . . . basically anarchic'.[11] In her dystopian novella 'The new Atlantis' (1975), the female hero comments: 'Some people love illegality for its own sake. Men, more often than women. It's men who make laws, and enforce them, and break them, and think the whole performance is wonderful. Most women would rather just ignore them' (p. 68). However, the laws in dystopia are notoriously difficult to ignore. The speaker, a cellist, has been, since the 'full employment act', an 'inspector in a recycled paper bag factory' (p. 67) (unemployment, like marriage, is illegal); her cello comes in handy for disguising conversations in her bugged apartment, especially when played in the marvellous acoustics of her bathroom.

The law in other dystopias is even more pervasive and oppressive, far from the consensuality prized by women in their eutopias, and in dystopia women are the powerless. Whether it is the brutal conquest of an entire planet by a militarist and authoritarian power (as in Le Guin (1972), Carr (1979), and Slonczewski (1986)), or police disruption of a small women's community in Texas (Arnold, 1973), the principle is the same; law is seen as the means of oppression, particularly of women.

The militarism of the dystopias is often explicitly associated with traditional religious beliefs. One of Sheldon's male astronauts wants to convert all of the 'unnatural' women of the future, and quotes to them: 'The head of the woman is the man . . . Let the women learn in silence and all subjection' (pp. 220–1). The community of women in Singer's *The demeter flower* (1980) has founded its secret retreat as a refuge from the main US society of the future, where a panic response to nuclear radiation has led to a fundamentalist religious revival and martial law, and each woman must be 'owned' and controlled by a man. Fundamentalism of different kinds (of Jewry and Islam) bring violence to the community of women in Broner's otherwise joyful *A weave of women* (1978). Le Guin's 'The eye of the heron' opposes the gentle Quakers to a strictly 'macho' patriarchal society on the same planet; the Quakers have been exiled from Earth for their non-violence; the others, ironically, are criminals, exiled for their violence.

This fear that, in a crisis, men will turn on women as scapegoats is most fully explored in Charnas's *Walk to the end of the world* (1974), where the men, after what is surely a nuclear war:

> rejoiced to find an enemy they could conquer at last . . . female vermin of all kinds spewed out millions of young to steal our food supplies and our living space! Females themselves brought on the wasting of the world! And the men, armed with staves and straps, reminded them and saw to it that these things were not forgotten again. (p. 4)

The same fear that, in a time of crisis, all that women have taken so long and fought so hard to achieve will be stripped from them is the basis of Elgin's *Native tongue* (1984) and its sequel, *The Judas rose* (1987), and Canadian Atwood's *The handmaid's tale* (1985). Elgin's women do manage to 'outwit' some of this through their linguistic abilities as translators who deal with aliens, creating for themselves a secret and subversive language which binds them together, and they subsequently gain autonomy through separatism within family compounds within the Women's Houses. Firstly claiming their own reality through language, they consolidate it in these Houses, and then oversee its gradual infiltration into society generally.

The bond with nature

Awareness of the natural world has never been so strong. The women of *Mizora* and *Herland*, for instance, identified with nature to varying degrees, but to Lane and Gilman a society of nomadic hunters would have seemed merely primitive. The feminist movement has underwritten some aspects of the change, the ecological movement others. Feminism's influence is chiefly through the spiritual affinity of women with nature in the separatist novels, which hallows both women and nature: she is the great mother, just as in *Herland*, but not a mother to transform through genetic interference — rather, one to live with in peace. The ecological movement has raised consciousness of the fragility of the natural world, and its impact has been broad (those few recent eutopias by male writers are outgrowths of the ecological movement). More often than not, the Big Brother of Orwell's *Nineteen eighty-four*, is replaced by the nightmare of the faceless military/industrial complex which declares its God-given right to ravage the planet. Whether this planet is Earth or Alpha Centauri, in works as different as Wilhelm's *Where late the sweet birds sang* (1974), Charnas's *Walk to the end of the world* (1974) or Le Guin's 'The eye of the heron' (1978), the subjugation of nature is identified with the subjugation of women; the rape of one is a metaphor for the rape of the other.

With this affinity established, the cities are increasingly viewed as centres of alienation, and loci of mental and physical illness. The city is associated with authoritarianism, alienation, violence — and male control. In Piercy's chilling future city, for instance, women are reduced to sexual and breeding functions. It is an artificial world of (male) killers and fems, so divorced from nature that, when questioned about the lack of windows in her apartment, the fem occupant replies: 'Light? How? From outside? Oh, I guess when you get up high enough. This is just the hundred twenty-sixth floor. But even up on the sun plaza what's to see except the sun?' (p. 295). The claustrophobia (and much else) of this scene is emphasised by its comparison with the natural (but not unsophisticated) eutopia with which the reader has already become acquainted. Gearhart's *The wanderground. Stories of the hill women* (1979) has a similar dichotomy: women's eutopian life in the hills is contrasted with the violent, male-dominated city, the only place where men are potent (p. 127), and where women's presence in public without at least one male as escort is prohibited. Even where there is a technological component to societies, separatist or androgynous, it is maintained in harmony with nature. Russ comments on Arthur C. Clarke's *The city and the stars* that it makes the point 'that a really sophisticated technology would *look like* "nature"' (original emphasis).[12] The world of Whileaway also does just that: as Janet explains:

Whileaway doesn't have true cities . . . Whileaway is so
pastoral that at times one wonders whether the ultimate
sophistication may not take us all back to a kind of pre-
Paleolithic dawn age, a garden without any artifacts except
for what we could call miracles. (*The female man*, p. 14)

Similar transformations are found in Sheldon's 'Houston,
Houston', where the women's spaceship is a marvel of hydroponics,
and has its own chickens, and Piercy's future Mattapoissett, where
the (fully automated) factories are underground. The miracles of
molecular biology on Slonczewski's planet, Ocean (1986), use none
of the paraphernalia of Earth sciences, and what the male scientists see they cannot identify.

With such an attitude to science and technology, it follows that
those women working in the sciences are not isolated in laboratories:
in fact, their appearance and many of their activities are similar
to those of the women in the wholly pastoral societies. Dressed in
shirts and shorts/trousers, working 'in the field', they have none
of the absent-mindedness or the pomposity of Le Guin's Professor
Higgins. By far the most imaginative and playful on the subject
of technology is Russ:

[The young] run routine machinery, dig people out of land-
slides, oversee food factories (with induction helmets on their
heads, their toes controlling the green-peas, their fingers the
vats and controls, their back muscles the carrots and their
abdomens the water supply) . . . They are not allowed to have
anything to do with malfunctions or breakdowns 'on foot'
. . . meaning in one's own person and with tools in one's
own hands, without the induction helmets . . . They do not
meddle with computers 'on foot' nor join with them via
induction. That's for *old* veterans. (p. 51)

The old have creative freedom: sedentary jobs 'mapping, drawing,
thinking, writing, collating, composing' (p. 53).

The women in other all-female societies have a range of non-
scientific occupations: they are horse-traders (Charnas), hunters and
healers (Gearhart), farmers and artists (Singer), and there are
agricultural androgynous societies (Bryant, 1971, Lynn, 1979). The
most unusual healer is the hero of McIntyre's *Dreamsnake* (1978),
who uses serpents for healing, as she travels a dystopian, post-
nuclear holocaust landscape.

One separate group are the space/time travellers. Sometimes they are diplomats, envoys, who travel from world to world, although the eutopian and dystopian societies in their backgrounds are usually subordinated to the adventures of the individuals: Holland (1976), Carr (1979), Vinge (1980). There are many others which properly belong to the strong subsidiary sub-genres of fantasy and sword and sorcery novels: sometimes they overlap with the utopias, but generally they lie outside its parameters. They overlap most when a traveller from eutopia crosses time to enter the present (as with Piercy).

Whether these active women are Amazonian hunters or biologists, they dress in remarkably similar styles of clothing. In shorts or trousers and shirts, engineers and hunters alike dress for comfort, for ease of movement, and for *work*. When these eutopian women encounter strangers, they are often taken for men. Luciente, in Piercy's *Woman on the edge of time*, for instance, is perceived as a young man because of her dress (trousers, shirt) and because of her body language: '[she] squatted, she sprawled, she strolled, never thinking about how her body was displayed' (p. 66). Women from Charnas's (p. 14) and Gearhart's Amazonian societies initially frighten women whom they encounter fleeing from male violence, and remove their shirts and expose their breasts to disarm these fears.

There is everything natural and nothing masculine about these eutopian women. How differently things are ordered in the artificial worlds of the dystopias, where women's occupations are restricted to those allotted to them by men, and their appearance signals this difference. Whether in decorative satin, in rags, or soberly modest, women's dress in dystopia is a sign of their lower caste, and their lower caste occupations. Charnas's (1974) dystopia has two roles for women — slave/breeder or house pet. Slaves have their heads shaved, and dress in smocks and sweat rags. House pets (prostitutes) also have shaved heads, tattooed with 'stripes, spots, even fine striations like the hair of beast pelts' (p. 112). In this post-holocaust society, there are no animals; 'men in *Walk* act like beasts while the women are treated like animals'.[13]

Charnas's women have reached the depths of degradation. Much more commonly women are sex objects or the demurely draped, submissive vessels of fundamentalist temptation. The women in Gearhart's dystopia of the city, for instance, are described as: 'the man's edition, the only edition acceptable to men, streamlined to his exact specifications, her body guaranteed to be limited, dependent, and constantly available' (p. 63). What this means for practical purposes is that trousers are outlawed for women; ambiguity is out, femininity is in. Piercy's dystopia presents a frightening view of the woman that men might wish to see: she is not merely dressed artificially, like a doll, but has been the subject of deforming genetic interference:

> her body seemed a cartoon of femininity . . . a tiny waist, enormous sharp breasts that stuck out like the brassieres Connie herself had worn in the fifties — but the woman was not wearing a brassiere. . . . her hips and buttocks were oversized and audaciously curved. She looked as if she could hardly walk for the extravagance of her breasts and buttocks. (p. 288)

This is particularly frightening when compared with Luciente's freedom, and with her honest sexuality; but not only is the woman of this future modified for a passive sexual role, the male, who has a grafted weapon hand, has been modified for violent action. In Le Guin's *The dispossessed*, the women of Urrasti dress in provocative, revealing dresses, profoundly embarrassing for the male visitor fron anarchist Anarres, who is unaccustomed to any form of gender distinction. Far different is the clothing imposed in the dystopias of patriarchal religious belief, where women wear the long, heavy dresses of the nineteenth century, inhibiting action, defining their purely domestic roles, and smothering their 'dangerous' sexuality (Le Guin, 1978, and Singer, 1980). When the female hero of 'the stone telling' in Le Guin's recent *Always coming home* (1985) enters a like patriarchal society (the Condor), her practical travelling clothes are burnt, and she must cover her head and wear dresses.

The alienation from nature in the dystopias is the alienation of women from themselves.

Quasi-tribal

Consensual agreement in these societies is supported by a range of informal sanctions that replace institutionalised laws. These sanctions may have a tribal or a mystic basis; what is important is agreement on how people will behave, and a tolerance of difference. Thus, Piercy's future society may go to extraordinary lengths to reach consensus, but can accommodate some difference; her 'winners' feast her 'losers' in recognition of this. Quite a few of these writers use similar rituals from tribal societies as their model, incorporating into their eutopias mechanisms of social cohesion, binding individuals into community through ritual and ceremony, rather than coercion and codified laws. Rites of passage, seasonal celebrations, menarche, conception or childbirth figure as events in the natural cycle of human life that unify society and continue tradition.

The separatist novels naturally celebrate the functions of women's reproductive systems. In Gearhart, one of the stories of the Hill Women, 'The deep Cella', is a celebration of implantment deep in the earth, where the hot currents of air fertilise the merged ova, after preparation with herbs. The ceremony is not private, but communal, a source of strength for the women. The menarche is an important rite of passage for women in Singer's *The demeter flower* (1980), which also communally celebrates conception (aided by the flower of the title), and for the women in Sargent's *The shore of women* (1986), where it is celebrated by parties, gifts, the choice of profession, and moving from the maternal home. The women in Charnas's *Motherlines* (1978) also celebrate, and the transition from girlhood to womanhood means a complete change of life: in an intricate ceremony that recreates their history, the women 'gave a child the plains':

> Some say that on such a day all elements of the world are placed fresh: living and nonliving, past and future, the spirits of animals and of grass and wind and time passing and even the spirits of stars. Each time we make again the web that is the inner pattern of all things, all things are balanced, the world is made steady. (p. 201)

Piercy's androgynous society has as rite of passage for boys and girls a period alone in the wilderness, during which the maturing individual chooses her or his adult name, and from which they return with an adult identity. Such passages as these draw on anthropology to find the networks for new worlds.

Another form of social cohesion is that of a collective consciousness that unites members of a society on a subconscious level of dreams, sometimes through practising communications through extra-sensory perception. Often this is an important element in social cohesion, and in some eutopias this ability to share thoughts and/or dreams takes on the significance of an alternative technology. The antithesis of the mind-control of some dystopias, it is closely integrated with the eutopian concept of nature. In the pastoral societies that have rejected technology, these manifestations of the paranormal provide long-distance communication networks using nature, rather than science, as their base. The 'mindstretching' abilities fostered by Gearhart's Hill Women, for instance, have been described in these terms: '[Their] language is extraordinary in its appropriation of vocabulary associated with technology, and high technology at that; these powers belong not to machines in Gearhart's fiction, but they are powers of human minds.'[14] In two of these societies, both off-world, only one recognisably human in shape, there are connections through dreams. Le Guin's *The word for world is forest* (1972), her allegory of the Vietnam war, a peaceful planet is colonised (by recognisable Americans), and the web of life torn, the earth uprooted. The people of this world have connections through a rich network of symbolism shaped by the sharing of their dreams. So, too, do the people of Bryant's *The kin of Ata* (1971), whose first act on waking is to share their dreams, and whose communal meetings centre on these dreams; whose simple, agricultural life sustains them physically, but whose rich dreams are their true, spiritual lives.

In other, and quite different, societies women's ability to heal and the development of their intuition to the level of an art and a science contrast the humane technology of women with the inhumane technology of men. This, too, is an extension of the interest in pre-technological societies. McIntyre's *Dreamsnake* (1978) tells of a woman, Snake, who travels a devastated post-holocaust world, healing with her serpents. Whether physical or spiritual healing is the focus of the novel, it is done in accordance with natural forces. The Comyn, telepaths of Bradley's Darkover novels, use their 'laran' (psychic) abilities to heal.

Among the pre-technological societies that American feminists have incorporated into their novels are, of course, the Amazons. Unlike the British Victorians, or Lane or Gilman, it is not their nationhood, and what that implies of ability to govern, that is important. Now they are most often restored to their roles as hunters and warriors, and their sexual orientation is explicitly lesbian. Suzy Charnas, in 'A woman appeared', describes the inception of her Amazon society: 'I was interested in the potentialities of an Amazon-like society unconstrained by our distorted and fragmentary notions of real, historic Amazons.'[15] Her Amazon Riding Women (*Motherlines*, 1978) are tribal plaindwellers in a post-nuclear holocaust America, nomads and horsetraders: their lives are defined in opposition to the hierarchical, militaristic society of men described in her earlier dystopia, *Walk to the end of the world* (1974). The novel reflects a strong sense of female bonding (lesbianism is part of the change), an association with the natural world and distrust of urban culture.

So, too, does Gearhart's *Wanderground*, whose women's lives consist of ritual hunting and are centred around pre-Christian matriarchal religions that have been part of a feminist rediscovery of her story.[16] However, place of honour, because they were the first, should go to Bradley's Free Amazons. Bradley has been at the receiving end of a deal of criticism from writers of separatist fiction (her Free Amazons do not take centre stage in the Darkover novels, but are one of a group of societies), which she discusses with some bitterness: 'they said I was "unable to deal with" an all-feminist Utopia. Damn right. I don't like a "final solution" for men any more than I liked Hitler's final solution about people *he* saw as undesirables.'[17] Her 'Guild of free Amazons' is an amalgam of the separatism of the legendary Amazons with lesbianism, and whose members associate (even if unwillingly) with members of two-sex societies, and have an impeccably feminist oath which concludes:

> And if I betray any secret of the Guild, or prove false to my oath, then I shall submit myself to my Guild-mothers for such discipline as they shall choose; and if I fail, then may every woman's hand turn against me, let them slay me like an animal and consign my body unburied to corruption and my soul to the mercy of the Goddess.

The Darkover series has led to a volume of stories about the Free Amazons, who lead a settled life, and enjoy a wide range of occupations (their organisation is centred on the medieval guilds), but are at home in the natural world where their physical endurance is legendary. While the differences between Bradley and writers like Russ and Charnas are unlikely to be resolved, her Amazons should not be relegated to the scrap heap on grounds of ideological impurity. Many of the separatist societies have nothing but gender and autonomy in common with the Amazons, however. Those of Russ and Sheldon live in highly technological worlds, those of Slonczewski are not even human, but amphibious aliens.

Sexual permissiveness

In Le Guin's *The dispossessed*, a woman pressed to enter a temporary relationship on the grounds that 'Life partnership is really against the Odonian ethic', replies, 'Having's wrong: sharing's right. What more can you share than your whole self, your whole life, all the nights and all the days?' (p. 48). The difference between sexual permissiveness on the one hand, and power and ownership on the other, is part of a spectrum of individual expression. While other writers are less sure about the durability of a life-long bond, the distinction between the possessiveness of 'having' and the equality of 'sharing' is common. In its dystopian form it takes on two aspects. The first is ownership of women's sexuality by men, as implied by the legalisation of a private relationship. The second is the ownership of women's reproductive capacities by men. Both are rejected in feminist utopias.

Let us look first at the dystopias, where we find the antithesis of what is desirable in private, as in public life: coercion, the misuse of power, and violence. In Piercy's dystopia, for example, the legal and commercial aspects of sexuality in dystopia are brought out by the complacent acceptance by the 'fem' of her own 'two year contract':

> Some girls got only a one-nighter or a monthly, that's standard. You can be out on your ear at the end of a month with only a day's notice . . . You can't get out of a contract unless you're bought out. (*Woman on the edge of time*, p. 290)

The 'permissiveness' of Piercy's eutopia, where there is general acceptance of a number of sexual relationships, but a constant awareness of responsibility and real sharing, is healthy and desirable when compared with this blatant attitude to sexuality. So, too, in a very different novel, that of the compared marriages in the 'Stone Telling' story of Le Guin's *Always coming home* (1985). Among the patriarchal Condor:

> wives were expected to have babies continuously, since that is what One made women for; one of the Daughters of Terter House had seven children, the eldest of them ten years old, and for this incontinence she was praised by men and envied by women. (p. 367)

In this society, 'Stone Telling' (whose name changes throughout the story) is married, but to face her wedding she gets herself drunk, as a response to a society that treats women like 'incontinent' animals, and where even the doctor who comes when she is ill is 'nervous and disgusted' when he finds that she is menstruating (p. 366). By comparison, in her own society, that of the more liberal-minded Kesh, virginity has no status, marriage is entered into with some ritual, but also gradually, so that, by the time her marriage there is confirmed by the singing of the Wedding Song, a relationship of trust and mutual understanding has already been entered.

In eutopia sexuality is given free play, and, apart from such taboos as those on Whileaway, which forbid any possibility of exploitation of the young, passes into the realm of individual choice. No one in these eutopias is defined or labelled by their sexual activities or by their sexual preferences, no one lives by their sexuality, whether in prostitution or in marriage. Above all, sexuality is free from any taint of violence of possessiveness. The women of Carr's *Leviathan's deep* (1979) cannot be raped, for instance, a magnificent physiological protection. There is general agreement among these writers that:

> sexuality should have nothing to do with issues of power or wealth, or one individual's advantage over another, and that violence has no place in the feminist concept of sexuality. It is natural for friends to love one another and to include sexuality within the larger boundaries of their caring and communication, and this phenomenon should hold true for all planets and times.[18]

Whether marriage is defended or dispensed with, the violence and coercion of the dystopias make their point. One of Le Guin's novels ('The new Atlantis') presents a world in which marriage is outlawed, and one character comments: 'it must have been easy to enforce the laws back when marriage was legal and adultery was what got you into trouble. They only had to catch you once (p. 69). The clear message, whether presented from a eutopian or a dystopian perspective, is that it is *not their business to catch you*, that sexual behaviour is a matter for responsible individuals to decide.

While violence and sexuality form a repellent combination, the possibilities of coercive reproduction are also feminist concerns. There is nothing intrinsically wrong with modern reproductive technology; it is the politics of its use that matter. Utopias by women often incorporate exogenetic birth in order to hurdle what earlier writers Clyde (1909) and Spotswood (1935) (see Chapters 1 and 4 respectively) envisaged as a biological barrier to true equality.

> Speculative fiction uses both positive and negative images of motherhood to denounce patriarchal control of birth. Regardless of whether the individual writer chooses to portray negative or positive aspects of pregnancy, each choice emphasizes the need to alter patriarchy's penchant for transforming women into powerless birth machines.[19]

In Piercy's dystopia, men have exclusive rights to the sexual services of individual women through contracts of varying duration, which cannot be broken without legal action, although women may be 'bought out' by another man. As well as the commercialisation of sexuality, children are also commercialised. A contract may specify a child, but generally this is for a small group of women, 'the moms' (p. 290). In Piercy's dystopia, as in her eutopia, marriage and family are things of the past. They have been replaced on the one hand by a system controlled by men and based on money and power, on the other by one in which the rights of individual and community are paramount, within a system of moral values that transforms one of the staples of previous dystopias, exogenetic birth, into an instrument of freedom.

> It was part of women's long revolution. When we were breaking all the old hierarchies. Finally there was that one thing we had to give up too, the only power we ever had, in return for no more power for anyone. The original production: the power to give birth. (p. 105)

The abdication of motherhood in the name of equality, and replacement of natural gestation and birth by a number of mothers (including males) for each child, with hormone injections for these male mothers so that they may suckle, reduce the barriers between the sexes to their lowest possible point. It seems as if what has come to pass in these novels is the transsexuality that Borgese had suggested might not be impossible in her 1960s essay. Borgese, in her *Ascent of woman* (1963), describes a 'personal' utopia, in which gender might change with age, so that each individual will experience life as female and male, being women (with older husbands) during the childbearing years, being men (with younger wives) after menopause. It is an interesting (to say the least) view of how human sexual and social behaviour might be transformed by science. Piercy's novel is the most outspoken on the subject of sexuality, contrasting the possessiveness of sexual relations in her dystopia with the openness of the pairings between 'sweet friends' in her eutopia: to Connie, the shocked visitor from the present, this seems like unbearable licence. After some time she comes to understand what this means: no more prostitution, no more exploitation, no more unwanted children, no more unhappy women forced into marriage for the sake of social conformity, but deep and abiding understanding.

Altogether, the view of reproductive technology in these novels is less dystopian than eutopian: the truly dystopian state is that of the 'fems' in Charnas's *Walk to the end of the world*, where women litter like animals, and their children are called 'cubs', or a society like that of the Condor in Le Guin's *Always coming home*. Constant indiscriminate childbirth is the dystopian horror; controlled childbirth, even if *ex utero*, is the eutopian dream. Perhaps the most ambiguous aspect of reproductive technology is that of cloning, which is only presented as a complete success by Sheldon, and is seen as an intermediate measure by Wilhelm (1974) and Sargent (1982).

There are few marriages in these novels, but many families. Families may be composed of married partners and their children; they may be composed of groups of like-minded people; they may or may not live togetheer. In Piercy's future there is no communal living: 'only babies share space. We live *among* our family' (*Woman on the edge*, p. 72). On Russ's Whileaway 'a family of thirty persons have as many as four mother-and-child pairs in the common nursery at one time' (p. 50). These families are not biological, but social groupings. Even in novels that include orthodox nuclear families (i.e. Le Guin's 'Eye of the heron', Slonczewski's *Still forms on Fox-field*), the pull is to community.

The feminist eutopias and dystopias of this modern period carry some diversity, notably on the separatist/androgynous split, but they all present similar values, differently interpreted, as desirable: non-violence, tolerance for individual difference and the need for individual voices to be heard, room for the free expression of sexuality, closeness to nature, and an end to power-games and repression. Perhaps it can be summed up in the word 'autonomy', and especially autonomy for women — the freedom to think, act, speak, and to live without fear. The dystopias spell out very clearly what that fear consists of — repression, violence, war, rape and powerlessness to control their lives. In the mid-1980s the tone is slightly changed. There is an even greater political awareness, and also signs in several works of a change from the separatism of the late 1970s. Forecasting future trends in utopian fiction is pitted with traps, but the tide of feminist utopias is still running strong in America; perhaps it will continue in these directions. Whatever circumstances might bring change, it seems unlikely that the tide will ebb, or that it will become darkened and overcast, losing its sense of visionary possibilities.

Notes

1. Lyman Tower Sargent, *British and American utopian literature 1516–1975. An annotated bibliography*, 1st edn (G.K. Hall, Boston, 1979), lists 23 eutopias, 65 dystopias, published in the US by male writers, 1970–5.

2. 'Recent feminist utopias' in Marleen S. Barr (ed.), *Future females: a critical anthology* (Bowling Green State University Popular Press, Bowling Green, Ohio, 1981), p. 76.

3. The number of critical works by one author, or of critical anthologies, continues to increase. The most recent single-author work, Marleen Barr's *Alien to femininity. Speculative fiction and feminist theory* (Greenwood, Westport, Conn., 1987), is a synthesis of selected feminist utopias with feminist theory.

.4. Mary Ann Tetrault, 'Feminist dystopias of the Reagan years: *The handmaid's tale* and *Native tongue*', paper presented at the annual meeting of the Society for Utopian Studies, 8–11 October 1987.

5. Linda Leith, 'Marion Zimmer Bradley and Darkover', *Science-fiction Studies*, vol. 7 (1980),pp. 28–35, discusses the changes in Bradley's fiction.

6. 'Escape routes' in *Language of the night. Essays on fantasy and science fiction* Susan Wood (ed.), (G.P. Putnam, New York, 1979), p. 203.

7. Betty King, *Women of the future: the female main character in science fiction* (Scarecrow Press, Metuchen, New Jersey and London, 1984), p. 108.

8. Joanna Russ, 'What can a heroine do?' in Susan Koppelman Cornillon (ed.), *Images of women in fiction: feminist perspectives* (Bowling Green University Popular Press, Bowling Green, Ohio, 1972), p. 5, discusses the comparative freedom of science fiction and the detective novel. She gives a more specifically feminist reason than Doris Lessing: like Angela Carter, she has not written in a realist mode, and also like her is a 'subversive' writer.

9. Harper and Row, New York, 1981, p. 71. See also her *Woman and nature* (Harper and Row, New York, 1978).

10. Carol Pearson, 'Beyond governance: anarchist feminism in the utopian novels of Dorothy Bryant, Marge Piercy and Mary Staton', *Alternative Futures*, vol. 4, no. 1 (Winter 1981), p. 126. See also Lyman Tower Sargent, 'A new anarchism: social and political ideas in some recent feminist

eutopias' in Marleen S. Barr and Nicholas D. Smith (eds), *Women and utopia: critical interpretations* (University Press of America, Lanham, Maryland, 1983), pp. 3–33.

11. 'Is gender necessary?' in Wood (ed.), *Language of the night* , p. 165.

12. Samuel Delany, 'The science fiction of Joanna Russ' in Jane B. Weedman (ed.), *Women worldwalkers: new dimensions of science fiction and fantasy* (Texas Tech Press, Lubbock, Texas, 1985), note to p. 113.

13. Marleen Barr, 'Charnas's feminist science fiction' in Barr and Smith (eds), *Women and utopia*, p. 47.

14. Patrice Caldwell, 'Earth mothers or male memories: Wilhelm, Lem, and future women' in Weedman (ed.), *Women worldwalkers*, p. 67, note 13.

15. Barr (ed.), *Future females*, p. 105. Charnas also discusses her Amazons in *Frontiers*, vol. 2, no. 3 (Fall, 1987), p. 77

16. For example, Merlin Stone, *The Paradise papers. The suppression of women's rites* (Virago, London, 1976, 1978); Abby Wetten Kleinbaum, *The war against the Amazons* (McGraw-Hill, New York 1983); Page du Bois, *Centaurs and Amazons: women and the pre-history of the great chain of being* (University of Michigan Press, Ann Arbor, 1982), as well as Monique Wittig, *Les guérillères* 1969; (first English translation, Viking, New York, 1971). There are also the Amazon anthologies edited by Jessica Amanda Salmonson.

17. 'Responsibilities and temptations of women science fiction writers' in Weedman (ed.), *Women worldwalkers*, p. 35.

18. Judith Spector, 'The functions of sexuality in the science fiction of Russ, Piercy, and Le Guin' in Donald Palumbo (ed.), *Erotic universe: sexuality and fantastic literature* (Greenwood, Westport, Conn., 1986), p. 207.

19. Barr, *Alien to femininity*, p. 128.

Bibliography of Primary Material

Note: * denotes works cited in other bibliographies, but not located or read.

Henderson, Zenna (1961) *Pilgrimage: the book of the people*, Doubleday, New York

Smith, Evelyn E. (1962) *The perfect planet*, Christopher, Boston

Borgese, Elizabeth Mann (1963) *Ascent of woman*, George Braziller, New York

Lawrence, Josephine (1964) *Not a cloud in the sky*, Avalon, New York

Mannes, Marya (1968) *They*, Doubleday, New York

Le Guin, Ursula K. (1969) *The left hand of darkness*, Ace, New York

Lightner, Alice M. (1969) *The day of the drones*, Norton, New York

Russ, Joanna (1970) *And chaos died*, Ace, New York

Bryant, Dorothy (1971; *The comforter;* 1976) *The kin of Ata are waiting for you*, Random House, New York

MacLean, Katherine (1971) *Missing man*, Putnam, New York

Le Guin, Ursula K. (1972) *The word for world is forest*, Putnam, New York

Russ, Joanna (1972; 1983) 'When it changed', *The Zanzibar cat*, Arkham House, Sauk City, Wisconsin

Arnold, June (1973) *The cook and the carpenter, a novel by the carpenter*,

Daughters, Inc., Plainfield, Vt.

Le Guin, Ursula K. (1973) 'The ones who walk away from Omelas' in R. Silverberg (ed.), *New dimensions 3*, Doubleday, New York

Charnas, Suzy McKee (1974) *Walk to the end of the world*, Ballantine, New York

Le Guin, Ursula K. (1974) *The dispossessed*, Victor Gollancz, London

Wilhelm, Kate (1974; 1981) *Where late the sweet birds sang*, Arrow, London

Le Guin, Ursula K. (1975) 'The new Atlantis' in *The new Atlantis and other novellas of science fiction*, Hawthorn, New York

Neeper, Cary (1975) *A place beyond man*, Charles Scribner, New York

Russ, Joanna (1975) *The female man*, Bantam, New York

Staton, Mary (1975) *From the legend of Biel*, Ace, New York

Bradley, Marion Zimmer (1976) *The shattered chain*, Daw, New York

Holland, Cecelia (1976) *Floating worlds*, Knopf, New York

Piercy, Marge (1976) *Woman on the edge of time*, Knopf, New York

Bradley, Marion Zimmer (1978) *The ruins of Isis*, Avon, New York

Broner, Esther M. (1978) *A weave of women*, Holt, Rinehard and Winston, New York

Charnas, Suzy McKee (1978) *Motherlines*, Berkeley, New York

Le Guin, Ursula K. (1978) 'The eye of the heron', in Virginia Kidd (ed.), *The eye of the heron and other stories*, Granada, London

McIntyre, Vonda M. (1978) *Dreamsnake*, Houghton, Mifflin, Boston

*Randall, Marta (1978) *Journey*, Pocket, New York

Sheldon, Alice [James Tiptree, Jnr] (1978) 'Houston, Houston, do you read?' in *Star songs of an old primate*, Ballantine, New York

Carr, Jayge (1979) *Leviathan's deep*, Doubleday, New York

Dodderidge, Esme (1979) *The new Gulliver*, Taplinger, New York

Gearheart, Sally Miller (1979) *The wanderground. Stories of the hill women*, Persephone, Watertown, Mass.

Lynn, Elizabeth A. (1979; 1979; 1980) *Watchtower; The dancers of Arun; The northern girl*, Berkeley, New York

White, Mary Alice (1979) *The land of the possible*, Warner, New York

Young, Donna (1979) *Retreat: as it was*, Naiad, Weatherby Lake, Missouri

*Randall, Marta (1980) *Dangerous games*, Pocket, New York

Singer, Rochelle (1980) *The demeter flower*, St Martin's Press, New York

Slonczewski, Joan (1980) *Still forms on Foxfield*, Ballantine, New York

Vinge, Joan (1980; 1981) *The snowqueen*, Futura, London

Wilhelm, Kate (1980) *Juniper time*, Hutchinson, London

Paxson, Diana (1982) *Lady of light*, Pocket, New York

*Petesch, Natalia (1982) *Duncan's colony*, Swallow/Ohio University Press, Athens, Ohio

Sargent, Pamela (1982) *The golden space*, Simon and Schuster, New York

Bradley, Marion Zimmer (1983) *Thendara house*, Daw, New York

Elgin, Suzette Haden (1984) *Native tongue*, Daw, New York

Forrest, Katherine V. (1984) *Daughters of a coral dawn*, Naiad, Tallahassee, Flor.

Thompson, Joyce (1984) *Conscience place*, Doubleday, New York

*Bluejay, Jana (1985) *It's time: a nuclear novel*, Tough Dove Books, Little River, Calif.

Bradley, Marion Zimmer (ed.) (1985) *Free Amazons of Darkover*, Daw, New York

Le Guin, Ursula K. (1985) *Always coming home*, Harper and Row, New York
*Reed, Kit (1985) *Fort Privilege*, Doubleday, New York
Sargent, Pamela (1986) *The shore of women*, Crown, New York
Slonczewski, Joan (1986) *A door into ocean*, Avon, New York
Elgin, Suzette Haden (1987) *The Judas rose: native tongue II*, Daw, New York

Bibliography

Note: What follows is a select bibliography of secondary sources. All references to primary material are incorporated in the text, and primary material bibliographies are located at the end of each individual chapter.

Albinski, Nan Bowman (1985) 'The vine and olive colony', *Journal of General Education*, vol. 37, no. 3, pp. 203–17

Amis, Kingsley (1960) *New maps of hell*, Harcourt, Brece and Co, New York

Anderson, Janice and Vonda N. McIntyre (eds) (1976) *Aurora: beyond equality*, Fawcett, Greenwich, Conn.

Armytage, W.H.G. (1968) *Yesterday's tomorrows. A historical survey of future societies*, Routledge and Kegan Paul, London

Atkinson, Ti-Grace (1974) *Amazon odyssey*, Links, New York

Atwood, Margaret (1985; 1986) *The handmaid's tale*, Houghton Mifflin, Boston

Auerbach, Nina (1978) *Communities of women: an idea in fiction*, Harvard University Press, Cambridge, Mass.

—— (1982) *Woman and the demon, the life of a Victorian myth*, Harvard University Press, Cambridge, Mass.

Babington-Smith, Constance (1972) *Rose Macaulay*, Collins, London

Banks, J.A. and Olive (1964) *Feminism and family planning in Victorian England*, Liverpool University Press, Liverpool

Banks, Olive (1985) *The biographical dictionary of British feminists*, Wheatsheaf, Brighton, Sussex

Banner, Lois M. (1974) *Women in modern America: a brief history*, Harcourt Brace Jovanovich, New York

Barr, Marleen S. (ed.) (1981) *Future females: a critical anthology*, Bowling Green State University Popular Press, Bowling Green, Ohio

—— (1987) *Alien to femininity. Speculative fiction and feminist theory*, Greenwood, Westport, Conn.

—— and Nicholas D. Smith (eds) (1983) *Women and utopia: critical interpretations*, University Press of America, Lanham, Maryland

Baruch, Elaine Hoffmann (1979) 'A natural and necessary monster — women in utopia', *Alternative Futures*, vol. 2

Beauman, Nicola (1983) *A very great profession: the woman's novel 1914–39*, Virago, London

Benford, Gregory (1984) 'In the wave's wake', *Foundation*, 30, pp. 5–9

Bowman, Sylvia E. (ed.) (1962) *Edward Bellamy abroad: an American prophet's influence*, Twayne, New York

Bradbury, Malcolm (1973) *Possibilities. Essays on the state of the novel*, Oxford University Press, Oxford

—— and David Palmer (eds) (1980) *The contemporary English novel*, Holmes and Meier, New York

Branden, Barbara (1986) *The passion of Ayn Rand*, Doubleday, New York

Bibliography

Brians, Paul (1987) *Nuclear holocausts: atomic war in fiction, 1895–1984*, Kent State University Press, Kent, Ohio

Brough, James (1980) *The vixens: a biography of Victoria and Tennessee Claflin*, Simon and Schuster, New York

Brownlee, W. Elliott and Mary M.Brownlee (1976) *Women in the American economy: a documentary history, 1675 to 1929*, Yale University Press, New Haven

Buhle, Mari Jo (1981) *Women and American socialism, 1870–1920)* University of Illinois Press, Urbana

Burton, Hester (1949) *Barbara Bodichon*, John Murray, London

Butler, Josephine E. (1869) *Woman's work and woman's culture*, Macmillan, London

Byrne, Janet (1982) 'Moving toward entropy: Anna Kavan's science fiction mentality', *Extrapolation*, vol. 23, no. 1, pp. 5–11

Campbell, Bruce (1980) *Ancient wisdom revived*, University of California Press, Berkeley

Carol, Avedon (1985) Review, *Foundation*, 35, pp. 96–99

Carter, Angela (1979) *The Sadeian woman: an exercise in cultural history*, Virago, London

Clapperton, Jane Hume (1885) *Scientific meliorism and the evolution of happiness*, Kegan Paul, Trench and Co., London

—— (1904) *A vision of the future, based on the application of ethical principles*, Swan Sonnenschein, London

Clare, Mariette (1984) *Doris Lessing and women's appropriation of science fiction*, Centre for Contemporary Cultural Studies, University of Birmingham, Birmingham

Clarke, I.F. (1966) *Voices prophesying war 1763–1984*, Oxford University Press, London

Cleghorn, Sarah N. (1936) *Threescore: the autobiography of Sarah N. Cleghorn*, Harrison Smith and Robert Haas, New York

Clyde, Irene (1934) *Eve's sour apples*, Eric Partridge Ltd at the Scholartis Press, London

Cobbe, Frances Power (1888) *The scientific spirit of the age and other pleas and discussions*, Smith, Elder and Co., London

Corea, Gena *et al.* (1985) *Man-made women. How new reproductive technologies affect women*, Hutchinson, London

Cornillon, Susan Koppelman (ed.) (1972) *Images of women in fiction: feminist perspectives*, Bowling Green University Press, Bowling Green, Ohio

Davidson, Jim (ed.) (1986) *The Sydney-Melbourne book*, Allen and Unwin, Sydney

de Bolt, Joe (ed.) (1979) *Ursula Le Guin: voyager to inner lands and outer space*, Kennikat Press, Port Washington, New York

Delamont, Sara and Lorna Duffin (eds) (1978) *The nineteenth century woman: her cultural and physical world*, Croom Helm, London

de Vos, Luk (ed.) (1985) *Just the other day. Essays on the suture of the future*, EXA, Anterwerpen

Dixie, Florence Caroline (Douglas) (1890) *Aniwee; or, the warrior queen: a tale of the Araucanian Indians*, Richard Henry, London

Doughan, David (1980) *Lobbying for liberation. British feminism 1918–1968*, London Polytechnic, London du Bois, Page (1982) *Centaurs and Amazons: women and the pre-history of the great chain of being*, University of Michigan Press, Ann Arbor

Edwards, Lee R. (1984) *Psyche as hero: female heroism and fictional form*, Wesleyan University Press, Middletown, Conn.

Eisenstein, Hester (1984) *Contemporary feminist thought*, Unwin Paperbacks, London

Evans, Richard (1979) *The feminists*, Croom Helm, London

Faulkner, Wendy and Erik Arnold (eds) *Smothered by invention: technology in women's lives*, Pluto, London

Firestone, Shulamith (1971) *The dialectic of sex: the case for feminist revolution*, Jonathan Cape, London

Flexner, Eleanor (1959) *Century of struggle: the women's rights movement in the United States*, Belknap Press of Harvard University Cambridge, Mass.

Fryer, Judith (1976) *The faces of Eve: women in the nineteenth century novel*, Oxford University Press, New York

Gerber, Richard (1955) *Utopian fantasy: a study of English utopian fiction since the end of the nineteenth century*, Routledge and Kegan Paul, London

Gilman, Charlotte Perkins (1923; reprinted 1976) *His religion and hers: a study of the faith of our fathers and the work of our mothers*, Hyperion Press, Westport, Conn.

—— (1935) *The living of Charlotte Perkins Gilman*, D. Appleton-Century, New York

Glendinning, Victoria (1983) *Vita: the life of V. Sackville-West*, Weidenfeld and Nicolson, London

Golding, William (1982) *A moving target*, Farrar, Straus, Giroux, New York

Gordon, Linda (1976) *Woman's body, woman's right: a social history of birth control in America*, Grossman, New York

Griffin, Susan (1981) *Pornography and silence: culture's revenge against nature*, Harper and Row, New York

Grumbach, Doris (1967) *The company she kept*, Coward-McCann, New York

Haldane, Charlotte (Franken) (1927) *Motherhood and its enemies*, Chatto and Windus, London

—— (1950) *Truth will out*, Vanguard, New York

Hamilton, (Mary) Cicely (1909; reprinted 1981) *Marriage as a trade*, Women's Press, London

—— (1910) *A pageant of great women*. The Suffrage Shop, London

—— (1935) *Life errant*, J.M. Dent, London

Hammerton, A. James (1979) *Emigrant gentlewomen: genteel poverty and female emigration, 1830–1914*, Croom Helm, London

Hardy, Dennis (1979) *Alternative communities in nineteenth century England*, Longman, London

The Harmony society in Pennsylvania (1937) Wm Penn Association, Penn.

Hartman, Mary S. and Lois Banner (eds) (1974) *Clio's consciousness raised: new perspectives on the history of women*, Harper Colophon, New York

Hayden, Dolores (1981) *The grand domestic revolution: a history of feminist designs for American homes, neighborhoods, and cities*, MIT Press, Cambridge, Mass.

Hill, Mary A. (1980) *Charlotte Perkins Gilman: the making of a radical feminist, 1860–1896*, Temple University Press, Philadelphia

Holcombe, Lee (1973) *Ladies at work: middle class working women in England and Wales, 1850-1914*, Archon Press, Hamden, Conn.

—— (1983) *Wives and property: reform of the married women's property law in nineteenth century England*, Martin Robertson, Oxford

Jackson, Rosemary (1981) *Fantasy: the literature of subversion*, Methuen, London

Jameson, (Margaret) Storm (1950) *The writer's situation and other essays*, Macmillan, London

—— (1969) *Journey from the north: autobiography of Storm Jameson*, Collins and Harvill, London

Jeffreys, Sheila (1985) *The spinster and her enemies: feminism and sexuality 1880-1930*, Pandora, London

Kagan, Paul (1975) *New world utopias. A photographic history of the search for community*, Penguin, Harmondsworth, Middlesex

Kelley, Mary (ed.) (1979) *Woman's being, woman's place: female identity and vocation in American history*, G.K. Hall, Boston

Kessler, Carol Farley (ed.) (1984) *Daring to dream. Utopian stories by United States women, 1836-1919*, Pandora Press, Boston

King, Betty (1984) *Women of the future: the female main character in science fiction*, Scarecrow, Metuchen, New Jersey and London

Kleinbaum, Abby Wetten (1983) *The war against the Amazons*, McGraw-Hill, New York

Lansbury, Coral (1985) *The old brown dog. Women, workers and vivisection in Edwardian England*, University of Wisconsin Press, Madison

Le Guin, Ursula K. (1979). *Language of the night. Essays on fantasy and science fiction*, (ed. Susan Wood) G.P. Putnam, New York

Leith, Linda (1980) 'Marion Zimmer Bradley and Darkover', *Science-fiction Studies*, vol. 7, pp. 28-35

Lemons, J. Stanley (1973) *The woman citizen: social feminism in the 1920s*, University of Illinois Press, Urbana

Lessing, Doris (1975) *A small personal voice*, Vintage, New York

—— (1986) *Prisons we choose to live inside*, Canadian Broadcasting Corporation Enterprises, Toronto

Le Warne, Charles Pierce (1975) *Utopias on Puget Sound, 1885-1915*, University of Washington Press, Seattle

Livermore, Mary A. (1891) 'Cooperative womanhood in the state', *North American Review*, 153, September, pp. 284-95

Manuel, Frank E. (ed.) (1965) *Utopias and utopian thought*, Houghton Mifflin Co., Boston

Marsh, Margaret S. (1981) *Anarchist women, 1870-1920*, Temple University Press, Philadelphia

Meyers, Walter E. (1980) *Aliens and linguists. Language and science fiction*, University of Georgia Press, Athens

Miller, George Noyes [1890] *The strike of a sex*, Wm Reeves, London

—— [1891] *After the strike of a sex*, Wm Reeves, London

Mitchison, Naomi (1975) *All change here: girlhood and marriage*, The Bodley Head, London

—— (1979) *You may well ask: a memoir 1920-1940*, Victor Gollancz, London

Negley, Glenn (1977) *Utopian literature: a bibliography with a supplementary listing of works influential in utopian thought*, Regents Press of Kansas, Lawrence

Norris, Christopher (ed.) (1984) *Inside the myth. Orwell: views from the left*, Lawrence and Wishart, London

Nott, Kathleen (1977) *The good want power. An essay in the psychological possibilities of liberalism*, Jonathan Cape, London

O'Neill, William (1967) *Divorce in the progressive era*, Yale University Press, New Haven

Palumbo, Donald (ed.) (1986) *Erotic universe: sexuality and fantastic literature*, Greenwood, Westport, Conn.

Pankhurst, E. Sylvia (1931; reprinted 1971) *The suffragette movement: an intimate account of persons and ideals*, Kraus Reprint Co, New York

Patai, Daphne (1981) 'British and American utopias by women (1836-1979)', *Alternative Futures*, vol. 4, nos. 2-3, Spring/Summer

Pearson, Carol (1981) 'Beyond governance: anarchist feminism in the utopian novels of Dorothy Bryant, Marge Piercy and Mary Staton', *Alternative Futures*, vol. 4, no. 1, Winter

—— and Katherine Pope (1981) *The female hero in American and British literature*, R.R. Bowker, New York

Perry, Ruth (1986) *The celebrated Mary Astell*, University of Chicago Press, Chicago

Pfaelzer, Jean (1984) *The utopian novel in America 1886-1896. The politics of form*, University of Pittsburgh Press, Pittsburgh

Punter, David (1980) *The literature of terror: a history of Gothic fictions from 1765 to the present day*, Longman, London

Roberts, Brian (1981) *The mad bad line. The family of Lord Alfred Douglas*, Hamish Hamilton, London

Robertson, Thomas A. (1964) *A southwestern utopia*, Ward Ritchie, Los Angeles

Roemer, Kenneth (1976) *The obsolete necessity. America in utopian writings, 1888-1900*, Kent State University Press, Kent, Ohio

—— (ed.) (1981) *America as utopia*, Burt Franklin, New York

Rohrlich, Ruby and Elaine Hoffman Baruch (eds) (1984) *Women in search of utopia, mavericks and mythmakers*, Schocken Books, New York

Rosaldo, Michelle Zimbalist and Louise Lamphere (eds) *(1974) Woman, culture and society*, Stanford University Press, Stanford

Rosinsky, Natalie M. (1984) *Feminist futures: contemporary women's speculative fiction*, UMI Research Press, Ann Arbor, Michigan

Rover, Constance (1967) *Woman's suffrage and party politics in Britain 1866-1914*, Routledge and Kegan Paul, London

Rowbotham, Sheila (1974) *Hidden from history. Rediscovering women in history from the seventeenth century to the present*, Random House, New York

Russ, Joanna (1983) *How to suppress women's writing*, University of Texas Press, Austin

Sage, Lorna (1977) 'The savage sideshow: a profile of Angela Carter', *The New Review*, vol. 4, nos. 39-40, pp. 51-7

—— (1980) 'Female fictions: the women novelists' in M. Bradbury and David Palmer (eds), *The contemporary English novel*, Holmes and Meier, New York

—— (1983) *Doris Lessing*, Methuen, London

Sargent, Lyman Tower (1976) 'English and American utopias: similarities and differences', *Journal of General Education*, vol. XXVIII, no. 1, Spring, pp. 16–22

—— (1979) *British and American utopian literature 1516–1975: an annotated bibliography*, 1st edn, G.K. Hall, Boston

Saxton, Martha (1977) *Louisa May: a modern biography of Louisa May Alcott*, Houghton, Mifflin, Boston

Scott, Sarah Robinson [A Gentleman on his Travels] (1762; reprinted 1986) *A description of Millenium Hall*, Virago, London

Sears, Hal D. (1977) *The sex radicals. Free love in high Victorian America*, Regents Press of Kansas, Lawrence

Segal, Lynne (1987) *Is the future female? Troubled thoughts on contemporary feminism*, Virago, London

Shelley, Mary (1826; reprinted 1965) *The last man*, University of Nebraska Press, Lincoln

Shinn, Thelma (1986) *Worlds within women: myth and mythmaking in fantastic literature by women*, Greenwood, Westport, Conn.

Showalter, Elaine (ed.) (1978) *These modern women: autobiographical essays from the twenties*, Feminist Press, Old Westbury, New York

—— (1982) *A literature of their own. British women novelists from Brontë to Lessing*, 2nd edn, Virago, London

Sinclair, Andrew (1965) *The better half. The emancipation of the American woman*, Harper and Row, New York

Smith-Rosenberg, Carol (1985) *Disorderly conduct: visions of gender in Victorian America*, Alfred A. Knopf, New York

Spender, Dale (1983) *There's always been a women's movement this century*, Pandora, London

—— (ed.) (1984) *Time and Tide wait for no man*, Pandora, London

Sprague, Claire and Virginia Tiger (eds) (1986) *Critical essays on Doris Lessing*, G.K. Hall, Boston

Staicar, Tom (ed.) (1982) *The feminine eye: science fiction and the women who write it*, Frederick Ungar, New York

Stern, Madeleine (1963) *We, the women: career firsts of nineteenth century America*, Schulte, New York

Stevenson, Catherine Barnes (1982) *Victorian women travel writers in Africa*, Twayne, Boston

Stone, Merlin (1976; 1978) *The Paradise papers. The suppression of women's rites*, Virago, London

Strachey, Ray (1928; reprinted 1978) *The cause*, Virago, London

Strauss, Sylvia (1976) 'Women in "Utopia"', *South Atlantic Quarterly*, vol. 75, pp. 115–31

Suvin, Darko (1979) *Metamorphoses of science fiction. On the poetics and history of a literary genre*, Yale University Press, New Haven

—— (1983) *Victorian science fiction in the UK. The discourses of knowledge and of power*, G.K. Hall, Boston

Taylor, Barbara (1983) *Eve and the new Jerusalem: socialism and feminism in the nineteenth century*, Virago, London

Taylor, Jenny (ed.) (1982) *Notebooks/memoirs/archives: reading and rereading Doris Lessing*, Routledge and Kegan Paul, London

Tetrault, Mary Ann (1987) 'Feminist dystopias of the Reagan years: *The handmaid's tale* and *Native tongue*', paper presented at the annual meeting of the Society for Utopian Studies, 8–11 October, Media, Penn.

Thompson, E.P. (1914) *The making of the English working class*, Penguin, Harmondsworth

Tyler, Alice Felt (1944; reprinted 1962) *Freedom's ferment. Phases of American social history from the colonial period to the outbreak of the Civil War*, Harper and Row, New York

Vassos, Ruth and John Vassos (1935) *Humanities*, E.P. Dutton, New York

Vicinus, Martha (1985) *Independent women: work and community for single women, 1850–1920*, Virago, London

Walsh, Chad (1962) *From utopia to nightmare*, Geoffrey Bles, London

Weedman, Jane B. (ed.) (1985) *Women worldwalkers: new dimensions of science fiction and fantasy*, Texas Tech Press, Lubbock, Texas

Wiggin, Kate Douglas [1924] *My garden of memory, an autobiography*, Hodder and Stoughton, London

Wittig, Monique (1969; reprinted 1971) *Les guérillères*, trans. Peter Owen, Viking, New York

Wolmark, Jenny (1986) 'Science fiction and feminism', *Foundation*, 37, pp. 48–51

Ziegler, Heide and Christopher Bigsby (eds) (1982) *The radical imagination and the liberal tradition*, Junction, London

Index

defined as female (feminist)
4, 8, 47-8, 50, 62, 163-4,
170-1
defined as female
(misogynist) 3, 4, 17, 79-81,
108, 133, 135, 143-4, 161
defined as male (feminist) *see*
barbarians; violence, male
see also culture
rejected by feminists 134-5
Neeper, Cary, *A place beyond
man* 164, 184
New Harmony (Owen) 53
New Harmony (Rapp) 51, 52,
70n13
Newton, Bertha, *My life in
time* 92-3, 104
Nichol, Mrs C.A. Scrymsour,
The mystery of the North Pole 43
Norris, Kathleen (Thompson),
Through a glass darkly 121,
125, 129
[Nostradamus, Merlin] *see*
Frances Power Cobbe
Nott, Kathleen, *The dry deluge*
95, 96, 103n32, 105
Nuclear pollution 136, 142,
145, 146-7, 162
Nuclear power, peaceful use
121-3
Nuclear war 7, 75, 95, 98-9,
100, 121, 123, 130-1, 136,
138, 140, 142-3, 162, 165,
172

Occupations, women's 31-3,
61-4
in dystopia; prostitutes 173;
sweated workers 144, 173
in eutopia;. artists 172;
biologists 48, 62, 173;
businesswomen, caterers
44, 62; diplomats 163;
doctors 61, 84, 95;
engineers, mechanics 48,
62, 163, 165;
horticulturists 62;
philanthropists 54;
physicists 163, 165, 172;
pilots 121, 122, 163;

professors 61; sailors 48,
62; scientists 62;
sociologists 62; teachers
32; warriors 163, 172
see also parliamentarians,
women
in real life; admitted to
professions 31, 48, 71n27;
prostitutes 57, 65;
sweated workers 32, 47,
63, 64
see also Society for
Promotion of Employment
for Women
O'Donnell, Margaret, *The
beehive* 144, 158
Oneida 45, 46, 64
Orpen, Adela, *Perfection city* 52,
53, 54, 73
Ortner, Sherry 3
Orwell, George, *Nineteen eighty
four* 6, 75, 139, 143, 171
[Owen, Caroline Dale] *see*
Caroline Dale Park Snedeker
Owen, Robert 53
Owen, Robert Dale 67

Paine, Thomas 138
Pankhurst, E. Sylvia 57
Parker, Dorothy 116
Parliamentarians, women 30-1,
32, 78, 89, 96, 115, 128n18,
143
see also Prime Ministers,
women
Patai, Daphne 29, 80, 81, 161
Patriarchy 17-18, 23, 52, 68,
79, 81, 90-1, 134-5, 141,
143-5, 161-2, 169-70, 173-4,
178-9
see also gender distinctions;
violence, male
Paxson, Diana, *Lady of light* 184
Peace 49, 64, 68, 86, 89, 92,
108, 110, 112, 114, 115, 118
Pearson, Carol 161, 167
Petesch, Natalie, *Duncan's colony*
184
Pettersen, Rena Oldfield, *Venus*
110, 112-13, 129

DATE DUE

Do not
circ.
until
10/16/91